W9-BBH-489
FC
2925.1
.F84
A3
Humber College
Lakeshore Campus
DISCARD
0 0 1 5 9 6 3 2 6
3/9
16.2
0552314
1996 05 13
16.2

HUMBER COLLEGE LIBRARY (LAKESHORE I)
DISCARD
T1

The Dangerous Delusion

The Dangerous Delusion

Quebec's Independence Obsession

as seen by former adviser
to René Lévesque
and Jean Lesage

Douglas H. Fullerton

McClelland and Stewart

ISBN: 0-7710-3217-X cl

0-7710-3218-8 pa

McClelland and Stewart Limited
The Canadian Publishers
25 Hollinger Road
Toronto Ontario, M4B 3G2

Printed and bound in Canada

Design: Michael van Elsen

Canadian Cataloguing in Publication Data

Fullerton, Douglas H., 1917-
The dangerous delusion
Quebec's independence obsession

Includes index.
ISBN 0-7710-3217-X bd. ISBN 0-7710-3218-8 pa.

1. Fullerton, Douglas H., 1917- 2. Quebec (Province) — Officials and employees — Biography. 3. Quebec (Province) — Politics and government — 1960- I. Title.

FC2925.1.F84A3 971.4'04'0924 C77-001593-X
F1053.2.F84A3

Contents

	Preface	7
Part I	**/ Early Years**	
	Chapter I Why Write This Book?	9
	Chapter II Montreal – where the French-English issue is joined, and where I grew up – absurdly separate	14
	Chapter III Ottawa: Government, Gordon Commission, Canada Council	27
Part II	**/ Adviser to Quebec**	
	Chapter IV René Lévesque and nationalization of the power companies (1962)	40
	Chapter V Success – but battle is joined on bond syndicates (1963)	53
	Chapter VI On to Hamilton Falls	62
	Chapter VII New Lesage initiatives, but Johnson elected (1964-1966)	75
	Chapter VIII Lévesque leaves the Liberals, and forms his own party (1966-1968)	87
	Chapter IX Parizeau Committee – and a few digressions (1966-1969)	99
Part III	**/ Ottawa Scene**	
	Chapter X Ottawa: Maurice Sauvé and Pierre Trudeau (1963-1969)	107

Chapter XI
The National Capital and the French Fact (1969-1973) 117
Chapter XII
NCC – the Quebec program and backlash 133
Chapter XIII
Bilingualism – the impossible Canadian dream? 143
Chapter XIV
Return to Montreal – following study of the Capital (1974-1977) 154

Part IV / November 15, 1976 - and after

Chapter XV
The péquistes come to power 167
Chapter XVI
The language legislation – launching pad for a holy war? 178
Chapter XVII
Separation – An emotional obsession collides with economic realities 192
Chapter XVIII
Good-bye, René . . . but I remember the good years 208

Appendix One
Letter September 1, 1962 to René Lévesque 214
Appendix Two
Memorandum, February, 1964, on Hamilton Falls 221
Appendix Three
Open Letter to Réne Lévesque, October 1967 224
Appendix Four
Summary of Bill 101, Language Legislation 229
Appendix Five
Weakness in Quebec Economy, June 1977 column 234
Index 237

PREFACE

In this book, largely written between mid-January and mid-July, 1977, I have tried to do three things: to write a personal memoir of my involvement with French Canada, including my early years in Montreal; to put on the record a history of Quebec events in which I participated, mainly as an adviser to the Quebec government during the quiet revolution of the 'sixties; and to express my views on the actions and statements of the Lévesque government, and the implications for Quebec and Canada, against a background of the history of the Parti Québécois and its independence objectives. Whether my attempt to combine autobiography, historical reporting, and editorial journalism in one book succeeds, I leave to the reader to judge.

Sections of the book were read in draft by friends, most of them with particular knowledge of Quebec, of the events which I describe, and of me. From them I received much good advice, notably of the need to excise material not directly related to the main theme of enabling the reader to develop a better understanding of Quebec and of the roots of its nationalism. However, I accept full responsibility for errors or omissions, and for the conclusions and judgments with which the final pages are rather freely laced.

I am grateful to the editorial staff of McClelland and Stewart for wise counsel. I am equally grateful to Mrs. Jeanette Schultz, who gave so much of her time during the spring and summer to keep the typed manuscript abreast of the continuing additions and revisions.

D. H. Fullerton

PART I
Early Years

I

Why Write This Book?

First, I suppose, because I must. Like Coleridge's Ancient Mariner, I have a story to tell, a story about my early years in Montreal, and my active involvement in Quebec's affairs these past fifteen years, a voyage of affectionate discovery about the French Canadians, as likable a people as one can find. A story that, I am afraid, is ending with my growing disillusionment with Quebec's Parti Québécois leaders, some of whom I have worked closely with in the past, whose efforts to take Quebec out of Canada can lead nowhere but to anguish and disaster, and whose methods to achieve their independence goal are becoming increasingly repugnant to me.

I am writing, too, because it seems to me there is no issue in this country today about which Canadians, English- and French-speaking, need to be better informed. The lack of knowledge of most English Canadians about Quebec is fully matched by Quebecers' ignorance about the rest of Canada. Both see each other now through cracked and distorted lenses. Within Quebec, the two groups are divided by language and by different interpretations of their separate histories. *"Tout comprendre, c'est tout pardonner"* is a French proverb that has stood the test of time. If it ever needed putting into practice, it is in the Canada and the Quebec of today.

I was brought up in Montreal, in the English community. Hugh MacLennan aptly used Rilke's "two solitudes" phrase as the title of his novel describing the Montreal of that era. We saw little of the French Canadians, never mixed with them socially; such contact as there was occurred mostly in the streets, tramways, or in stores, with the milkman or the breadman. And I'm not just speaking of the wealthy Montrealers, the Westmount-dwellers, but of the rest of us at every level of society. I did meet several French Canadians in school – they had been sent to learn English – but to the best of my memory I was never a guest in a French-Canadian home, or a French-Canadian friend in mine, until my mid-twenties, in Ottawa.

Yet when I did get to know French Canadians better I was instinctively attracted to them, and generally they to me. In the 'fifties I began to build up a circle of French-Canadian friends in politics, government and business in Ottawa, Montreal and Quebec, and these connections were a prelude to my first important job with the Quebec government. In 1962, as a consultant, I became an adviser to René Lévesque on the nationalization of the power companies, and served as a member of the small task force which brought it about. For the next seven years I was appointed to a succession of similar task forces, usually as the only anglophone, working with Jean Lesage and Daniel Johnson, as well as with Lévesque, and getting to know many of the people who now either are leaders of the Parti Québécois or other political parties, or prominent in Quebec business or the law.

In 1969 I became chairman of the federal National Capital Commission, charged among other things with the task of developing the Quebec side of the National Capital Region. This brought me into direct contact not only with the Quebec government on a rather different basis than before – confrontation and negotiation, usually but not always amicable – but also into closer contact with Quebec politicians in Ottawa. In 1973 I resigned to do a study on the governing of the capital, and in September, 1974 was appointed by Premier Bourassa to head a provincial task force studying commuter rail transit in the Montreal region. My right hand man, Denis de Belleval, left in September 1976 to run and win as a Parti Québécois candidate, and to become a member of Premier Lévesque's first cabinet. I resigned in February 1977, partly to free myself to write this book.

That, briefly stated, is the story of my involvement with Quebec. What I learned about the province, its people and the rising separatist movement is recounted in the chapters which follow. The story may also throw some new light on Quebec events which have not been adequately covered by the press or by other memoirs or revelations.

Terminology

Every field of study has its own special vocabulary. So it is with the study of Quebec. The way that Quebecers think of and describe themselves, and the English Canadians, not only changes over time but has more subtleties than most English Canadians imagine. Going back to the eighteenth and nineteenth centuries, people from Quebec of French ancestry, the originals, called themselves *"les Canadiens,"* and the others, the latecomers, as *"les Anglais."* After union in 1841 of Upper and Lower Canada, the phrases "French Canadians" and "English Canadians" gradually came more into use; in my youth these were the words, sometimes shortened into "French" and "English," that we and they used. As the Canadian national consciousness grew, and "Canadians" became the word for us all, the Quebec French started looking for alternatives – "French-speaking," later "francophone," became the preferred words they used to describe themselves.

Since 1960 there has been a further switch to "Québécois" – Quebecer – signifying the growing importance of territoriality in the Quebec consciousness; the word originally meant a resident of Quebec City. A francophone Québécois, however, has a special perception of the word – it means someone who speaks French, has adapted to the culture, and accepted the point of view of the majority of "Québécois."

This has had some unfortunate racist connotations; the restrictive use of the phrase Québécois in the preamble to the Lévesque government's Bill One – Charter of the French Language – left the impression that English-speaking residents of Quebec don't qualify as Quebecers, or don't even exist; this was corrected in the successor Bill 101.

Puzzled by it all? I vary the choice of words in the book, although I do try to match the word to the times – use "French Canadians" more in the early period, "francophone" later, and still later "Quebecer" – someone from Quebec – occasionally qualified by "francophone" or "anglophone." But to use one word again and again is tedious, and once in a while I switch for the sake of variety. I hope no one will be offended by my refusing to take all the fine distinctions entirely seriously.

Another sensitive area concerns "separatism." This word has been officially expunged from the vocabulary of the separatists, and has been replaced by *"indépendantisme."* It all depends on how one looks at it – we federalists view the act of Quebec leaving Canada as "separating" the country into two parts. Members of Lévesque's PQ party – the word in common use to describe them is "péquistes" (from the French pronunciation, pay-keu) – see it differently, more like freedom from bondage. Quebecers describe their premier as "prime minister," partly because there is no French equivalent to premier, but also, according to many Quebec nationalists, because they see their government leader as the equal of the man in Ottawa. I use the two words interchangeably in the text.

Finally, a word about that great bogey of all writers of memoirs – the dangers of self-justification, of seeking revenge, or of over dramatizing one's own role in the scheme of things. There are some classic examples of this in Canadian political biography of recent vintage. I've tried to avoid these pitfalls, without complete success, but in the process of trying I'm beginning to understand one of the reasons why it is so easy to fall into the trap. No one participating in an event knows all the facts; a person has to take decisions on what is known or assumed. In recounting the story afterwards, how can he tell it "as it was," unless he bases it on his own limited view of the circumstances? Yet I must confess to a few guilty twinges as I tell my side of the story. I rather like former Quebec Liberal leader and cabinet member Georges-Emile Lapalme's apologia – if you can call it that – in his memoirs. *"Mais ces Mémoires sont* Mes *Mémoires. J'oublie ce que j'oublie; j'oublie ce que je veux oublier; je n'oublie pas certaines petitesses provenant des faux grands hommes."*[1]

A few personal notes

This is *not* a full story of my life, but rather that part of it which involved me with Quebec and Quebecers. I admit to digressing from time to time to refer to extraneous events, either to keep the chronology straight in the reader's mind, or because they have a bearing on events later in the book. Some friends of long standing will find it puzzling that they are not mentioned, but I have made a conscious effort to stay on the central theme – Quebec – and this has forced me to drop entirely, or barely touch, the story of my non-Quebec activities. A further problem is that in discussing some organizations in which I was involved, such as the Canada Council, the narrative is not balanced or well rounded, but dwells rather on how the experience affected my relationships with Quebecers, and my knowledge of Quebec's affairs. For all those who might feel slighted, I beg pardon.

A reader of this book will no doubt form an impression of me from it. Some of the things I say may be unintentionally revealing of the kind of person I am – as opposed to my persona, the face I want seen. But one thing about me has to be laid on the table right now, the fact that since earliest childhood I have been a stutterer. It affects my manner of speaking, which, direct enough as it is, seems even more blunt and aggressive as I hurry through or garble my sentences. I look back on my childhood and adolescence with horror – I see myself in school, stabbing my hand desperately in the air to show the teacher and class how smart I was, and at the same time praying I wouldn't be asked for the answer to the question, and forced to display my stutter, once again, to all. A stutterer lives with fear, with shame, with embarrassment, with frustration, with guilt. Periods of fluency make it worse; because of them he or she can never become fully reconciled to the ailment.

Enough of this self-pity; like most handicaps, stuttering has provided some compensations. I've been drawn to writing, pushed to it, to communicate more clearly than I can orally, which is of course another reason for writing this book. I think also, in a curious way, it may have helped me relate to French Canadians. Many of them have inferiority feelings with *"les Anglais"* – they may feel more at home with a flawed anglophone, someone who, like most of them, is not perfectly fluent in English.

Notes

1 Georges-Emile Lapalme, *Le Paradis du Pouvoir* (Mémoires, Tome III, Montréal: Leméac, 1973), p. 143.

II

Montreal – where the French-English issue is joined, and where I grew up – absurdly separate

Where did it all begin, my fondness for French Canadians? Could it have been my first remembered contact with them, that smiling conductor on the Cartierville car, who so carefully looked after the five-year old boy placed daily in his care? Certainly it must have been in Montreal, where I grew up, a city divided then even more than now between the English and French cultures.

Montreal is today a great and cosmopolitan city of nearly three million people, two-thirds of them francophones of Quebec origin, one-third mostly anglophones, of various racial origins. The city proper is on Montreal Island, but there are large and growing suburbs on the south shore of the St. Lawrence, in the City of Laval on Ile Jésus on the north side of the Rivières des Prairies, and in a scattering of other suburban centres around the periphery.

A city in which the residential pattern reflects the language division: the western part of the Island largely English-speaking, the centre mixed, with Montreal Island east of St. Lawrence Main Street almost exclusively French, as are many of the off-island suburbs. It is a city, however, in which the balance of economic power probably still lies with the anglophone group, although in recent years there has been a steady displacement of it towards the francophones. It is mainly in the English controlled industries and offices of Montreal that the French-English struggle – the new battle of Quebec – has been taking place.

Few French Canadians I have met did not have at least one story to tell me, or emotional bruises to display, resulting from their own experience with the dominant and domineering English in Montreal. A job missed because of imperfect command of English, or even just because of being a French Canadian. Business lost because the English dealt only with other English firms in a massive closely-knit network that included the wealthier clubs and golf courses, the legal firms that serviced the companies, the investment firms that raised money for them, the English banks on whose boards few French Canadians sat, and McGill University, whose graduates had priority.

But above all it has been the language question. Having to learn English to get work, having to speak it, day in day out, because so few English, even fourth or fifth generation English, "bothered" to learn the language of the majority. Rarely being able to function in English as well as in French – and being judged unfairly because of it. The wounds are there in every French Canadian, even the most federally minded, and they are deep. It is not just péquistes who are keen to change things, by coercion if necessary; French Canada feels that English economic power has been used and abused to discriminate against the French Canadians. These deeply-held feelings provide the roots of nationalist power in Quebec, and win strong support for the péquistes among the bourgeois, well-educated French Canadians in Montreal.

There have been changes, of course, and the situation I have just described was much more valid ten or fifteen years ago than it is today. The growing self-confidence and pride of French Canadians, the moral, political, and economic pressures that they and their leaders have exerted on English business, the toughness of new legislation to compel the use of French as a language of work, yes, and the federal bilingualism program, have all combined to induce business to accept "francization," as it is called, more readily than before. More French Canadians have been promoted to senior levels, and more English Canadians are learning to function in French; more French Canadians sit on boards of directors and belong to the Mount Royal and St. James's Clubs, and the largely francophone Club St. Denis has gained steadily in relative prestige. If English is still the main language heard in the Montreal corridors of power, French is a great deal more commonly used than it was even five years ago.

For the péquistes, however, the rate of change has been much too slow. Their language policy, elaborated in the PQ white paper issued on April 1, 1977, led to Bill 1, introduced into the Quebec Assembly on April 27. This new legislation contained restrictive and coercive measures to bring about francization more quickly. Towards the end of the book I will be commenting extensively on Bill 1, its successor Bill 101, and the language question, but it is in many respects a reaction to the historic anglophone role in Montreal.

In their analysis of this anglophone domination of Montreal, however, some French Canadians have a tendency to regard it more as a product of a malevolent conspiracy to keep French Canada in its place than a natural development of history. Montreal's growth was not mainly a by-product of the rising population of Quebec – a result of the "revenge of the cradle" hymned so often by Quebec nationalists. Montreal grew because Canada grew: it profited from its role as the chief railroad terminus in Canada, and as a port, and from the head offices and businesses which it acquired as a result. A second major stimulus was Prime Minister John A. Macdonald's national policy of protective tariffs, which brought about the expansion of manufacturing industry in the Montreal region to serve the Canadian market. When one considers the capital imported to make this growth possible, from the rest of Canada, England, the U.S., and the anglophone managerial talent that ran the businesses, one can begin to understand that there is a solid anglophone claim to special status in Montreal. Yet seldom do I see any péquiste references to this, or to the fact that, at the time of the Union of Upper and Lower Canada (Ontario and Quebec) in 1841, *half* of Montreal's 40,000 inhabitants were English-speaking. I commented on this in an article early in 1977, writing, "A language policy that does not take these (Canadian) roots and their consequences into account is denying the city's origins, and denying the facts of history. Montreal . . . is a special case and merits special treatment."

But in the Montreal to which I came as a baby, in December 1917, these issues were but dimly perceived. A crisis surrounding the proposed conscription for military service had blown up that year – the English for it, the French opposed – and it bitterly divided the two peoples. But the cause was more on the one hand a reflection of the loyalty and devotion of English Canadians to the British Crown, and support for British wars, and on the other to the attachment of the habitant to his farm and parish, and to his opinion, not dissimilar to that of many Americans, that it was a war in which he should not get involved. Looking back, I think the French Canadians took the more logical position – even if Canada is supposed to have "come of age as a nation at Vimy Ridge."

My father, Roy Fullerton, had come to Montreal in 1911 from his farm home near Sackville, New Brunswick. Gold medallist at Mount Allison, he received a scholarship to Harvard, where he obtained his M.A. in mathematics. He lectured briefly at McGill, and then, like so many other Maritimers of his generation and background, he took a teaching job with the Montreal Protestant School Board.

In 1914 he met and married my mother, Effie Henderson, of St. John's, Newfoundland. In the summer of 1917 she went down to her St. John's home to await the arrival of her first child, and, no doubt, to give it what she believed to be the best possible start in life, a Newfoundland birthplace. Three months after I was born she returned with me by train to Montreal. It proved to be a memorable trip; the Halifax disaster occurred after we left North Sydney for Truro. After waiting in the Truro station for twenty-four hours, while the relief trains went by, we finally made it to Montreal.

We lived then at 111 (now 3493) Hutchison Street, at the corner of Milton, just outside the area demolished recently to make way for a redevelopment project. In 1920 my father became the first principal of Devonshire elementary school on Clark Street, just above Pine, and several blocks west of St. Lawrence Main Street. It lay in the centre of the region immortalized by Mordecai Richler, directly in the path of the Jewish migration northward in the strip between the Main and Fletchers Field. A few blocks away was Baron Byng High School. Duddy Kravitz would likely have gone to Devonshire; Saul Bellow almost certainly did.

In the Montreal school system, the Jews and other non-French and non-Catholic groups were lumped in under the Protestant School Board; by 1925 some 95 per cent of the students at Devonshire were Jewish. My father communicated with parents who spoke only Yiddish by drawing on his graduate school German. He seemed to get along fine with them and with his Jewish teachers.

One of the interesting aspects of that very Jewish region near the Main was that it served as a buffer zone between the English and the French. It's still that today – as the Greek, Portuguese and other migrants followed the Jews up the same path from the waterfront, and have maintained their own particular ethnic individualities, and sense of neighbourhood.

I digress. In 1922 the family of four (my brother Robert was born in 1921) moved to 60 Bellingham Road, at the corner of Maplewood. It was in Outremount, but just across the street from Montreal. The house is gone now, and it is perhaps indicative of the trend of recent times that Bellingham is now called "Vincent-d'Indy," after a French musician, and Maplewood is "Boul. Edouard-Montpetit," for the former secretary-general of the Université de Montréal.

It was decided that I would go that year to kindergarten at Devonshire, held in the mornings. My father took me down with him on the streetcar, but each noon he would walk me up to Mount Royal Avenue, to rendez vous with the big yellow-orange Cartierville car which left always at the same time, 12.20 or so – and with the same French-Canadian conductor, in whose care my father would place me.

I can still see that conductor and his wide friendly smile; he had a gold tooth or inlay which must have intrigued me. The car stopped at the Maplewood corner some 100 feet from my home; he would hold the car until I was safely in the house. One day I tried to copy the big boys, and leaped off the open back platform before the car had stopped. Unfortunately, I slipped and fell, knocking myself out. He got out and carried me into the house, waiting until he saw that I had recovered. I remember the incident as clearly as if it had happened yesterday.

Still, it's a wonder to me how anyone of my generation, brought up in the nineteen twenties and 'thirties in Montreal, ever got to know a French Canadian, let alone form a friendship with one. We heard French in the street and on the streetcars, had our milk delivered by J. J. Joubert, were served in Eaton's by pleasant French-Canadian clerks – in English of course. All this no doubt conditioned us to think of French Canadians in a subservient role – and conditioned them to see *us* as people with lots of money. But the division was accentuated by the fact that we English Montrealers lived in different parts of town from the French Canadians, went to different schools, attended different churches, socialized among our own.

We rented the Bellingham house from the Soeurs des Saints Nom de Jésus et de Marie; it was situated at the western edge of the wide lawn surrounding the nun's convent school. In the early evening we would see the hooded sisters walking up and down alone or in pairs, praying or reading. The convent boarders were a bit more lively in their recreational periods, but my memory of that lawn is overwhelmingly one of solemnity, quietness and decorum. Occasionally I had to deliver the rent cheque to the bursar or nun designated to meet the public, and I never entered the convent without an uneasy sense that, as a male, I was violating some strict rule for which I might be held accountable. It seldom occurred to us then, but there we were, right alongside an important part of French Canada, and yet had no real contact with it.

My childhood playmates were almost all like myself – Anglo Saxon Protestants with names like Perham, Powell, Bryson, Howard. Most of us attended Strathcona Academy in the first two grades; mixed in with the predominant Protestants were a scattering of children of other immigrant families, mainly Jews. One incident recalls very clearly the climate in which we lived. After school one day, I brought little Emile Boosamra, presumably of Syrian extraction, home to play. I then thought he should stay for supper, and asked my mother, who to my surprise refused, saying "Douglas, you should play with your own kind."

Now she was a good, generous, God-fearing, church-going woman, who gave of her time and money to help the church missionaries convert the heathen. Yet probably the inconsistency never crossed her mind. It was just that God and circumstances had ordained us to be Presbyterians and British; we should stay within the boundaries of that heritage.

She had a pecking order of acceptability. At the top were the Scots Presbyterians (us); Methodists were one notch down, although she had married one (he switched). But the Roman Catholics she viewed with suspicion and fear. Newfoundland was a hotbed of religious divisiveness –

every sect, for God's sake, had its own schools – and the Catholics were dominant. In her eyes, the Pope, then at perhaps the zenith of his power, was a proselytizing holy warrior leading an army whose main goal was to convert the Protestants. As children we were regaled with stories of the iniquities inherent in mixed (Protestant-Catholic) marriages, with the sorrowful children being forced to be brought up as Catholics.

My father was more tolerant and open-minded on religious matters – his school experience having undoubtedly helped – but he too was active in the church. Most family friends were either Protestant school principals and teachers, church associates, or Newfoundlanders.

The religious war game we played was not atypical of the world in which we moved. Religion was much more important in those days than it is now, and it bred intolerance of other religious groups. A Jewish friend who lived in Outremont at that time told me how pained a Catholic friend of theirs was to hear his priest rail against the Jews, "the Christ-killers." If the Catholic clergy were more anti-Semitic than anti-Protestant, in the working world of Montreal French Canadians seemed to get along better with Jewish businessmen than with the Gentiles. Maybe it was because the Jews had taken more trouble to learn to speak French.

The Montreal school structure was an equally potent instrument of division; some of the municipal walls between schools have since been broken down, but it still consists of four separate systems: French Catholic, English Protestant, English Catholic, and French non-denominational. In February, 1977, after three years of intensive study, the Island of Montreal School Council voted to leave the system unchanged, as it has been largely for 100 years – all this in spite of strong support for a simple split along non-denominational English-French lines. Religious and language prejudice dies hard.

Even if school and church divisions had not kept us apart from the French Canadians, the tendency of each group to live with its own has proved to be an effective barrier. There was some mixing in the wealthier and boundary areas – notably Outremont and centretown before World War II, and Mount Royal and Westmount after the war – but the great mass of the proletariat lived, and continues to live, in remarkably unilingual areas.

What did I as a child think of all this? No doubt some familial and neighbourhood prejudices rubbed off on me, but I think I was saved from much of it by my own rebellious nature. For one thing, I became skeptical early in life about religion; this made it difficult for me to accept religious differences as of any relevance in making up my mind about someone. But I was never really put to the test, because until high school I had little exposure to French Canadians on a personal basis. And, to be honest, I was so immersed in my own stuttering problem in the 'twenties and early 'thirties, that I never gave much conscious thought to the matter of English-French relations.

In the fall of 1927, my parents transferred me to the elementary school (one class of each grade) at the downtown High School of Montreal – the school was regarded as a cut above average, and drew students from all over the city. Here I encountered my first French-Canadian class-mate, named Lagacé, from Cartierville. Several years later, in my final years at Montreal High, I was to meet three more – Alcide Ethier, Fernand Dugal and Jacques Pelland. All had been sent there to learn English, a frequent practice of ambitious French-Canadian parents.

We moved again in 1930 to 4701 Victoria Avenue, still Montreal but near the Westmount boundary. The area was predominantly anglophone, although there were several French-Canadian families living near us. Again my friends in the neighbourhood were almost exclusively English-speaking, although my brother had a good friend – perhaps his closest – named Bob Le Moyne, who has remained his close friend to this day.

One experience with rural French Canada is worth recounting. I spent the summers of 1930 and 1931 at the Eastern Townships' farm of John Cowan (father of a family friend) at the village of Gould near Scotstown. The area had been a centre of Scottish immigration, so much so that the service at the Presbyterian church was still carried on in the Gaelic (I was allowed to skip church by reading the collected sermons of evangelist Billy Sunday).

But the French-Canadian population explosion was at its peak, and farm after farm was being picked off by the advancing hordes of French-Canadian farmers with their large families. Gould still held fast, but the next township, at Lingwick, was solidly French. The Scots-Canadians not unnaturally felt threatened, and relations between the groups were strained. At election time, however, the divisions were along different lines; in the 1930 election I remember being, like Cowan and my parents, a rabid Conservative, even making speeches along the thirteen mile mail route, which he and I drove every day in a horse and buggy. Such electioneering was absolutely illegal, of course. Our man was Sam Gobeil, a garage owner from Lapatrie; he was the first politician I ever met. I can't say I was that impressed by him, but he was elected as one of the few Quebec Conservatives, and became Postmaster General in R. B. Bennett's government. Cowan kept his mail route.

In June 1933 I graduated from high school with my junior matriculation. Like most of my class-mates whose parents could afford it, I applied for entry to McGill University, just across University Street from Montreal High, and was accepted. The distance between high school and college, however, was to prove for me a good deal wider than the street itself. Things just didn't work out. I'd picked the wrong faculty for one thing, pursuing a romantic idea about research gleaned from such books as De Kruif's *Microbe Hunters.* Science soon palled on me, and the year turned into a disaster. Like so many present-day students I was in a mood of rebellion against the course, against my parents, against the frustration caused by my stuttering, against God knows what else. I skipped most classes after January to play bridge and billiards in the McGill Union. The university authorities called home to find out why I had "dropped out," and there was a culminating horror scene in early April, when my parents marched into the Union to find me cue in hand, about to take a shot!

Retreat from McGill

In disgrace, and out of work at seventeen, in the depths of the depression, things looked rather bleak. The family was not in financial difficulties; my father's job was secure, although his pay was cut by 10 per cent. We never had an automobile, electric refrigerator or washing machine, but because of my mother's poor health we managed a maid, Flossie, from the outports of Newfoundland. Still, for me to be idle was out of the question, and every connection we had was approached in the family effort to open some kind of a door for the errant boy.

Finally a relative working in Canadian Industries Limited lined me up a job as a messenger in the Montreal head office. I started in September at $30 a month. Success in this would bring promotion to the clerical staff, but a week or so before Christmas I was called into the sanctum of the personnel manager, Cyril Kossatkine, a former Russian prince. He told me that because of my stuttering, I had no future with CIL, and I was thereupon fired, with two weeks' notice. I protested, and he graciously allowed me to work the two weeks – to see if I could "get over" the stuttering!

I can now look back on the experience with equanimity, but it certainly confirmed a view I had slowly been acquiring, as the depression deepened – that businessmen were a bunch of bastards. Perhaps I was unfair; the government had been as much to blame for the depression as anyone. But I'm sure my developing attitude towards business made me a good deal more understanding and sympathetic toward French Canada's feelings about Montreal's English ruling class. Moreover, I suspect that my views were shared by most of the 90 per cent of English-speaking Montrealers who did low-level work for big business in the city. It's a pity that this fact has never been grasped by many French Canadians, who perceive English Montreal solely in terms of a stereotype – a wealthy boss, living in Westmount, growing rich by exploiting their labours.

Still, the French had quite a case. English was then overwhelmingly the language of business. French, like stuttering, was a very considerable handicap. Moreover, the English at least were more upwardly mobile; as my experience showed, many of us had a few connections who could help us find work. For the better educated, the ladders from the heights of Westmount were dangling down into our midst. If we earned the passport of graduation from McGill, we could aspire to climb and be received at least into the antechambers of the Montreal great. It was not so easy for the French Canadians.

Before finding my way back to McGill, and a chance to earn that essential passport, I still had some hurdles to surmount. Stuttering now being perceived as a major obstacle, my parents sent me to a school in Toronto to be cured. William Dennison (later to become a CCF member of the Ontario legislature, and still later mayor of Toronto) ran it, and we stutterers boarded at his home. If I was not cured of stuttering, at least I did learn for the first time to look at my ailment with more objectivity; my mental attitude improved, and with it came some lessening in the severity of my spasms.

I returned home in the spring of 1935, still looking for a job. A neighbour worked in the Whittall Can Company in Point St. Charles. (One of the owners lived farther up the street, and I knew his son.) He got me in there in June, working in the factory, seven in the morning to six at night – only six hours on Saturday – all for 15 cents an hour. It was my first brush with the realities of factory life – so noisy that I went home deaf every evening, exhausting (I lived an hour away by streetcar and bus from the factory), and deadly, deadly dull. Yes, $8.40 for a fifty-six hour week – excluding travelling time; weekly car fare cost 75 cents. A far cry from today, even if a dollar then had real value.

The job was, however, my first real encounter at a working level with French Canadians, although little communication with them was possible, except at the lunch break, because of the noise. I was regarded somewhat sourly by them and by the francophone foreman; I had been "parachuted" in from above, depriving one of their own people of a job – and in the depression. Furthermore I was not very adept at the work, cutting myself frequently on the tin sheets. Finally, a month and a half later, I was asked to work on a hot Saturday afternoon in July, without overtime pay; having other plans I told the foreman (*en français*) where he could stick his job, just as he told me to get the hell out. I informed my parents that I had decided to go back to take my senior matriculation at Westmount High, equivalent to repeating first year university. They were relieved. After passing my year, I found myself back at McGill in the autumn of 1936, in the second year of the four year Commerce course.

Return to McGill

McGill, Canada's second oldest university, had been founded by royal charter in 1821 out of a bequest of land and money from the will of James McGill. He had been a prominent Montreal merchant and member of the provincial legislature. As a university, McGill was noted more for its medical school and science faculty than for arts or commerce, but for us English Montrealers it was the place to go if one hoped to crash the gates of downtown business.

The links between McGill and that business establishment were broad and deep. The ultimate accolade denoting arrival at the top of Montreal's business community was an invitation to join the Board of Governors of McGill – a much more exclusive club even than English Montreal's finest, the Mount Royal Club, a few blocks west along Sherbrooke Street. The presidency of some of the more important Montreal institutions, such as the Bank of Montreal and the Canadian Pacific Railway, carried with it automatic election to the McGill Board. That great figure in CPR history, Lord Strathcona, was McGill chancellor from 1889 to 1914. Sir Edward Beatty, who became CPR president in 1918, was chancellor from 1920 until his death in 1943. During Beatty's term of office, every McGill board meeting, until his serious illness in 1941, was held in the CPR boardroom at Windsor Station. And Sir Edward ran McGill as he ran the CPR – with a tight rein.

In those days, of course, McGill was greatly dependent on donations from wealthy Montrealers for scholarships, for building construction campaigns, and for additions to its endowment funds. The businessmen came through, too, particularly before the 1929 crash. Most generous of all were the Macdonalds, of tobacco fame, whose name adorns a number of McGill buildings, as well as the agricultural college at St. Anne de Bellevue on the western tip of Montreal Island. The need for a continuing flow of funds from well-to-do graduates, and from other sympathetic Montrealers, undoubtedly helped shape the university's policies and student structure.

The McGill I went back to in the mid thirties was in many respects a replica of the downtown business establishment. The Greek-letter fraternities – an American import to be sure – rivalled in their social structure the men's clubs of business. Most of the sons of the wealthy became members of the wealthiest fraternities such as Zeta Psi, Alpha Delta Phi, Kappa Alpha, or Delta Upsilon. It was not only money these students had in common; most of them had attended private Canadian schools like Upper Canada College, Lower Canada College, Trinity College School, Ashbury; only Westmount High, of the local public schools, was at an acceptable level. Friendships were forged that were to serve them later in life, not least in landing positions downtown in the best law firms, in the investment business, or in the large corporations.

The French Canadians with some justification perceived McGill to be a key element in the anglophone structure which controlled business in Montreal and Quebec. Their attitude towards McGill may have been subtly influenced too by its location. On the slope of the mountain, but adjoining the downtown area, it seemed to gaze out benevolently and possessively over Montreal's commercial and business districts. The French Canadians not only saw McGill's physical place daily in the scheme of things in Montreal, but also observed with some bitterness the steady stream of McGill graduates, mainly WASPS, who each year collared most or all of the jobs in Montreal which led eventually up to the executive suite. McGill was a symbol, all right, to most French Canadians – that of Anglo Saxon Protestant domination.

A considerable number of French Canadians did attend McGill, but with the conscious primary goal of improving their English in order to get ahead in business or in their chosen profession. Most of them in fact were fairly anglicized by the time they reached the university level, and functioned in English as well as we did. So far as I am aware, in their job-hunting later they found little overt discrimination, although in those depression days jobs of any kind were hard to find.

If McGill accepted French Canadians who were prepared to take their courses in English, it is unpleasant to have to record another kind of discrimination at the university, one which reflected the prejudice of big business in Montreal against the Jews. Jews faced a variety of obstacles on entry to McGill, unwritten but nevertheless real. One was that a Jew needed 75 per cent to enter Arts and Science; another was a Jewish quota on medical school entrance. There were very few Jews in engineering; one reason I heard put forward was that there were no jobs in Montreal for Jewish engineering graduates.

There is still anti-Semitism in our society, I regret to say, but in those days it was widespread. The banks, the insurance companies, the investment houses, the law firms, and many of the large corporations, with very few exceptions, simply would not hire Jews. Such discrimination was not exclusive to Montreal of course – Toronto was probably as bad – but in Montreal it seemed more virulent, perhaps because its Jews were a larger minority within the English group.

It was not much consolation to French Canadians to know that the Jews were a notch below them in the scale of acceptability to downtown business but it did reflect the deep divisions then existing in Montreal society. Not just French-English, but WASP-Jew, rich-poor, establishment-outsiders, foreigners-us. The Jews fought back by working harder, becoming more adventuresome and more aggressive, by clawing their way into the upper levels of business – even finally breaching slightly that last bastion of all, the financial and investment community. The French reaction to the primacy of the English WASP establishment in Montreal, if in many ways as tribal as the Jews, was less individualistic. Not accepted into English law firms or businesses? Build our own, but continue to work through political and nationalistic organizations to achieve a reconquest of the levers of power. But if there has been a significant breakthrough of both Jews and French Canadians in Montreal's economic life – and if Jews, WASPS and French Canadians appear together today at the big society functions in support of the arts, or charity, or whatever, the social divisions remain – at least three solitudes, if not six or seven.

If French Canadians viewed McGill with a somewhat jaundiced eye, they were remarkably slow in adapting their own universities to supply the needs of business. There were only two French-Canadian universities, Laval, in Quebec, and Université de Montréal. Both were dominated by the Roman Catholic clergy who set the courses and provided most of the staff in undergraduate faculties. The priesthood was overwhelmingly the favourite choice of Quebec francophone parents for their children, with law, medicine and teaching the only competing professions. McGill may not have been very strong in social sciences, or in the commerce course which I took, but in the Quebec universities the teaching in such courses was more from a Catholic or humanist point of view. Our orientation was considerably more practical.

Certainly there was very little contact between McGill and U. of M. at the academic level, nor did we see much of each other on the field of sport. I can think of only one team contact sport in which McGill and U. of M. were rivals – hockey. I played a bit of football, but the college teams we competed against were either the Quebec anglophone institutions, like Bishops or Loyola, or, at the senior level, Toronto, Queen's, and Western.

One source of French-English dissension in the Montreal of the late 'thirties was the authoritarian régime of the government of Maurice Duplessis. In March 1937 it had passed a piece of regressive legislation, called "the padlock law," curtailing freedom of speech and placing considerable powers of arrest and seizure in the hands of the premier himself. Duplessis was a powerful figure, who could be vindictive towards his enemies. We reacted violently at McGill against the padlock law, organizing speeches and parades of protest. Most of the Catholic clergy supported Duplessis, and one day it was rumoured that the U. of M. students were going to "attack" the McGill Union. We readied our fire hoses (I was on the Union board), but nothing came of it. Still, the climate of English-French student relationships at that time probably could be described as unfriendly, if not hostile.

Yet I must admit that if these impressions of Montreal, of McGill, of the relations of the English with the French Canadians and the Jews, were making some subconscious impact on me, like most young men of my time I was much more interested in personal problems, and in the overhanging shadow of Hitler and war. Most of us by this time had become fully aware of what a waste of lives the Great War had been, and we could all see ourselves as coming to adulthood just in time for the next great slaughter. As Housman put it, "Life, to be sure, is nothing much to lose; But young men think it is, and we were young."

Hitler came through more or less on schedule, and my twenty-second birthday opened with a bang – the radio announcement that we were at war with Germany. I had decided earlier in the summer to stay on at McGill for a year's graduate work in economics, and, feeling no urgency about enlisting, went ahead with my plans. It was an uneasy academic year – our studies went on against the background of recruits marching up and down the campus to military tunes. In Europe the only military action to speak of, following the initial German *blitzkrieg* into Poland, was the Russian invasion of Finland; everyone was holding his breath about the western front. Whether this general air of tension affected me or not – or was just an excuse for me to avoid my studies – I couldn't concentrate, and just scraped by with an undeserved Master of Commerce degree. On May 23, 1940, I went to Ottawa to work in the statistical section of the Foreign Exchange Control Board (FECB), drawn to that city and war work by my growing interest in the economic problems of wartime finance.

III

Ottawa: Government, Gordon Commission, Canada Council

If one had to pick the single most important cause of the current separatist movement in Quebec, it would have to be the French-Canadian perception of and reactions to the dominance of anglophones and the use of the English language in the business affairs of Montreal. Yet not far behind this in importance would be the failure of English Canada to accept, until very recently, that French Canadians had a right to share in the administration of the federal government in Ottawa. Certainly the Ottawa in which I arrived in 1940, fresh from university, was in outward appearances a very anglophone city. English was *the* working language of government; bilingualism was a word used only in academic circles. In wartime Ottawa, as during the seventy-five years since Confederation, the unchallenged assumption was that French Canadians should be glad to serve their country in the language of the majority.

There were many French Canadians in the region; if Hull and the other communities on the Quebec side were taken into account, they made up over 40 per cent of the population of Ottawa's metropolitan area. If most of the French in Ottawa worked at menial tasks, there was a fairly well-to-do professional class, and the city's one institution of higher learning was the bilingual, but strongly francophone, University of Ottawa, run by priests of the Oblate Order.

But the French in Ottawa were not very visible to the new arrivals, come to town to get jobs and help themselves while helping win the war. In a strange way, like the anglophone existence in Montreal, we knew the French were there but had little contact with them. One exception was the main cultural event of the city – the Tremblay series of concerts.

Antonio Tremblay and his wife had built up the series during the depression, and attracted to Ottawa most of the great artists of the time.

The economic disparity between the French and English was perhaps not as great as the social gulf. Most English civil servants were not well paid – salaries then were well below those in the business world – but they had job security in the depression, most owned their own homes, and they were in a white-collar occupational class. I never noticed much animosity between the two groups, except perhaps over the conscription issue (the French opposition struck some sympathetic chords among my friends of military age). It was just that we lived mainly in different worlds. We, the English, accepting without much thought our economically superior role; they, the French, quietly resentful, nursing their historic grievances, focusing their attention on their church and on efforts to keep their language and culture alive in eastern Ontario.

Our feelings about the place of French Canadians in the scheme of things Canadian were reinforced when we looked across the Ottawa River at Hull. That city appeared to be filled mainly with ramshackle tarpaper houses – which we found out later was partly due to the fact that municipal assessment was based on the external appearance of the property. But Hull had two redeeming features. One was night life – booze, shows, girls, dancing and all that – of which there was little in strait-laced Ottawa. The other was Café Henri Burger, run by Madame Burger, a Swiss; it was the only decent restaurant (the Château Laurier Grill Room perhaps excepted) within fifty miles of the Peace Tower.

My next thirteen years were largely spent in Ottawa, and the story of those years is not particularly relevant to this book. Four years were in the army, largely in staff work at National Defence Headquarters, but including a nine-month stint in England. After the war I joined the federal civil service, working mainly in the Finance Department in the field of economics and statistics. I hardly heard a word of French at work from one year's end to the next; of all the departments, Finance was perhaps the most anglophone. A few French Canadians joined the staff about 1950, but they worked exclusively in English.

Most of our friends were English, but we did know some French Canadians. My wife Maudie, whom I had met early in the war when she was convalescing from a severe case of tuberculosis, had made friends with many French-Canadian patients in the sanatorium. She had been largely in the care of an excellent French-Canadian doctor, Jean-Paul Paris, without whose skill and concern she felt she might not have survived. Maudie had become a particularly close friend of Claire Menard, a fellow patient, and we visited often at the home of Claire's mother, Florida Sigouin, in Embrun, a village just east of Ottawa. This was my first introduction into French-Canadian family life, and the warmth and kindness shown to us by Mrs. Sigouin and her family was something we have never forgotten. When Claire married Dr. Jean Vigneau, after the war, their wedding reception was held at our home. Claire and Jean now live outside Montreal, and are still close friends.

In 1953 stuttering was again posing difficulties for me in my work. Government is run by committees – departmental and inter-departmental – both at the official and ministerial levels. A bureaucrat's progress up the ladder tends to be a function of how his performance at committee meetings is judged by his peers and by his superiors. Being bright and informed helps, but the game also involves quickness in dashing into a pause and grabbing the conversational ball. A stutterer finds this as difficult as presenting long, carefully reasoned, arguments; the flow is often chopped up by the stutter. There were even a few unprincipled bastards who moved in on me when I was in the middle of a speech spasm!

I went to Toronto to work on the stuttering (with Ernest Douglass), and while there took a part-time job with an investment firm, Harris and Partners. I liked the job and the people, and left the government. By 1955, however, I was again becoming restive. As luck would have it, one of my clients was Walter Gordon, a friend of Bill Harris. Gordon was a prominent chartered accountant and management consultant, who played an important role in government finance during the war years. He had a patrician bearing, and appeared a bit aloof, but in our discussions about his investments he was very straightforward – "Don't ask me, just go ahead and buy it if you think it's right" (I've always been attracted to good delegators!). Certainly he had a reputation of being a cool customer – and tough. He was still practising his profession, but was working behind the scenes with the Liberal party – and was increasingly drawn towards a more active role in politics himself.

In early 1955 Gordon showed me a speech he was planning to make, urging the federal government to examine the long term economic prospects and potentialities of Canada. The idea sounded interesting to me, and apparently struck a responsive chord in Liberal circles in Ottawa, notably with Gordon's good friend Mike Pearson (C. D. Howe, Minister of Trade and Commerce, his influence still great but waning, was reportedly not very enthusiastic). Out of it all emerged the Royal Commission on Canada's Economic Prospects, with Gordon as chairman. One thing led to another, and Gordon offered me a job on the research staff of the new Commission. I resigned from Harris and Partners and in May 1955 began my work with Gordon.

Royal Commission on Canada's Economic Prospects

Our Commission was to last over two years; what we produced at the end is still available in libraries in thirty-six or more volumes, in both official languages. The research staff was heavily weighted towards university professors; we had had a few recruiting problems, because it was widely believed that Gordon had protectionist and nationalist leanings, neither very popular among professional or academic economists.

Doug LePan, a scholarly diplomat from External Affairs, as well as a poet and writer, was Secretary and Director of Research; a good part of the writing of the Report was to fall on his shoulders. He also had the unenviable job of acting as a buffer between Gordon, a very strong-minded fellow when he wanted to be, and the research staff, a rather fractious bunch, headed by four assistant directors of research. I was one, the others being two bureaucrats, my friends Simon Reisman from Finance and Jack Davis from Trade and Commerce, and Bill Hood, a very bright economics professor from the University of Toronto. Davis was later to become a federal minister in Trudeau's cabinet, and still later to be a minister in the BC provincial government of Bill Bennett, Jr.

Like the economic departments of the federal government, we were pretty thin in French Canadians. Maurice Sauvé was one of two assistant secretaries, who organized the hearings in Quebec, and was ultimately responsible for getting out the translation of the report. Of the eighteen or so full-time researchers, the only French-Canadian economist was Yves Dubé, a professor from Laval, who had the adjoining office to mine. Dubé was intelligent, but suffered a bit from his inability to express himself in English as precisely as he could in French.

Maurice Lamontagne was involved in the final stages of the Report. A tall, lean, academic type, he was one of the few senior French Canadians in the public service at that time, having joined the Privy Council (cabinet) Office in 1955 as an economic adviser. He had graduated from the faculty of social sciences at Laval and then taught there between 1943 and his 1954 Ottawa appointment; while there he had been closely associated with Father Georges-Henri Lévesque, whose key role in the quiet revolution in Quebec will be discussed later in this chapter. Lamontagne was a confirmed federalist; in fact his 1954 book, *Canadian Federalism, Evolution and Problems* (Laval University Press), had challenged the traditional Quebec clerical and isolationist approach, and had sent shock waves through Quebec nationalist circles. In 1957, as our Commission was winding down, he left government – having been too closely identified with the Liberals – and went back to teaching economics at the University of Ottawa. The following year he became adviser to Mike Pearson who was then Opposition leader. Lamontagne ran unsuccessfully in the 1958 and 1962 campaigns in a Quebec City riding (his approach was a bit too high-brow, some people said, for the voters), but he won the safe Outremont-St. Jean riding in 1963 and entered the first Pearson cabinet.

I respected Lamontagne, and saw something of him during the next few years, but I became much closer to Maurice Sauvé. He was entirely different from Lamontagne – bulky, aggressive, impatient, blunt, with thinly veiled political and personal ambitions that didn't win him many friends – not the traditional charming French-Canadian politician at all. He had joined the Canadian and Catholic Confederation of Labour in 1952, following a degree in law and a Paris Ph.D. in Economics; he was on loan from them to the Commission.

While with the Commission he became involved with *Le Rassemblement,* an anti-Duplessis coalition movement in Quebec, which was established in 1956 to try to bring about democratic reform in the province. Its 600 members ranged across a wide spectrum from right to left, from federalists to separatists. They included Pierre Trudeau, Jean Marchand and Gérard Pelletier, as well as such well-known CCF members as Thérèse Casgrain and Eugene Forsey, and Jacques-Yvan Morin, later péquiste and prominent member of René Lévesque's first cabinet.

Le Rassemblement was too diverse in its structure to become an effective political instrument, but it was to help pave the way for the triumph of Jean Lesage's Liberal government in June 1960. When his work with the Commission came to an end early in 1958, Sauvé became active in the Quebec Liberal party as public relations director. He left that in 1962 to run in the federal constituency of Iles de la Madeleine (the Magdalen Islands) in the Gulf of St. Lawrence, won, and eventually became a minister in the Pearson cabinet.

Sauvé and his wife Jeanne did much to widen my Quebec horizons. I had never really given much thought to why the Quebecers were different than we were, why they viewed the federal government through different eyes, why they clung to their language and culture with such tenacity. Most of us in the Ottawa bureaucracy had acquired a rather stereotyped view of Quebec – priest-ridden, acquiescent to the rule of authoritarian leaders like Duplessis, inward-looking, too dominated by history. We viewed their intransigence in federal-provincial relations more as perverse, a wilful display of hostility towards Ottawa, than as representing a totally different view of federalism as a pact between two nations, French and English.

My understanding of French Canada grew with my next move. Early in 1957 I began to give some thought to what I would do when the Commission ended. In April, Brooke Claxton, former federal cabinet minister and then Canadian head of the Metropolitan Life, called to ask me if I would be interested in becoming treasurer of the Canada Council. This new Crown agency was being set up to "foster and promote the study and enjoyment of, and the production of works in, the arts, humanities and social sciences." Claxton was to be its chairman and my main

exterior; his inner fires had not been extinguished by the loss of his Laval deanship. Every one of us, members of the Council and the permanent staff, became very fond of him – not because of his symbolic role in Quebec, but simply because he was such a fine person. I remember when many Council members and staff, some with families, were going out by train in 1958 to a Council meeting in Vancouver, and the patience and humour he showed in handling the worshipful attention of our daughter Kate, aged four, who followed him constantly up and down the train for most of the trip.

The 1957 federal election campaign was taking place at the time the Council was launched, and Louis St. Laurent had lent his Parliamentary office as temporary Council headquarters for the director, Albert Trueman, and the associate director, Eugène Bussière. Trueman, originally from a small village in New Brunswick, five miles from my father's old home, was in fact a distant cousin. He had headed two universities and the National Film Board before his Council appointment. Eugène Bussière was a former student and associate of Father Lévesque's at Laval, and had been working in senior positions in the federal government, universities and at UNESCO in Paris in the field of adult education. He was a close friend of Maurice Lamontagne, and became a good friend of mine.

The Council received its $100 million on May 1, half as an endowment fund for the arts, humanities, and social sciences; the other half to be disbursed in university grants for construction. Towers and I invested it the same day in short term securities bought from the Bank of Canada. Our real work then began, to establish a long term investment program and to carry it out. I found immediately a significant difference between the English and French investment communities. All the large English firms descended on me like a horde of locusts, anxious to tap the new source of business. I must have been called on by twenty-five or thirty fairly high level Toronto investment types that first week or two.

Of the French-Canadian dealers in Montreal I heard from one only, Rodolphe Casgrain, son of the widely known Thérèse. I found out later that most of the other French-Canadian dealers (if they had heard of the Council) assumed that the road in lay through their political connections, and several M.P.s did call me on behalf of X or Y from Montreal. I was determined from the beginning to do something about this lack of contact in Montreal, and discussed it one day with Casgrain at his office. There was a City of Montreal bond issue coming up, and Rudy gave me, rather unselfishly, the names of the six largest French-Canadian investment dealers – all his strongest competitors – Lévesque Beaubien, Crédit Interprovincial, Geoffrion Robert, René T. Leclerc, and several others. I called on each firm that morning, asked to see the head man, and promptly gave him an order for $100,000 of the new Montreal issue – with my card. This was a most unusual procedure, since the institutional bond business is done almost entirely over the telephone, and it is the dealer who initiates most of the calls. They were all startled, but unquestionably pleased.

However, Montreal Mayor Jean Drapeau withdrew the issue from the market that afternoon, nullifying any orders, but my point had been made. I was canvassed regularly after that, not only by the firms I had visited, but by others as well; the story got around. I made many good friends in the Montreal investment community in the next months and years, enjoying their company socially as well as in business discussions. Among the group were Roly Giroux, who was later to head Hydro-Québec, Jean Ostiguy, Ginger Gingras, Louis Gélinas (later Senator), Jacques Boulanger, Michel David and Hubert Godin.

Other Council activities*

The Council members and staff became natural targets for every cultural organization in the country seeking money – and I have yet to discover any such body that was not always short of funds. This led to many invitations to openings, special events, concerts, mainly in the Montreal-Ottawa-Toronto triangle, but also in other Canadian cities. The Council believed it important to carry its message outside the somewhat ingrown eastern concentration of culture, and every year scheduled one or two meetings away from Ottawa, across the country from St. John's to Vancouver. The social functions accompanying these meetings formed part of the "spreading of the word," and senior staff members were always included. This naturally brought us into contact with many people prominent in the arts all over Canada. Of the francophones, I remember particularly the painters Jacques de Tonnancour and Alfred Pellan, musician Gilles Lefevre, who headed Les Jeunesses Musicales and almost singlehandedly ran its summer school for the young at Mount Orford, opera singer Louis Quilico, and Jean-Louis Roux and Jean Gascon of the theatre and TV.

The late Peter Dwyer, an enormously gifted Englishman who at one time had been prominent in the British Secret Service, joined the Council early in 1958 as Supervisor of the Arts Programme. Coming to Canada in 1950, he had worked first in the security division of the Privy Council

*I must warn readers that the emphasis in this recounting of the early days of the Council is much more on the role it had in broadening my connections with Quebec, and my awareness of Quebec issues, than in providing a comprehensive story of the Council's activities. The roster of French names might give the impression that the Council was heavily preoccupied with Quebec's affairs when in fact it did its best to allocate its resources equitably across the country – subject to the one overriding consideration that the principal cultural bodies it backed were centred in the largest cities, notably Toronto and Montreal.

Office, but his interest in the Arts led him into that area, and he had played a leading role in drafting the Canada Council Act. Urbane, witty, and bilingual, Dwyer was the right man at the right time for the Council, and we became fast friends. I wasn't much of an accountant, but I became involved often in appraising applications from organizations for grants, looking at them with a critical eye from the point-of-view of creditworthiness or just common sense.

One project in which Dwyer and I had a particular interest was the establishment of the National Theatre School. It was to be co-lingual, the brainchild of many Canadians prominent in the theatre, including actors and directors Jean Gascon and Jean-Louis Roux, and Pauline McGibbon (now Lieutenant Governor of Ontario), Mavor Moore and David Gardner. The Council members were not very enthusiastic – new mouths at our sparse table tended to be scrutinized pretty carefully – but this was an occasion when both Dwyer and I, with the solid backing of Eugène Bussière, were 110 per cent convinced of the merits of the school, and pushed hard for it. I think the clinching argument was that it would bring together in one place English and French drama students, all to be exposed to the rather different approaches of the English-language and French-language theatres.

The Council finally came through with $40,000; there was an initial grant from Quebec of $50,000, and it was with a considerable sense of satisfaction that we attended the opening of the school on November 2, 1960, in the decrepit old Knights of Columbus Hall on Mountain Street, in Montreal. The inaugural address was by Michel St. Denis, the great French director and teacher, who was the Honorary Artistic Director of the school. The school has since been a great success, thanks to the calibre of such people as Jean Gascon, its first executive director.

The French-Canadian members of the Council were particularly adept at opening windows for us all into the Quebec cultural world. Father Lévesque knew everybody; I remember one delightful impromptu concert at Maison Montmorency when tenor Richard Verreau sang for us, and other Quebec artists performed. A particularly close friend was Council member Andrée Paradis, director and editor-in-chief of the art magazine *La Vie des Arts* in Montreal. A charming woman, she was a great hostess; one lunch she entertained my family, including our son John, then ten. He somehow managed – while we were all enjoying the very lively conversation – to down a little too much wine. We had to walk him around in their garden for an hour or so to get him sober enough to drive off with us in the car! My essential point is that there was a "family" aspect to the Council at that time. Regardless of the changes in the Council's composition, as terms expired and new members were appointed, barriers between French and English, between east and west, seemed not to exist.

The Quebec City contingent of Council members included at various times Dr. Eustace Morin, Ginette Trépanier and Raoul Jobin. It was at Mme Trépanier's home in Quebec that I was later to have a memorable evening with Daniel Johnson. Jobin, former tenor at the Metropolitan Opera, headed the Conservatoire de Québec. His daughter married Jacques Pigeon, a friend of mine and son of lawyer Louis-Philippe Pigeon, who is to figure prominently in the next chapter of this book.

Marc Lalonde

One way the Council tried to get closer to the grass roots of Canadian artistic and intellectual life was through conferences which brought in experts or artists from all over Canada to discuss how the Council could best spend its money. One of these, on the humanities and social sciences, was held in Kingston at the end of December 1958. At one session I was greatly impressed by a twenty-nine year old law professor from the Université de Montréal named Marc Lalonde. He had a strong face, with a high forehead and a prominent Roman nose. He was clearly very bright, spoke and argued with great logic and precision – and in both languages. A few days later at home I was talking to Davie Fulton, who lived next door. He was then Minister of Justice in the Diefenbaker cabinet, and he told me he was looking for a good French Canadian to serve as an executive assistant. I told him about Lalonde and he checked him out, finally offering him the post. Marc took it and worked about a year and a half with Davie. I got to know Lalonde then, and indeed worked with him later when he came back to Ottawa, first as an adviser to Pearson, and then as secretary and adviser to his old friend Trudeau. Lalonde ran federally in 1972, was elected, and entered the cabinet.

Marcel Faribault

One of the most impressive Council members was the late Marcel Faribault, who had been appointed by Diefenbaker in 1959. A heavyset, powerful looking man of impressive bearing, he was a notary, president of the Trust Général, and a well-known Catholic Conservative. A man of scholarly interests, he reportedly preferred, for his bedtime reading, the Greek classics in the original. He was very much interested in constitutional issues, and his stand on Quebec, although moderately nationalistic, was more in the direction of "provincial rights" than separation. He felt deeply about the problem of Confederation, and one day had some Council members in tears as he spoke movingly about the need to hold the country together. In 1963 he and his good friend Bob Fowler, a prominent Liberal, jointly produced a book *Ten to One,* or, as they put it in the subtitle, "The Confederation Wager." In this book they proposed a new Canadian constitution and spelled it out in considerable detail.

The Duplessis ban on federal grants to Quebec universities had caused some $15 million to accumulate to their credit in our University Capital Grants Fund. Faribault had been working with his old friend, Paul Sauvé, who had followed Duplessis as Quebec Prime Minister, to free this money. Formerly secretary-general of the Université de Montréal, the *de facto* lay head, Faribault knew how strapped the Quebec universities were for funds. The matter was largely resolved by the time Jean Lesage became Quebec Prime Minister in June 1960 and the first grants were paid in 1961.

One problem we faced from the delay in payments to Quebec concerned the allocation of interest earned on the Fund's investments. Faribault argued, convincingly, that this income should be allocated on the basis of each province's undrawn balances, as in a trust fund for beneficiaries of an estate. This "hotch-pot" concept, although it clearly favoured Quebec because its share of the fund was still intact, made sense to Council staff members, and we adopted it. Maxwell Henderson, the Auditor General, challenged this approach, arguing that the Act said that interest as well as capital had to be divided according to the basic "provincial population" formula. Our legal adviser supported us; Henderson stood fast. I was instructed to get another legal opinion, and went to Marc Lalonde, who had by then left Fulton and was in legal practice in Montreal. He gave us a second supportive opinion, so we stood fast. For several years, Max kept sniping at us in his annual reports to Parliament, but finally gave up, if only because by that time most of the money had been paid out to the universities.

Meetings with Quebec politicians

A federal-provincial conference had been scheduled in Ottawa a few days after the Quebec election in June 1960. I knew that Maurice Lamontagne had been hurriedly drafted to help the newly-elected Jean Lesage prepare his speech for the conference, and I volunteered to help. I also wanted to meet Lesage and give him my views on Quebec's bond financing, and also to sound him out on the possibility of my going to Quebec in some advisory role, perhaps even as a bureaucrat in the debt management field. Lamontagne accepted my help – I prepared several pages on investment and economic matters – and lined up a meeting for me. Jean Lesage, a good looking, confident man, was finding his first few days in office somewhat hectic. He hadn't much time for general discussion, and our talks were inconclusive. We parted, amicably enough, not to meet again for several years.

In my Canada Council capacity, however, I later met several of his ministers in Quebec. Paul Gérin-Lajoie, years later to become a federal official in Ottawa as head of the Canadian International Development

Agency, was then Lesage's Minister of Youth and later the first Quebec Minister of Education. Surprisingly, he was then one of the most nationalistic members of the Lesage cabinet; if we at the Council had been expecting a change in the wind with Duplessis dead and the Union Nationale defeated we were soon disabused. Gérin-Lajoie's reception of our Canada Council group in Quebec was correct, if formal, but the atmosphere was icy.

Minister of Cultural Affairs, Georges-Emile Lapalme, also did not go out of his way to make us feel at home. This may have been due as much to his offhand, almost distracted, manner, as to his nationalism. Like Lesage he had been a federal member (1945 to 1950), and had been Opposition leader in Quebec from 1953 (following George Marler) until replaced by Lesage in 1958. Certainly his interests seemed to be more intellectual and cultural than political; his memoirs from which I quoted in the first chapter[2] are delightfully written – a kind of self-interrogatory, stream-of-consciousness approach. He too figures in the nationalization story in the next chapter.

Another move

Early in 1962, after five years with the Council, the need for a fresh challenge was becoming stronger. I was in the process of writing a textbook on the bond market[3], and was interested in putting into wider practice an approach to bond investing that I had been following in the management of the Council's portfolio – that of actively trading bonds, instead of putting them away and forgetting them. Jack Mackenzie, a bond man with an investment firm, had similar ideas, and in March 1962 we formed Fullerton, Mackenzie and Associates (FMA), offering our bond advisory services to institutional investors and to individuals. I resigned as treasurer of the Council, but we kept the Council as a client. Resignation from the Council did free me in another way; it allowed me to branch out and take on work other than simply handling or advising on bond transactions. Within a month, in fact, I was to meet René Lévesque, and to begin shortly thereafter nearly fifteen years of direct contact with the Quebec government.

Notes

1 Conrad Black, *Duplessis* (Toronto: McClelland and Stewart Limited, 1977), pp. 474-486. See also Robert Parisé, *Georges-Henri Lévesque, Père de le renaissance Québécoise* (Montréal: Alain Stanke Ltée.).

2 Lapalme, *op. cit.*

3 Douglas Fullerton, *The Bond Market in Canada* (Toronto: Carswell Company Ltd., 1962).

PART II
Adviser to Quebec

IV

René Lévesque and nationalization of the power companies – 1962

The business of Fullerton, Mackenzie and Associates did not develop as quickly as we hoped it would. Naturally we were out looking for clients, and my study of provincial financing, for purposes of my bond book, led me to conclude that Quebec could profitably use our services as bond advisers. Although I had respect for A.E. Ames and Company and the Bank of Montreal, the province's principal bond underwriters and financial advisers (I had good friends in both places), I believed that they had been unimaginative in tapping new sources of funds for the province. I was also opposed in principle to the idea, cherished by most large bond houses, that regular borrowers would benefit by restricting themselves for advice to one firm or group of underwriters – theirs! Since this chapter and the next touch frequently on bond underwriting matters, it is perhaps appropriate for me to outline briefly how the system works.

The underwriting of bond issues may sound complicated to the uninitiated but it is simpler than it appears. Groups of investment dealers band together as "syndicates" to underwrite – guarantee the sale – bonds issued by government and corporate borrowers. They do this because seldom is one firm large enough, or financially strong enough, to accept the risks inherent in buying for resale a large amount of bonds, sometimes $100 million or more, from the issuer. Moreover, the more firms that are involved, the greater the prospective coverage of potential buyers, normally large financial institutions, such as insurance companies and pension funds, but often including individual retail buyers.

The investment dealer with the largest syndicate share is normally the manager, and carries out regular liaison with the borrower about the terms of new issues. This naturally gives him a continuing and preferred relationship with the client, for rarely is one syndicate dropped and replaced by another. One weakness in this system is that it limits competition and restricts the sources of advice available to borrowers, a particularly important consideration for Canadian provinces which have to go frequently to the market.

A role for us in Quebec?

Well, we were ready to help Quebec out on advice. But what was the best way to make contact? My meeting with Jean Lesage after the June 1960 election had not been very fruitful, and all premiers or prime ministers soon develop a protective circle around them that is difficult for outsiders to penetrate without invitation. I talked to Maurice Sauvé, and he offered to line up an appointment for me with René Lévesque, the Quebec Minister of Natural Resources, whom he felt would be sympathetic to my thesis. For some time Lévesque had been beating the drums inside the cabinet, and publicly, for the nationalization of the privately owned power companies. The main opposition from his colleagues, one gathered later, usually took the form of the question, "But, René, where will the money come from ?"

The nationalization issue had several roots. One was economic. There were two main electric systems functioning in Quebec: one publicly owned, Hydro-Québec; the other a bevy of private companies, of which Shawinigan Water and Power, and its Quebec Power subsidiary, were by far the most important. Hydro-Québec was a wholesaler of power to the private companies, but also had a large retail market in the Montreal area. Shawinigan was also a primary producer, but its main income came from industrial and retail markets outside of Montreal. The growth of demand in Quebec was causing all kinds of problems – who should expand, where, and at what prices. The lines connecting producers and consumers were in danger of becoming a tangled web. Shawinigan, for example, constructed a steam generator at Tracy, with power costing seven mills, double the cost of Hydro-Québec's new hydro development at Manicouagan.

Something had to be done to rationalize the system. Ontario had set up its own publicly owned system in 1906, and its role expanded steadily until virtually all production and distribution in the province came under its control. The model was established; why shouldn't Quebec follow the same path? In fact, had there been no nationalization, developing conflicts would have forced some kind of a restructuring and co-ordination of the industry. Strong further arguments in favour of the provincial ownership route were that the private companies paid income taxes to the federal government, and that wide differences existed in electricity rates charged across the province, damaging the competitiveness of the poorer regions.

But there were other, more nationalistic arguments as well. The largest of the private companies were controlled by the Montreal English establishment. Hydro-Québec had become an important element in the picture only in 1944, when it had been created by the Liberal Godbout government to take over the Montreal Light Heat and Power Company, and begin a program of rural electricification. The battle against the "electric trusts" had been carried on for years before that, led by two doughty political warriors, Dr. Philippe Hamel and Télesphore-Damien Bouchard. Hamel, a dentist, was a nationalist in the Quebec clerical tradition, and had joined the Union Nationale in the expectation that Duplessis would take action on nationalization. However, it was Bouchard, former journalist, a strong anti-nationalist, and a very independent member of the Godbout cabinet, who finally succeeded in bringing it about – less on grounds of nationalism than of populism and common sense.

It is interesting that in René Lévesque's pantheon of Quebec heroes in his 1967 book *Option-Québec,* he names Hamel but not Bouchard.[1] Perhaps he recalled Bouchard's first speech as a Senator in 1944, which Conrad Black says was "the most controversial in the history of the federal Upper House . . .[it was] a résumé of all his anti-clerical, anti-isolationist, liberal, Liberal, views." Bouchard is quoted as saying that after leaving school "I learned that Canadians of English descent were not all cloven-footed and did not all bear horns . . . Why had I been led to believe these sillinesses? . . . Since my infancy I had been taught that everything the French Canadian had to suffer came from the fact that he was of French and Catholic descent." We must "stop a subversive propaganda . . . which could bring us before long to mob rule and even civil war, prompted by a racial hatred insidiously instilled into the souls of French Canadians by a wrong teaching of Canadian history . . . The worms are gnawing at the roots of the tree of our liberties."[2]

Bouchard is high on my list of Quebec heroes. We could use a few like him these days – his vigorous statement could hardly be more topical. Yet he paid for his frankness; several days after his Senate speech, when he was attacked by all the nationalists from Duplessis down for having "denigrated Quebec in the eyes of outsiders," he was fired as Hydro-Québec president.

René Lévesque

Anyway, at 11.00 AM, on April 30, 1962, I called on the Hon. René Lévesque at his office on the seventeenth floor of the new and impressive

Hydro-Québec headquarters on Dorchester Street. I knew a bit about Lévesque's alleged antipathy towards the English community, and was expecting a rather wary and cool reception – much as I had encountered with the few Quebec ministers I had met during my days as Canada Council treasurer. My experience had also taught me that even the most human of ministers develop an increasing sense of self-importance and isolation from the herd after a few years in office.

What did I find? About as warm a welcome as I could imagine – no prefatory or formal words in French to put me in my place just, "Come on in, Maurice has told me all about you, have a cigarette (as he lit one from his butt). Coffee? Fill me in on the bond market." Fifteen years later it is difficult to recall much of the detail of the discussion, except that I gave him some draft chapters of my book which touched on provincial financing, told him where I thought Quebec's borrowing approach had been deficient, and offered our firm's services. We may have talked briefly about nationalization of the power companies, but one thing he did make clear to me was his own dissatisfaction with the Ames-Bank of Montreal underwriting monopoly. I sensed that some of this may have been because they represented the quintessence of the old Montreal Anglostocracy for which he had little respect or liking. He asked me to put something on paper about my view on Quebec and Hydro-Québec financing, and I agreed.

Memory may play tricks about our discussion, but what remains very clear to me today is that I left the meeting feeling that a good rapport had been established, that he was a direct and honest man whom I could trust, and that he was simply loaded with that appeal which these days we call charisma. Put another way, I suppose, he charmed me out of my boots.

After seeing Lévesque I dropped in downstairs to touch base with an old McGill classmate of mine, Ed Lemieux, who was then Director General of Finance with Hydro-Québec. We talked briefly about financial markets, and I gathered that he too was not entirely happy with the existing underwriting situation. We agreed to maintain contact; during the next few years we worked together on a number of things, including attempts to open up the syndicate monopoly. But of that more in the next chapter.

On May 2, I wrote Lévesque a letter with my comments about problems facing Quebec in the market, including the sharp increase in its borrowings, the fear of conservative buyers about the radicalism of the Lesage government (including threats to take over Shawinigan Water and Power!), and, I added, "Separatism is a distant shadow still, but a consideration in the eyes of some buyers."

I criticized some aspects of the present underwriters, including the excessive dependence on the Canadian market and on long term bond issues. Although I did say that Ames and the Bank of Montreal had "done a good job of distribution of new issues," I suggested experimenting with new types of short term instruments (Treasury Bills, Savings Bonds, etc.), more competition among the underwriters, and proposed the co-ordination and centralized direction of all provincial sinking and pension funds to make a better market for Quebec bonds once the initial distribution of a new issue had been completed. Finally I said that these proposals required further elaboration and study, suggesting that we were just the people to carry it out and to provide professional management for the various funds referred to above. I have no record of receiving a written reply, although I seem to remember a 'phone call thanking me for the information.

Lac-à-l'Epaule

Towards the end of August, Maurice Sauvé called me. Jean Lesage had asked him to try to find an independent opinion about the province's capacity to borrow. The cabinet debate on nationalization had become increasingly bitter with René ranged at one extreme, former Liberal leader and Montreal notary, George Marler at the other, and Jean Lesage himself in-between but strongly influenced by the caution of Marler and the underwriters. Sauvé said the matter was urgent, because the cabinet would be meeting at Lac-à-l'Epaule on the Labour Day weekend (September 1 – 3). He asked me to dine a few days later, August 31, at his Outremont home. Lévesque would be present, and would I bring along a memo stating my professional opinion on the capacity of the province to raise the additional sums needed to finance the proposed take-over of the private electric utilities in the province, with the new money required (additional to outstanding company bonds) put tentatively at $350 million? You bet I would, but for some reason – perhaps because I wanted the arrangement to be clearly official – I asked that the request for my services be put in writing.

I prepared a letter, in part based on my letter to Lévesque May 2, which covered every aspect of the question I could think of, and concluded ". . . we are firmly of the view that the Province could raise the money needed to purchase the private utilities, providing (a) it is prepared to undertake some changes in the sources of its borrowing; (b) the nationalization is carried out in such a way as to minimize the effect upon buyer attitudes; and (c) that sinking funds and other funds available to the province are mobilized to support the market for Quebec issues." Off I trotted to dinner, clutching the letter dated September 1 (the following day), arriving at the appointed time.

René didn't turn up for an hour, but I had a good chat with Maurice and Jeanne while we waited. When he came we dined and then discussed the contents of the letter, after he had formally presented me with his written request, as Minister, for my professional advice, "... on the bond market implications of increased borrowing by the Province of Quebec, with particular reference to the possible effect upon the Province's credit of the nationalization of a number of private electric power companies." Both letters are in Appendix One.

He seemed to like my line of argument, and left about 11.00. As he walked down the path, he turned towards us waving and still talking – only to fall ass-over-teakettle into the excavation for a new sidewalk. He came back in, embarrassed, one arm bleeding profusely. Jeanne doctored him up, we all had another drink, and away he went, this time safely.

The Lac-à-l'Epaule meeting was held, and the rest, as they say, is history. After a further bitter debate, the cabinet decided unanimously not only to go ahead with the nationalization, but to call an election based on it. Stories of the meeting are a bit conflicting, but Georges-Emile Lapalme, former Liberal Opposition leader, whom I had met in Canada Council days, provides some fascinating glimpses in his memoirs.[3]

Lapalme compares René Lévesque's pursuit of nationalization to Mao's Long March. He cites René's lack of cabinet discipline in debating the issue publicly, but told how he was followed around by journalists as he lectured them on the merits of his proposals. Lapalme said "Electricity had become an adorable political fairy." He noted that although Jean Lesage had been strongly opposed "until the last minute," Lapalme says that he himself had become convinced by Lévesque several months earlier. Yet at Lac-à-l'Epaule, the question finally only came up the middle of the second day – everyone had been dodging it – when Lapalme asked Lesage bluntly "What are we going to do with René's proposal? Do we, or do we not, nationalize Shawinigan Water and Power?"

Lesage, caught off guard perhaps, gave Lévesque the floor and he made an impressive pitch, although the $600 million total cost had given some ministers pause. Finally Lesage asked Lapalme "Georges, what do you think? If you agree with René, what would you say to an immediate election based on it, if everyone agrees?" "It was the answer to a virgin's prayer," says Lapalme, and he gave his support – and everyone went along, even Dr. Couturier – who said he would be beaten by it in his own riding!

Since the opposition had centred around the cost question, my letter may have strengthened Lévesque's case – but I doubt if I'll ever know. I'd like to think I influenced this important decision in Quebec's history – a tiny footprint of mine in the sands of time? – because I was whole-heartedly behind the decision.

The election was called for November 14, and the campaign slogan chosen was *"maîtres chez nous"* – masters in our own house. Lévesque in particular promoted the power issue during the campaign, although I would have preferred a less emotional and nationalistic line of argument. As I noted earlier the more I looked into it, the more I became convinced of the economic logic of nationalization. But economic logic seldom wins elections, which the politicians sense more keenly than I.

Nationalization proved to be a good election issue, and on November 14, the Liberals won sixty-three of the ninety-five seats, a gain of twelve. On the morning of November 23, my 'phone rang; it was René Lévesque, "Would you be able to join a task force under Lesage's legal adviser, Louis-Philippe Pigeon, to begin work immediately on nationalization?" Would I? I'd been building to this moment since spring! He then suggested that I meet Jacques Parizeau in Montreal the next morning (Saturday), and then go to Quebec City to talk to Michel Bélanger, his director general of planning. Parizeau had done a report on which the $600 million overall cost estimate had been based.

I had met Jacques a few months earlier when Jack Young and he, as staff members of the Porter Commission, had interviewed me about the impact on the bond market of the Bank of Canada's administration of monetary policy. I had been impressed by him, had found him bright and informed if a bit intense, although I sensed in him then a certain feeling that he should have been assigned a more important role in the scheme of things than he had been given at the Commission. He was to find a more satisfying niche fourteen years later as Minister of Finance in the Lévesque government.

We hadn't much time to talk that morning, however; he simply gave me a copy of his report. I had to dash off almost immediately, along with my partner Jack Mackenzie, to catch the plane for Quebec to meet Bélanger. The three of us had a good discussion over lunch at the Georges V across from the Parliament Buildings, and Jack went back to Montreal.

I found Bélanger, then thirty-three, very *sympathique* – direct, sensible, with a clear idea of our prospective course of action, and a good understanding of the internal workings of the Lesage government and who was who in the power structure. He had spent some time with the federal government in Ottawa, in the Finance Department and on the Borden Committee on Energy. Like Parizeau, he too was destined for high places in Quebec; he later became deputy minister of a number of provincial departments, and then left government in 1973 to become president of the Montreal Stock Exchange and, in 1976, president of the Provincial Bank.

Michel had also been one of Father Lévesque's students, and had been influenced by him. He had nationalistic feelings, of course, but I never sensed in him the same commitment to the cause that I had found in some others with whom I worked in Quebec. He had a great facility for getting on with people – never seemed to jar them, as Parizeau sometimes did. In fact, in a *Financial Times* story on him (February 21, 1977), Joan Fraser cites a former colleague as describing him as "lovable" – a most unusual phrase to describe a bank president – and who said "He inspires loyalty, enthusiasm and confidence, but at the same time he is a humble and modest man with no complexes and no hot air." A good description, to my way of thinking: I have met no one in government or business I liked more.

I had arranged through Father Lévesque to stay during the week-end at his order's Maison Montmorency, a few miles east of Quebec, and I went into a kind of retreat there to study Parizeau's report and all the documents about Shawinigan and the other power companies that Jack and I had hurriedly collected the day before. But I still felt uneasy about my meeting with Pigeon on Monday, since I sensed it would be crucial. Michel Bélanger had spoken highly of his talents, but suggested that some people found him formidable.

In any event, I did my homework as best I could and turned up Monday after lunch to meet Maître Pigeon. I had a general idea of how I thought the affair should be handled: my notes list a number of topics and principles which I proposed to raise:

- A public offer for stock was the only sensible approach; any direct deal with Shawinigan and the others based on asset or replacement value was to be avoided at all costs.
- If the offer was to be successful it had to be measurably above current quotations; this meant we had to move quickly and in total secrecy; any leak would frustrate our objectives.
- "Value" had to be based on earnings, and probably on earnings only, but it also must be judged fair by majority of shareholders, and by U.S. financial markets; it would help if the values set were attacked, but not too violently, by the directors of the affected firms, and were mildly criticized as "too generous" by the opposition in the Assembly.
- Litigation and expropriation were to be avoided except as last resorts – bad for the province and for shareholders.
- Nothing should be done to disturb the status of the outstanding company debt (some $235 million at an average interest rate of about 4 per cent); if it had to be paid off, it would add to interest costs and raise the borrowing requirements substantially.
- The method of value should be consistent, but built around the Shawinigan calculation; that company's worth was approximately two-thirds of the estimated $600 million total for the eleven companies combined.

Pigeon received me on November 26 in a businesslike if formal way;

we wasted no time in getting to the heart of things. I was pleasantly surprised to find that he knew a great deal about financial markets, and that he had thought out the approach and had come to almost identical conclusions. He said that the task force would be called together shortly; meanwhile he related to me his discussions with Jack Fuller, president of Shawinigan, and other company representatives. Fuller had put forward proposals to the government for the purchase (or expropriation) of its assets; we both felt that, if only as a smokescreen, his talks with the Shawinigan people should continue.

I was to work closely with Pigeon over the next few years, and to discover what a remarkable person he was. His legal career speaks for itself: early years with Louis St. Laurent's firm, legal adviser to Premier Adélard Godbout during the war, and to the Opposition between 1944 and 1960, when the Union Nationale was in power; defended labour in many celebrated cases during that interregnum; legal and principal adviser to Premier Lesage, 1960-66; professor of law, Laval, 1942-67; bâtonnier of the district of Quebec 1960-61, all leading ultimately to his Supreme Court appointment in 1967.

Yet Pigeon was much more than an outstanding lawyer. He had an incredible catholicity of interests, and was particularly proud of his engineering skills. He prepared the plans for and built his Quebec home, and had wired it for sound, had built his own stereo system, had his own photographic studio, had built a 200-foot electric train system with his boys – in many ways, I think he felt he had missed his calling. Once, when the Duplessis Bridge at Three Rivers developed some cracks, Pigeon inspected it and told George Marler, then Liberal Opposition leader, that it would fall. It did, several months later.

But even that misses the real Pigeon, which is conveyed more by the stories about him which still circulate among Quebec lawyers – his foibles and mannerisms. His voice would go up a full octave when excited – "But you seeeeee . . . (his voice rising) . . . Mr. Fullerton . . ." This is one of my favourite stories: while a junior in his law firm, he was in charge of the file of an important client, but Louis St. Laurent himself thought he should take it over for a meeting. As his senior partner presented the firm's views, Pigeon busied himself at the end of the table balancing a heavy ashtray on a piece of string, held between his hands. Annoyed, St. Laurent stopped abruptly, asking Pigeon to carry on. Without missing a beat – and still balancing the ashtray – Pigeon made a masterful presentation.

One contact with English Canada had bruised Pigeon badly. While with St. Laurent, he had done a good deal of work for one of the large English law firms of Montreal; feeling the need for some more experience in English, he enquired through a contact about entry into the firm, only to be told "they don't hire French Canadians."

The task force

I was given the green light to go ahead as quickly as possible on the valuation of all the common and preferred stocks; Mackenzie had already been busy quietly seeking out market analyses or opinions of the value of Shawinigan and the other companies, and we enlisted the co-operation of the Montreal Stock Exchange to obtain data about transactions going back six or seven years. Eric Kierans, then president of the Montreal Stock Exchange, told me years later that he had guessed what was going on, but had kept it to himself. Kierans was soon to be in the Lesage cabinet, and became a close friend.

I had one other valuable source of information; I had recently been an expert witness in a British Columbia court case involving Premier Bennett's take-over of the B.C. Power Company, appearing for the holders of the convertible bonds. I knew that a great mass of material on valuation of power companies had been collected during that trial, along with relevant judgments, and was able to obtain this from Charles Locke, the lawyer who had retained me in the BC case.

The task force which met a few days later was composed of six people: lawyers Roger Létourneau of Quebec, and Claude Ducharme of Montreal (both active in the Liberal party hierarchy); Lucien Bélair, senior partner of the Samson, Bélair firm of chartered accountants, and Bélanger, Pigeon and myself. The two outside lawyers, able as well as personable, were assigned the specific task of following up the legal implications of the prospective offer, such as provincial and federal laws, stock exchange requirements, position of U.S. and other non-residents, and so on. Bélanger was to liaise with Hydro-Québec, keep René Lévesque informed, and in general to represent the bureaucracy; Pigeon filled in Premier Lesage, met representatives of the companies, and co-ordinated the work of the task force.

The group worked very well together as a team; if Philippe Pigeon dominated it by the force of his intellect and his relationships with Lesage, he was a good listener – and none of the group was particularly shy about putting his ideas forward. The others spoke French most of the time. Usually I stuck with my English; whenever I felt I had missed the precise meaning of the French dialogue, they would summarize it in English for me.

It was my first real baptism in a francophone working group, and I found it tiring. Two things eased the burden. One was the warmth with which I was received by all members of the group. Nothing was kept from me, even in my first discussion with Bélanger and Pigeon; they assumed that I was committed to their goal as much as they were. There was no swearing of oaths of secrecy (a bit different from Ottawa); it was taken for granted I could be trusted. I was to encounter the same warm reception and trust in similar situations later. Often the sole anglophone member of a francophone task force, I half-expected to receive an occasional snide comment. I was kidded a bit from time to time, but everyone went out of his way to make me feel welcome and at home.

The urgency and excitement of the task also made things easier. We were working in secret and against the clock, and there was a conspiratorial atmosphere surrounding our discussions. Only the six of us, plus Lesage and Lévesque, knew what was going on. Even my colleagues in FMA, however much they guessed the approach, were always kept aware of the possibility of alternative courses of action which might have to be taken at the last minute.

As the December days went by the excitement mounted. One thing we all feared was a leak that would send up the price of the stocks. Shawinigan was a special concern, because of its overwhelming importance, and because its eight million common shares were widely distributed and traded actively. Meanwhile I had been working feverishly, with the help of my colleagues, in putting together a draft report covering procedures and valuation; by December 16, I had a draft ready, and had it typed and circulated. The group discussed it on Tuesday the 18th; revisions were made, but nothing of substance was changed.

Meanwhile, Shawinigan common had been steady as a rock. From November 28 to December 21, almost every trade was in the $24 to $25 range. We had made arrangements to be kept informed of any bids for blocks of stock, and to be given the names of brokers who were active on the buying side of Shawinigan. Nothing of note happened; the other stocks were similarly stable.

Although the subject is now academic, our method of valuation took account of all the usual approaches – price-earnings and cash flow ratios, physical assets, book value, earnings trends, dividend yields, market performance. We placed the greatest emphasis on past and current earnings performance and future earnings prospects. As one investment analyst noted at the time, "A battery of accountants, appraisers, lawyers and politicians will throw figures into the ring, concerning future potential (who knows), as well as such items seldom considered by the stock market, such as depreciation and replacement value. Earnings *under ordinary circumstances*, are worth about ten times as much as all other considerations put together."

However, I tested the results of our valuation against a sampling of investment opinion, and the conclusions of published studies where these were available. These figures tended to cluster around those reached by us independently, giving a reasonable measure of confidence in the recommendations. In the report I put forward specific price recommendations for the eight listed stocks. The price put on Shawinigan common was $30, with shareholders given the right to buy a share in the non-power assets, which Quebec did not propose to acquire, at $5. Among the assets Mr. Lesage insisted on retaining, however, was Shawinigan's 20 per cent interest in the Hamilton Falls Power Company; the reasons for this were to become clearer later.

Preferred shareholders were to be offered short term discount bonds, in a few cases supplemented with a cash bonus, in order to give them a bit more than the net return, after taxes, on their shares. Nothing was to be done about the bonds, except to try to ensure that the trust deed could not be invoked to force us to call them – adding to the financing difficulties.

The task force accepted our recommendations and on or about December 20, the report went forward to Premier Lesage, with additional recommendations about the form of the offer. One hitch, however, developed at this last moment. Lesage felt he should put his colleague George Marler in the picture because of his previously expressed concern about financing, and our task force met with Marler, who was accompanied by Doug Chapman, head of Ames. Marler, supported by Chapman, reiterated the view that the $300 million or so cash needed should be borrowed *before* we made an offer to the shareholders. "What if we can't raise the money?"

I took it upon myself to reply saying (as I recall) "The election was fought on nationalization, and the financial risks accepted by the government at that time. Moreover, every prospective bond buyer in Canada and the U.S. knows nationalization is coming. How can you sell a bond issue to them, or even write up the offering prospectus, without revealing full details of the prospective method of acquiring the power companies and probably the offering prices? How could such an offer to shareholders then possibly succeed? The stock market quotations would immediately rise to reflect the method of acquisition – even if prices were not revealed – and the incentive to sell to the government would be gone."

Lesage and the others supported the logic of this position, and we agreed to shoot for an announcement after the markets closed on Friday, December 28. This would give investors the week-end to think things over. A meeting was called for Boxing Day, in Quebec, and the group, along with New York counsel, met together and then, later in the evening, with Jean Lesage and René Lévesque in the cabinet room.

We were to meet the cabinet and Hydro-Québec Commissioners at 3.00 o'clock on the 28th for a full presentation. On the 27th and 28th, I received reports every half hour of trading in Shawinigan; there were worrying signs of buying pressure, and the price slowly edged up. It touched $25⅝ in the early afternoon of the 28th, up ½; I arranged for the closing quote to be passed in to me at the cabinet meeting: $25⅜! I breathed a sigh of relief and passed it over to Lesage, who announced that our security system had held tight – at the same time justifying to his colleagues why they had not been told sooner.

In retrospect I am puzzled that more speculators had not followed the same reasoning process that we had, and gambled on a respectable provincial offer for the stock. One reason may have been that our discussions with Shawinigan continued right to the end, and this fact was known in the street. Another may have been that few people expected such quick action. Most of all, I suspect, was that many investors did not believe that the government would be "fair," and that it would use its weight to bulldoze the companies into submission.

The cabinet meeting was more or less a formality and at 4.00 o'clock Jean Lesage advised the party caucus of the decision. The press had been alerted to stand by for something big at 6.00 o'clock, and Premier Lesage made his historic announcement to them. By this time I had left on the government plane for Montreal and flew back to Ottawa in time for a party of our Ottawa mandarin friends at Jim Grandy's. We all watched the TV coverage of the event on the 11.00 o'clock news, my natural glow of pride having been enhanced, as I vaguely remember, by a considerable amount of booze.

It had been quite a year: resignation from the security of my government job at the Canada Council to venture again into the private sector; the completion of the *Bond Market in Canada* and its publication; my involvement in one of the most controversial and important events in the history of Quebec. I had made a host of new friends in Quebec, and had found out that working with a French-Canadian team was not only intellectually satisfying but a source of fun.

Could 1963 match the year just ending? Not quite, but it had its moments, as we shall see.

Notes

1 René Lévesque, *Option-Québec* (Montréal: Les Editions de l'Homme, 1968), p. 20. (English version, *An Option for Quebec* (Toronto: McClelland and Stewart Limited, 1968), p. 14.
2 Black, *op. cit.*, pp. 277-278.
3 Lapalme, *op. cit.*, pp. 163-184.

V

Success – but battle is joined on bond syndicates (1963)

Our year-end offer for the power company shares had been launched by Premier Lesage with appropriate fanfare, and we were confident that it would succeed. The initial newspaper comments were favourable, and the published and private views of brokerage houses provided a good deal of vindication for the prices we had set. One firm said that in spite of the complaints from Shawinigan management "The $30 price, however, looks like it will stick. It's fair, and compared to the Bennett butchering of the BC Power deal, this smells like a garden in June."

On January 3, 1963 we met to plan the details of the next step, the drawing up of the official offering letters, and the consideration of the myriad of legal questions which surrounded the prospective purchase. Claude Ducharme had primary responsibility for drafting the offering documents, with considerable help from Pigeon and Létourneau. My role consisted mainly of feeding in all available material on other purchase offers, of keeping a watchful editorial eye on the texts, and generally helping out.

We were also bracing ourselves a bit for the expected counter-offensive from Fuller and his Shawinigan board. It was not long in coming. On January 7, the presidents of British American Oil (now Gulf Canada) and Shawinigan announced jointly that BA had bought control of Shawinigan Chemicals from Shawinigan Water and Power, for $25 millions; Shawinigan's holding in the subsidiary dropped from 75 per cent to 33⅓ per cent, BA's rising from 25 per cent to 66⅔ percent. The news release said a partnership "buy, sell" agreement had existed, and that this had led to "earlier negotiations" which gave BA the right to move in should "unknown and possible incompatible interests" threaten to take over control. The Quebec offer for Shawinigan shares had included placing Shawinigan Chemicals in the new Shawinigan Industries package, to be offered to Shawinigan shareholders for $5. This raised the possibility of an outsider moving in and buying control of Industries, since many, perhaps most, holders of Shawinigan would have little interest in retaining the residual shares.

We were upset about this move for several reasons. One was that no mention of these earlier negotiations had been made in the discussions between Shawinigan and the province; we suspected that the decision had really been taken at the last minute, in part to embarrass us and possibly mess up the main offer itself. Secondly, control of Shawinigan Chemicals was to be the crown jewel (if a slightly tarnished one) in the Industries package; without such control the attractiveness of Industries was considerably diminished. We felt that the B.A. Oil purchase had in fact been at the expense of Shawinigan shareholders. This was confirmed by the drying up of interest in the rights to buy Shawinigan Industries stock, which had traded up to $1.60 following Lesage's announcement.

Our third concern was this transaction had violated a condition of the offer, that "no company may take, or allow a company under its control to take, any action other than acts of current administration in the ordinary course of business." However, as Premier Lesage noted in a statement on January 9, there was not much the province could do about the sale since Shawinigan Chemicals had a federal charter. *Faute de mieux,* he said that the offer of $30 would be maintained, and reiterated the government's resolve "to afford all possible protection to shareholders and purchasers of rights." There the matter rested; there appeared nothing much more we could do – but the details of the BA transaction would prove useful to us later.

On January 18 the Shawinigan board sent out a news-letter to shareholders, stating that "the internationally-known Stone and Webster organization" (presumably compared to the unknown provincial advisers!), "after months of intensive work," had submitted a "comprehensive" report to the company which provided a "sound and impartial basis" to judge the Quebec offer. Not surprisingly the report produced a figure of $40 per share, $10 above our offer. The report said all relevant factors had been taken into account including "reproduction cost new, less depreciation" which produced a higher figure of $47 per share. The letter went on to urge shareholders "defer final judgment" until they had received the official offer from Quebec.

On January 11, Fuller had sent a long letter to Lesage, but written in

English. He conveyed the conclusions of the Stone and Webster study, suggested that Shawinigan had been hard done by in relation to the other companies, and proposed that the terms of our offer be submitted to a tribunal – with the astonishing suggestion that whether shareholders accepted our offer or not, they would be entitled to any higher price that the tribunal would set! Since we had based our whole approach on setting a price that shareholders would find attractive, avoiding lengthy expropriation or arbitration procedures (which would likely benefit no one except the lawyers, and the management of the companies), we found this new Shawinigan tack slightly ridiculous.

I helped draft the reply for Premier Lesage, which was dated January 24; both letters were released by him to the papers. The premier rejected any reconsideration of our offer. In one paragraph we made effective use of the BA deal: ". . . how dare you tell your shareholders that the offer is insufficient because it amounts to only 125 per cent of the book value of your utility assets, when you have just disposed of a controlling portion of the shares of Shawinigan Chemicals, at the base book value, without consulting them at all?" In the English draft I had used "could" rather than "dare"; my colleagues felt however that the only appropriate French verb was "oser", admittedly a little stronger, and in it went. "Comment osez-vous. . .?" brought headlines in the French press. Lesage also accused Mr. Fuller of not telling his shareholders of all the hazards and tax problems inherent in the expropriation alternative. He ended his letter by saying "For your convenience, I am enclosing an English translation of this letter." Zap.

The company passed both letters to their shareholders on Feburary 11 complaining about the decision, but made no recommendation. However, the ball game was as good as over, although our offering letters did not go out until late February. The investment community, a few dealers commenting wryly about the difficulties of taking on the government in battle, recommended to their clients that the offers be accepted. On March 21, Shawinigan advised their shareholders by letter that the directors would be accepting the government's offer "mainly on the basis that, while the offers are inadequate, the alternatives to acceptance, obscure as they are now, might produce a more unsatisfactory net result."

Our letters went out on schedule, and most of the stock of the eight companies had been turned in by the end of April. There remained simply a mopping-up operation. The Shawinigan Industries' offering to shareholders concerned us a bit, because of the danger that the rights would not be taken up (if the market viewed the residual company as worth less that $5 per share). However, Power Corporation came through with a bid for stock or rights placing the new company's value at just over the $5 figure.

Raising the money

While all this was going on, Premier Lesage, in his role as Minister of Finance, was preoccupied with the question of where and how the money would be raised. The Ames syndicate had proposed a large issue in the U.S. and, presumably with the blessing of Lesage and Hydro-Québec authorities, were busy lining up a $300 million private placement in New York. In this they worked in association with First Boston Corporation, one of the largest American underwriting firms. The group was successful, (Prudential Life alone being prepared to take $100 million), and brought the deal to Lesage on or about January 25.

He consulted our task force, and I opposed the proposal for several reasons. A month earlier I had given Lesage a memo in draft form in which I had reiterated the views I had expressed in my first letter to Lévesque, about the need for broadening Quebec sources of funds by tapping the short term market, and borrowing in the U.S. On this latter question I said the following: "We believe it essential that a substantial amount be borrowed in the U.S. market in 1963, but do not believe that this borrowing should be overdone, for two reasons. One is the possible impact on the rate, the other is that the U.S. government for balance of payments reasons has been attempting to slow down borrowing in the U.S. by foreign governments. Although we are advised by senior officials in Ottawa that it is most unlikely that Canada would be affected by any action that the U.S. Government takes to impose restraints on foreign borrowing, the tactics would appear to suggest that Quebec's U.S. borrowing should be moderate. We believe that a total of $200 million would be so regarded, and suggest further that if necessary $50 million of this be short term debt, to be refinanced in 1964 and 1965."

However I sensed Lesage was committed to the Ames' proposal. There was certainly a good deal in favour of a well publicized big U.S. bond deal – it would provide an investor seal of approval on the take-over, remove all public doubts about Quebec's ability to finance the purchase, and quiet the concern of any of his colleagues, such as Marler, who might have some lingering doubts. Besides, Lesage liked being associated with big deals – the bigger the better. However, he asked Ducharme and me to attend a meeting with the syndicate in Montreal on Monday, January 28.

Lesage chaired the meeting; Doug Chapman of Ames and Ed Townsend of First Boston spoke for the underwriters. I sensed an understandable degree of hostility from them – what the hell was I doing trying to mess up their deal? – but I pressed on anyway with my view that the issue was too big, was too closely identifiable with the take-over, and that its very size would lead to problems for all Canadian borrowers in the U.S.; the Europeans had already been warned to cut down their dependence on the New York market. Townsend countered by saying that he had cleared the issue with Treasury officials in Washington, who did not oppose it. Obviously, I had lost, and the deal was closed a few days later, a $300 million, 5 per cent, twenty-five-year Hydro-Québec issue.

I did feel vindicated that summer when President Kennedy brought in the Interest Equalization Tax, a graduated tax on long term foreign borrowing in the U.S. market. The U.S. felt itself to be in balance of payments difficulties at the time. Many Wall Street observers believed that the very large Quebec loan, for those days, had been the last straw which led to the imposition of this tax. It brought about crisis conditions in the Canadian bond market until the Americans relented and exempted us from the tax – on condition that we would not build up our exchange reserves with proceeds from borrowing in their market.

Syndicate sensibilities and the short term market

Premier Lesage was much more amenable to my suggestions about Quebec entry into the short term money market – that is, borrowing with a term of three years or less. I lined him up all the information I could about such borrowing by other provinces, including savings bonds, Treasury Bills, and bank lines of credit. I also proposed that he meet with John Abell of Wood Gundy, a friend of mine and an acknowledged expert in the money market. He agreed, and arranged lunch for the three of us at the Garrison Club in Quebec on February 5. This was to lead to another episode in my running battle with Chapman.

Abell and I turned up at the premier's office at 12.45, and we went directly to the Club. To our surprise we found Wood Gundy's Quebec manager waiting there, with a message for Abell to call his Toronto office *before* lunching with Mr. Lesage. Abell phoned, and then we went ahead with our lunch and our briefing of Lesage about the money market.

Abell told me the story later. Because of Ames' role as syndicate manager, out of courtesy Wood Gundy had informed Ames about Abell's trip to Quebec. Doug Chapman was home sick in bed, but was so incensed that he got dressed and called on senior Gundy officials, and urged them to stop Abell from seeing Lesage (presumably because he felt the adviser should have been someone from Ames). The Gundy people were so worried about a rift with Ames, that Abell was told that if the luncheon date could not be broken, at least he should make it clear to Premier Lesage that he was not speaking for the syndicate, and that Wood Gundy was not really trying to move in on Ames' territory!

I referred to this in December in a letter to Lesage, proposing new syndicate arrangements, saying "This all sounds just as childish in the recounting as it did to me at the time, but it does illustrate, I think, how jealously a syndicate manager guards his monopoly position with an account" (Letter of December 27, 1963). For me, it was just one more example of why Quebec needed to broaden out its syndicate arrangements from the existing Ames-Bank of Montreal monopoly.

Shortly thereafter the province began issuing Treasury Bills, and Ed Lemieux at Hydro-Québec was authorized to sell short term notes and paper in the money market. Both forms of borrowing have continued since to play a useful role in meeting Quebec's borrowing needs.

In February, Premier Lesage had come under public fire from a number of sources about the province's underwriting arrangements, including the limited part played by francophone dealers in the group – many Quebec dealers had complained to me about their inadequate allotments – and about the length of time, thirty years or more, that the Ames-Bank of Montreal group had managed the province's bond issues. Another concern was that the system strengthened the anglophone establishment in Montreal.

One example is the choice of lawyers to pass on the legality of the bond offering. Each bond issue is backed by a "prospectus," which contains all relevant facts about the company (or government), its financial affairs, and the issue itself. Corporate legal work related to these bond prospectuses is extremely lucrative, and up until 1962 was almost exclusively the preserve of English firms. There is validity in the argument that strength begets strength – buyers vastly prefer the opinion of well-known, established firms to that of unknowns, often making it a decisive factor in turning an issue down. But how could francophone legal firms ever get to be recognized and accepted unless they were given a chance? Quebec bond issues appeared a good place to start. The arguments of Quebec nationalists that there was a conspiracy at work to keep the French Canadian subjugated are far-fetched, but the incestuous nature of the Montreal anglophone establishment had somewhat similar consequences.

Early in July 1963 I had lunch with Eric Kierans, who was then president of the Montreal Stock Exchange. I had met him a few times, had liked him, and had been particularly impressed by the forthrightness of his attack on Walter Gordon's unfortunate June 13th budget. I may have had some ulterior motive for the lunch, since Claude Ducharme had asked me my opinion of Kierans, and of his potentiality as possible Quebec cabinet material; Jean Lesage was on the look-out for a good English-speaking minister. I don't remember if the lunch was connected with this, but certainly it marked the beginning of a close relationship with Kierans. On August 8, he was named to the Lesage cabinet as Minister of Revenue, and won a seat shortly thereafter in a by-election. He was to prove an invaluable ally in the next – and culminating – round of the syndicate affair.

In September, the syndicate brought out a Quebec twenty-five-year issue on a 6 per cent basis. I felt that the issue was badly timed, was sold too cheaply, and was based on a wrong forecast of Quebec's prospective demands on the long term market over the ensuing twelve months. I wrote this in a letter to Claude Ducharme, his firm having by then become involved (jointly with a large anglophone firm) in drawing up the prospectuses on some Quebec issues. I hoped he would pass it on higher up. By this time, I was beginning to suspect that Jean Lesage was getting a bit edgy about my continuing complaints.

A new syndicate

On November 15, I lunched with Ed Lemieux to discuss our common interest in shaking up the syndicate's monopoly. That night I dined with Kierans, who I knew shared our views and had agreed to help out. Early in December, we decided to test things with an issue through a new group, but one in which members had little to lose because of their relatively small share in the Ames syndicate. It included Royal Bank, Banque Canadienne Nationale, Greenshields and René T. Leclerc. Kierans played a key role in bringing this group together. Premier Lesage was vacationing in Florida – making Eric acting Minister of Finance. I helped out through my contacts among the dealers.

The Ames-Bank of Montreal group heard of the threat, and responded by sending out their annual syndicate letter to all members of their group, asking for acceptance of their participation in the syndicate to deal with all Quebec, Hydro-Québec and Quebec Autoroute borrowing in 1964. Included in the letter was the normal provision that no member of the syndicate could function in any other syndicate on Quebec issues with a term exceeding one year. There was a reference also to some rearrangement of member participations – and I was told that there were discreet 'phone calls urging that the agreement be signed quickly and returned before "the other bastards get their toe in the door." Kierans blew his stack at this letter, issuing a public statement after Christmas saying, "group managers would be well advised to withdraw their letters" arguing that no mandate to an underwriting syndicate had yet been given by Quebec for the year 1964. He added that syndicate members might find themselves involved "in restraint of trade" proceedings.

There was a considerable and lively press interest, particularly in the French papers. They were our natural allies, and I remember keeping Michel van Schendel of *La Presse* pretty well briefed – he wrote a story every day. As I have noted, francophone resentment of the Montreal financial oligarchy ran deep. Meanwhile, George Marler apparently warned Lesage that things were getting out of control. I wrote a long letter to Lesage on December 27, expressing my views on the syndicate battle, beginning my letter: "In the controversy swirling around the appointment of a new syndicate for Hydro-Québec, I find it difficult to remain a detached observer." (Perhaps I should have been more forthright about my own contribution to the swirl).

I put my reasons forward under three headings:

"(a) The need for increased competition in Quebec financing, and for broadening the sources of financial advice open to the province.
(b) The importance of increasing the participation of French-speaking dealers in the syndicate.
(c) Shortcomings in the past performance of the Ames-Bank of Montreal syndicate."

Lesage came back and held meetings in Quebec on January 7, 1964, with some of his colleagues, and with the leaders of the old and of the proposed new syndicate. The press and photographers were outside the cabinet room in full force. Doug Chapman, annoyed, told the *La Presse* photographer – "Get out of here, no picture! . . . It's not a Roman holiday" – but his picture was taken anyway, with a hand out, half covering his face. Nobody had much to say after the meeting.

On January 8, Arnold Hart, Bank of Montreal president, issued a statement which was regarded in all the papers "as a veiled warning to avoid a drastic break with tradition." Hart defended the performance of the syndicate, citing particularly the $300 million U.S. loan early in 1963. On January 10, *Le Devoir* had front page headlines, referring to Hart's pronouncement: "Les Ministres sont indignés: C'est une gifle à la face du gouvernement" (The Ministers are indignant: it's a slap in the face for the government) – going on to quote some ministers as saying "The prestige of the government is at stake . . . The government can't accept the status quo without losing face." Another minister praised Kierans for his stand: "after thirty-five years of monopoly, in which the government had no choice but the one syndicate, Mr. Kierans had rendered a great service to the province."

We were winning the battle of the press, but nothing had been settled at the cabinet level. On Saturday morning, the 11th, I was called at my home in Ottawa by Jean Lesage, who asked me if I could do anything to "clean up the mess." I told him I'd try, and would report to him in Quebec early Monday morning. I got busy on the phone, and by Sunday afternoon had logged some fifty long-distance calls to key people in the underwriting business. By late Sunday I had put together a proposal that Kierans and I thought was a reasonable compromise, and flew to Quebec. The only ominous note was a late call from Bruce West of Ames that he had just heard that the matter had been "settled" at the highest level. However I worked until 1.00 AM writing my report – and then got up at 4.00 to finish it. I turned up at 9.00 in Lesage's office with my handwritten document, including a draft press release – only to find that the syndicate matter had indeed been "settled" – and not along the lines I was recommending.

What Kierans and I had been shooting for was two separate syndicates, with individual shares appreciably different; this would not preclude some overlap, for example, senior members of each group would participate to a lesser degree in the others' issues. It was only through this kind of wholesale revision of the syndicate structures that the share of francophone dealers could be appreciably increased. My proposal suggested that either the syndicates could alternate on all Quebec issues, or one group could handle straight Quebec's and the other Hydro-Québec. Eventually the province might move to competitive bidding.

What Lesage announced on Monday, was the setting up of two management groups, one headed by the old group, Bank of Montreal, Ames and Lévesque Beaubien, and the other by a new group, Royal Bank, Wood Gundy and René T. Leclerc. The share of the more junior members would remain substantially unchanged. The managers would alternate on all Quebec issues.

The syndicate change did achieve at least one of the objectives I had been working for all year – broadening the list of financial advisers on whom the province could draw. As for the rest, I suppose the "rotating heads" approach was the best compromise one could expect, given the long-established relationship with the old group. I was also pleased that Premier Lesage made a considerable reference in his statement to broadening the province's sources of financing, referring to the forthcoming second Quebec savings bond campaign, to Hydro-Québec's short term notes, to a possible issue of Quebec Treasury Bills, and to further recourse to the U.S. market – all of which I had been pushing from the time of my first meeting with Lévesque in April 1962 down to my December 27 letter.

My satisfaction in this partial victory was somewhat muted when Mr. Lesage, in reply to a press question as to who had handled final details, said "I did it all myself, on the telephone; I had no emissaries." It made me feel rather foolish about my own frantic week-end, and I wondered what the people I had talked to would think. My pique passed quickly – perhaps because that same day I began work on a new Quebec task force to be concerned with the negotiations over power from Hamilton Falls. The group included Roger Létourneau, Michel Bélanger and Lucien Bélair, from our old nationalization group, with Ed Lemieux added from Hydro-Québec. It was to prove quite an experience.

VI

On to Hamilton Falls!

Desultory and at times discordant discussions had been held in the 1961-1963 period between Quebec and Newfoundland – the main spokesmen were Premier Smallwood and Prime Minister Lesage – about the possible development of Hamilton Falls in Labrador. Originally Grand Falls, they had been renamed in honour of an early governor of Newfoundland. In 1965, after the death of Sir Winston Churchill, Smallwood renamed the falls and the river in his honour.

The prospective power from the Hamilton Falls basin, then probably the largest and most economic undeveloped hydro-electric power site in the western world, had been the prize element in the 1953 deal between Smallwood and a British consortium of investors, the British Newfoundland Corporation (Brinco). In return for a twenty-year concession covering power, mineral and timber rights in Newfoundland and Labrador, Brinco had agreed to spend $1,250,000 on development in each of the four successive five-year periods.

The story of the negotiations over the Brinco concession, and the events leading up to and during the discussions with Quebec is told in detailed and entertaining fashion by Philip Smith in *Brinco: The Story of Churchill Falls.* [1] My discussion of these negotiations is limited largely to my participation in them, and to my interpretation of events surrounding the harnessing of Churchill Falls, and the effect on the relationship between Quebec and Newfoundland of the Labrador boundary issue. Indeed one can only begin to understand the emotional tangle surrounding the power negotiations against the background of the boundary question, which had bedevilled relations between Quebec and Newfoundland for decades.

In 1927 the British Privy Council, having been asked by the

Photo reproduced by permission of Louis Gale.

thought, and on Sunday, February 2, I put together a memorandum in longhand. Jean Fournier, then my next door neighbour in Ottawa, had just joined the Quebec public service as cabinet secretary, and was still commuting between the two capitals. He took the memorandum back with him to Quebec City that night, had it typed, and gave copies to my committee colleagues, and to Lesage and Lévesque.

In essence, the memorandum suggested that Quebec and Newfoundland should get together and buy out Brinco's interest, and develop the project jointly. The main reasons were these: as a private company, Brinco had to pay income tax; its costs of raising capital were higher, both on equity money and on its borrowing; we estimated the cost differential at close to one mill per KWH. We added that the risks normally associated with private ownership and equity financing were not present, and such risks as were associated with the project appeared to lie with the buyer of the power, Hydro-Québec; all such developments throughout the world were in this day and age done by governments; because of the boundary issue, a deal for Hamilton power would go over better with the Quebec public if its own government was involved.

The proposal was discussed in the Quebec cabinet a day or so later, and became an integral part of the government's negotiating posture – apparently Lesage and several of his colleagues had had thoughts along similar lines. Because most of the references to this aspect of the negotiations which have appeared in book form have been either from the Brinco point of view by Smith or more sympathetically but truncated in Richard Gwyn's book,[4] I think the memorandum merits publication in full, and it is included as Appendix Two.

On February 11, our committee submitted its preliminary report to Lesage, Lévesque and Lessard. The report not only contained an abridged version of the memo above, but also included many other reasons militating against the project at the three mill price. In summary, we felt the price should be in the 2.1 to 2.3 mill range, that this price would probably not be acceptable to Brinco, and that the government should consider the public enterprise approach, given the higher costs involved in the private ownership route.

On February 13, Lessard conveyed the substance of this in a letter to Winters, which I helped draft. According to Smith, "Winters immediately got in touch with his old friend Walter Gordon, the federal Minister of Finance," seeking changes in the income tax, which obviously discriminated against provinces with privately owned utilities. Winters, says Smith, apparently felt that something would be done, and he was confident enough to bring his price down to 2.85 mills.[5]

On February 13, Winters also sent an urgent letter to Smallwood, suggesting he meet Lesage, who wanted to see him to talk about the

Labrador border, "but I believe even more important is that he would like to consider with you some basis for developing Hamilton Falls as a joint operation between the Quebec and Newfoundland governments so as to avoid the Federal Corporation Tax . . . "[6]

On February 17, Lévesque, with Létourneau, met Winters and John Kirwan-Taylor of Brinco; we were seeking more detailed information about HFP Co operations and financing costs. Winters referred to his talk with Walter Gordon, but kept making the point that Hydro-Québec was being offered power at a price cheaper than any alternative open to it. He added that he thought Brinco could finance the project as a private company cheaper than Hydro-Quebec could (which was ridiculous, particularly because Quebec could borrow as work progressed, while any private company would have to commit itself for the whole borrowing program at the beginning). Létourneau sounded out Winters on the possibility of Brinco selling its shares in HFP Co to Quebec and Newfoundland. Winters replied that "he was carrying the flag of private enterprise."

Meanwhile Con. Ed. was still interested in buying part of the energy. However, its position was complicated by one engineering problem; to make economic use of Hamilton power required that it take it without interruption, and this required some form of storage. The only feasible solution appeared to be the contemplated Storm King project on Hudson River; it would pump water up into a reservoir one thousand feet above the river in off-peak periods, drawing generating capacity from it in peak periods. But the environmentalists were solidly against it, and the project was stalled. The Con. Ed. people also had unrealistic expectations about nuclear alternatives (everyone had in those days), and they would not budge from the four mill price at the Quebec-New York State border. This added to the unattractiveness of the Brinco price, from our point of view, given all the added costs and technical hazards involved in transporting power across Quebec and linking it into the New York system.

On February 18 Winters met Smallwood in London to fill him in on developments. Both Smith[7] and Gwyn[8] refer to Winter's attempt to kill the Crown corporation idea, (Gwyn: "Winters noted happily (in his diary), 'He [Smallwood] will resist any attempt by Jean Lesage to operate Churchill Falls as a crown company.' ")

On March 1, Smallwood and Lesage met in Montreal. Lesage put a package of proposals to him, including joint development (with Brinco out), use of Quebec labour and materials, and Labrador boundary changes. This latter issue had been on Lesage's mind for some time, because of the power potential of the five rivers cut by the southern Labrador boundary; to exploit them economically would require the backing-up of water onto Labrador territory. Smallwood said "No"[9] and the talks broke off. Winters saw both in Montreal a week later, but they wouldn't talk to each other; as a go-between he apparently succeeded in persuading Smallwood to consider some exchange of land – headwaters of rivers emptying into the St. Lawrence for land along the border north of Schefferville.

A federal-provincial conference opened on March 31 in Quebec City, and Smith reports that the first evening, in a private talk, Lévesque tried to persuade Smallwood to take over the Brinco operation and "do it yourself." Next day there was a further discussion involving Lesage, Smallwood, Lévesque and Newfoundland Attorney General Carter about the proposal to adjust the Labrador boundary, to give Quebec the headwaters of the five rivers flowing into the St. Lawrence.

Before Smallwood could broach the issue in the Newfoundland legislature, *Time* magazine broke the story, saying that Quebec would get "a substantial chunk of Labrador." Smallwood denied it, saying only discussions were being held. He was attacked by the press and he backed off, suggesting that any land deal with Quebec would be submitted to the people of Newfoundland for approval, that no one could *force* Newfoundlanders to agree to a change in the boundary.[10]

We continued to meet with the Brinco people through April. Winters came down to 2.65 mills; we stayed at two mills, although agreeing among ourselves that we might go as far as 2.45 mills. Finally we agreed to meet with them in New York on May 14 and 15. These talks did not prove very fruitful, unless one considers the unexpected bonus of the Chateau Haut Brion '54 (as Bélanger reminded me recently), produced at dinner at the Brussels. None of us found the Brinco or Morgan Stanley group very congenial – perhaps because they felt the same, particularly about me. But let Philip Smith describe it:

> . . . it fell to Mulholland's lot to explain them to Lesage's committee and field their many questions. Even though he had lived with the figures now for many months, he remembers the experience as the most gruelling two days he ever spent. As one of the architects of the now-abandoned policy that Hydro-Québec had no right to know Brinco's costs, Ed Vollmers viewed the proceedings with barely concealed impatience. On the Quebec side, his mood was matched by Douglas Fullerton, perhaps the most implacable opponent of the Brinco proposals . . .[11]

Our committee met again on May 27 and on June 5; Yvon De Guise, engineer and Hydro-Québec commissioner, had been added to it. Obviously things had reached an impasse. We submitted our final report to Lesage, Lévesque and Lessard. In it we attempted to show the remaining differences between Quebec and Brinco, including Newfoundland's unwillingness to consider nationalization, a $58 million difference in capital cost estimates, a gap of ½ of 1 per cent on allowable return on investment; we concluded it was pointless to carry on further discussions, at least at our level. On July 8 Premier Lesage issued a statement regretting that "it is impossible at the present time to reach an agreement."

His final paragraph is relevant:

> On March 19 last, I noted that we continued to believe that the development of Hamilton Falls was eminently desirable for all, particularly the people of Newfoundland and of Quebec. We are still of this opinion, provided that all means are taken to make the most of the possibilities offered by Hamilton Falls for the production of low cost power. In this connection, it should be pointed out that, at the present time, in Canada, large scale power production projects are generally undertaken by publicly owned corporations.[12]

A new approach

In spite of the gloom cast by Lesage's statement, the project did not fade away. Smallwood kept pushing his new "Anglo Saxon" route for Churchill power – transmission lines down to the Strait of Belle Isle, then a fifteen mile submarine cable to Newfoundland, across the island to Cabot Strait, then a seventy-five mile submarine cable across to Cape Breton, then by land onwards to the New England States. A mad idea, hopelessly uneconomic, and soon shot down by the engineers. But early in 1965, Winters kept trying to persuade the government to change its taxation of private utilities, to put them on an equal footing with those in public ownership. His efforts finally met with success. Walter Gordon announced in July that the government planned to amend the Public Utilities Income Tax Transfer Act, under which it would rebate to provinces 95 per cent of the corporation tax received from the private utilities. He expressed the hope that this would be passed on to consumers, and that it would help get the Churchill Falls development going.

In March 1965 Premier Lesage agreed to having "talks" (not negotiations) resume, and named a new team, exclusively from Hydro-Québec; Létourneau, Bélanger and I were no longer directly involved (although I was working on other Quebec task forces). Jean-Paul Gignac, a Hydro-Québec commissioner and friend of René Levesque, became the leading spokesman on the power question. Louis-Philippe Pigeon was simultaneously having quiet discussions with Newfoundland representatives about the boundary question and the headwaters of the five rivers. I understand that by the spring of 1966 a package power-boundary deal was ready for signing, but the election intervened. However, the discussions carried on. Yves Pratte*, a Quebec lawyer who was to become a close friend later,

*On September 29, 1977, Pratte was appointed by Prime Minister Trudeau to the Supreme Court of Canada.

negotiated the tough letter of intent for Quebec, and Premier Johnson raised no new obstacles. In October the twenty-three page letter was signed – but the completion of the final agreement was still dependent on Brinco's ability to raise the money.

Nearly two more years of negotiations were to pass before July 10, 1968, when the Johnson government authorized Hydro-Québec to sign the contract. However, work at the site had been going on all through the period, as had negotiations about the prospective sale of the bond issue. The $500 million placement had been made possible only by the two special forms of assistance. One was the federal waiver of the normal 15 per cent withholding tax on the issue, placing it on the same basis as a provincial bond. The other was Hydro-Québec's guarantee to complete the project if it proved necessary, its agreement to pay for the power available whether it could use it or not (the so-called "take or pay" provision), and its $100 million investment in junior Brinco debentures.

The questions that must be asked of the 1964 negotiations are really these: "Why did negotiations break down when a deal was so close?" "Who was responsible?" Is it true, as Gwyn quotes Winters as saying, that the failure to reach an agreement to develop Churchill Falls in 1964 was "one of the worst blunders of Canadian economic history"?[13]

To deal with the last question first, any agreement in 1964 would have required the onward sale to Consolidated Edison of half or even more of the power on a long term basis at a bargain price. Would such a sale have been in Canada's interests? I don't think so. One may argue that Quebec benefited by the delay, not Newfoundland – but Quebec is still part of Canada, despite November 15, 1976. And the added costs of delay only served to raise the power cost by less than half a mill.

As to responsibility, it must certainly be shared. The federal government could have settled things in 1964 by abating to the provinces its income tax on private utilities. Smith[14] quotes Bill Mulholland as saying that, with the tax off, the price could have been 2.2 mills (we had priced the tax in our calculations at .4 to .5 of a mill). But the feds didn't act until later.

Personality clashes didn't help. Smallwood and Lesage mixed like oil and water. As I have noted above, we didn't find Winters or his team very congenial. Lévesque found it particularly distasteful to deal mainly with titled Britishers and American financiers – and with their leader, Winters, who preferred to talk to Lesage and Lessard. They didn't find us that congenial either – with Lévesque and me cast as leading S.O.B.s. Winters left Brinco in 1965 to join the federal cabinet; it was made clear to me by several of my friends and acquaintances in cabinet that he regarded me as the main architect of the breakdown of the talks in 1964. Well, *de mortuis nil nisi bonum.* Having new teams on both sides, from 1965 on, helped smooth things over – particularly with the accession to the Brinco team of personable Don McParland, who was later to die tragically in a plane crash at Wabash in Labrador.

Joey Smallwood could have settled things earlier by going along with the Quebec joint ownership proposal. Winters certainly did his damnedest to fight it. In his memoirs, however, Smallwood explains his reservations (Gwyn had quoted him as saying "one elephant, one mouse"[15]):

> I think it quite likely that Lesage was being pushed hard by Lévesque. They definitely wanted us to cut BRINCO out of the picture and Newfoundland to nationalize the Churchill project. They gave me figures of their own compilation to convince me that we would profit more from nationalization than through development by BRINCO. I gave the figures to BRINCO, without revealing their source, and asked for a reply. I was convinced that if we nationalized the project and entered into the partnership with Quebec, Newfoundland would truly get the rotten end of the stick. I was convinced that Quebec would show neither scruple nor conscience in its treatment of Newfoundland – that we would be victimized at every turn. . . .
>
> Why wouldn't I fall in line with the proposal to nationalize? I wouldn't as long as there was a reasonable alternative. It was not merely because some members of the Royal Family, and Winston Churchill, and other great personages in England were shareholders in BRINCO, though obviously that was no insignificant aspect. Rather, it was because it would represent a vile piece of treachery on Newfoundland's part. I had gone to England asking help and had offered the British this opportunity, and they had spent many millions working up the project. If we were to nationalize BRINCO now, the English-speaking world would denounce our conduct, and rightly. I felt that financial circles on both sides of the Atlantic would never trust Newfoundland again; that Newfoundland's name would stink in the nostrils of business people everywhere. I was convinced that never again would we be able to induce an industrial or commercial concern to take us seriously.[16]

The irony of the final deal is that it was accomplished by turning Brinco in effect into a public utility, as a result of the federal government concession on utility taxes, its removal of the withholding tax on the bond issue, and by many Hydro-Québec guarantees. Nothing can take away from Brinco's engineering accomplishments at Churchill Falls – they were magnificent – but events showed the phoniness of the original concept, and which was the main source of our opposition, that the Churchill Falls project could really be carried out as "private enterprise."

In 1974, I was to become an adviser to the Newfoundland government following their take-over of Brinco's interest in Churchill Falls and other hydro rights in Labrador; early in 1975 I became first chairman on Newfoundland and Labrador Hydro. I resigned from both at the end of 1975 "for personal reasons." Everything that happened during that period and since convinces me that Newfoundland today would be infinitely better off in its negotiations with Quebec over Labrador power developments had it become a partner then in Churchill Falls, rather than watching power from the Falls sold to Quebec by a private company, on a very tough and tightly drawn contract. I remain convinced that the only sensible answer for Labrador development is for Quebec and Newfoundland to do it together as equal partners. Almost every problem that comes up between the two provinces can trace some or all of its roots back to the emotional way in which the people and politicians of both provinces view the Labrador boundary issue.

I noted earlier some of the Quebec concerns about the 1927 decision. In 1968 I chanced upon a new book on the issue by Robert Bédard, *L'Affaire du Labrador*, which built a strong case that Quebec had really been hard done by.[17] Bédard had done extensive work in the archives in London, as well as in Canada, and argued that

- Canada and Quebec had carried out many acts of government in the interior of Labrador, between 1867 and 1926, including the geological survey that discovered the iron ore;
- Quebec had never agreed to Privy Council adjudication of the case, but only to seeking its "juridical opinion";
- the British government was judge and party in the case, its Trade Facilities Board in 1923 having guaranteed a loan of £2 million to Newfoundland Power and Paper, based in part on the security of resources in the Labrador interior. The company failed in 1925, and the boundary case placed the security in jeopardy; and
- two of the five justices of the Privy Council sitting on the case, Lords Cave and Haldane, had been members of the British cabinet approving the loan.

In 1968 I devoted two of my weekly press columns to presenting the Dorion and Bédard arguments, since both books were available only in French. The St. John's *Evening Telegram* carried my columns, and so far as Newfoundland reaction was concerned the heading of the July 3 lead editorial in the *Telegram* told the story: "Not Bloody Likely, Mr. Fullerton." It said in effect, don't confuse us with facts, the Privy Council has spoken, the case is closed.

The strong Quebec stand on the Churchill contract unquestionably reflects in part the feelings of most Quebecers about the boundary; if they were robbed in 1927, by God, it was only simple justice to get some of their own back from the lowest possible price on the power, and a tough contract. Correspondingly, Smallwood's intrasigence on the public ownership issue reflected the fear of many Newfoundlanders that Quebec "would take Labrador over" through the back-door of a partnership arrangement – "the elephant and the mouse." Newfoundland feelings now about Labrador, and its fears about Quebec's designs upon it, are reinforced by its view of the Churchill Falls power contract; it believes it sold its power birth-right for a mess of pottage. In 1976 the Newfoundland government launched a suit against the Quebec government for a re-opening of the contract.

To those in Quebec who still aspire to take over Labrador completely, I can only say "forget it" – however valid they feel the claim to be. Fifty years have passed since the Privy Council decision, and the entry of Newfoundland into Confederation validated its claim. Quebec would not likely get very far in an international court – Premier Lévesque suggested in 1976 that an independent Quebec would seek a hearing before it – because both sides must agree to adjudication. Any Quebec attempt to move into Labrador in force would probably lead to bloodshed, as Newfoundland called on Canada for help. These are unlikely developments, to be sure.

What is, however, crying out to be done is for Quebec and Newfoundland, now, to forget their grievances, and to get together on the development of Lower Churchill power, and on the power from the other five rivers along the St. Lawrence. If they do, both provinces will end up winners – and will have taken a long step towards coping with theirs, and Canada's growing energy shortages. It is encouraging that on July 13, 1977, Premiers Lévesque and Moores met in Quebec City to discuss this very issue, and set up a committee, chaired by ministers to study the joint development of energy in Labrador and Northeastern Quebec. Mr. Lévesque was quoted as saying that "feelings of some Quebecers that Labrador rightly belongs to Quebec" will not enter into the energy development studies. Premier Moores said that Newfoundland will continue to press its case in court for a re-opening of the Churchill Falls contract.[18]

Feelings in Newfoundland about the Churchill contract continued to run high, however, and on October 25, 1977, the Newfoundland Action Committee put a full page ad in the *St. John's Daily News* calling on Premier Moores to "cut off the power" if Premier Lévesque could not negotiate a "mutually satisfactory deal." The appeal apparently stemmed from the September breakdown in the transmission line from Churchill Falls, which had blacked out Montreal for several hours and had caused widespread disruption; the implications had been widely commented on in Newfoundland. Moores himself appeared to give some support to the idea in a speech he made to the Newfoundland Progressive Conservatives, late in October.

Notes

1 Philip Smith, *Brinco: The Story of Churchill Falls* (Toronto: McClelland and Stewart Limited, 1975).
2 Henri Dorion, *La Frontière Québec-Terreneuve* (Québec: Les Presses de l'Université Laval, 1963).
3 Smith, *op. cit.*, pp. 176 *et seq.*
4 Richard Gwyn, *Smallwood; the unlikely revolutionary* (Toronto: McClelland and Stewart Limited, 1968).
5 Smith, *op. cit.*, p. 176.
6 *Ibid.*, p. 177.
7 *Ibid.*, p. 178.
8 Gwyn, *op. cit.*, p. 263-264.
9 See Smith, *op. cit.*, and Joseph Smallwood, *I Chose Canada* (Toronto: Macmillan Company of Canada Ltd., 1973), p. 457.
10 *Ibid.*; and Smith, *op. cit.*, p. 179.
11 Smith, *op. cit.*, p. 191.
12 *Ibid.*, p. 191.
13 Gwyn, *op. cit.*, p. 265.
14 Smith, *op. cit.*, p. 214.
15 Gwyn, *op. cit.*, p. 264.
16. Smallwood, *op. cit.*, pp. 459-460.
17. Robert Bédard, *L'Affaire du Labrador* (Montréal: Editions du Jour, 1968).
18 *Montreal Star*, July 13, 1977.

VII

New Lesage initiatives, but Johnson elected (1964-1966)

Nationalization of electricity had been the most striking initiative of the Lesage government in its efforts to bring about a greater degree of Quebec control over its own destiny. Other moves were taking place simultaneously, of which the most important occurred in the area of government pensions. In the fall of 1962 Jean Lesage had set up an interdepartmental study committee on retirement funds, with its ultimate object the establishment of "a public and universal retirement plan on the basis of actuarial calculations and of contributions." There was an implicit further objective, not very far below the surface, of providing a large source of investment funds which could serve to reduce the dependence of Quebec capital from outside the province.

But at an even earlier date, January 1962, Lesage had created a "Comité de sidérurgie" (Steel Committee) to co-ordinate studies on the establishment of a steel industry in the province, studies begun some months earlier under the aegis of the Quebec Economic Advisory Council. One committee member was my friend Michel Bélanger; another was René Tremblay, who was to leave the Quebec public service in March 1963 to run as a federal member, to win a seat, and then to become a minister in Pearson's first cabinet in 1963.

The lack of a primary steel industry in Quebec had for a long time been a sore point with Quebecers of all shades of political opinion. They could see neighbouring Ontario with three huge complexes, Steel of Canada and Dofasco in Hamilton, and Algoma in Sault Ste. Marie. Nova Scotia had the Dominion Steel and Coal (DOSCO) primary mill at Sydney, even if it was old and run down. These steel mills not only created jobs directly, but there were secondary and tertiary benefits as other manufacturing industries were built up around the primary plants. Yet Quebec had to go on importing most of its steel, losing out on a major source of employment in manufacturing industry.

The Steel Committee, in a preliminary report submitted in the fall of 1963, concluded that a viable, medium-sized but fully-integrated steel industry, selling mainly to domestic markets, was feasible. A site was picked, at Bécancour on the south shore of the St. Lawrence, just downstream from Trois-Rivières, and optioned. In December 1963 the cabinet approved the purchase of the site, and it was acquired through the Societé Générale de Finance (SGF); the SGF had been formed by the Quebec government in 1962 to promote, finance and assist the development of Quebec industry; it had, however, some private capital invested in it.

As my work on Churchill Falls came to an end, I was asked by Premier Lesage to attend a meeting in Quebec City on June 12, 1964, at which "steel" would be discussed. It turned out to be a rather different scheme than the proposal of the Committee. In August 1963, Lesage had been approached by Ted Emmert, president of DOSCO, about the possibility of DOSCO's substantial steel finishing and fabrication facilities at Contrecoeur, Quebec, becoming the nucleus of an enlarged Quebec steel industry. A meeting was held on August 15, 1963; I don't know what transpired then or subsequently, but DOSCO set up a separate Quebec subsidiary, DOSCO Steel Ltd., and continued to expand its Contrecoeur mill. DOSCO also co-operated in the work of the Steel Committee, working through Committee chairman, Jean Deschamps, then deputy minister of Industry and Commerce, and in 1977 appointed Quebec's delegate-general in Paris.

Our June 12 meeting was not with DOSCO officials, however, but with Paul Desmarais, then head of Provincial Transport, destined soon to become president of Power Corporation, and emerging rapidly as one of the top financiers in the country. He was accompanied by Jean Parisien, his right hand man. There were three on the Quebec team: Jean Deschamps, Michel Bélanger, and me. Desmarais had proposed to Lesage a joint private-public venture involving the purchase of a controlling interest in DOSCO from the owner, Hawker Siddeley, along with most of Hawker's other manufacturing investments in Quebec. Ownership would be split 60-40 between a Desmarais company and the SGF. The Quebec government would be asked to supply or guarantee the loan capital required.

Desmarais, tall, lean and persuasive, put on a great performance, charming us thoroughly. But we weren't launched very long into the discussion before he and I looked at each other and started to laugh. We discovered that we shared a common complaint, stuttering. It was a strange way for a friendship to begin, but it did that day: I've seen a lot of Paul since and have found him to be one of the most direct, honest, and unpretentious persons I have met. Financial ogre? Bloody nonsense, just a corporate builder with a natural talent for fitting potential pieces of a financial empire together, the guts of a high wire artist, and a great capacity for persuading important people – like bankers – to lend him the money he needed to carry out his plans.

The meeting produced no very fruitful results, except to confirm our view that the somewhat decrepit DOSCO empire might conceivably be the quickest and cheapest way into the steel business for Quebec. Although the tone of our meeting with Desmarais had been most cordial and constructive, we faced some obstacles in working out a deal. One was that the government would have to put up most of the money (or guarantee bonds) without any clear indication of actual or ultimate control over the projected operation. How could the province justify publicly its role as banker, and in effect silent partner, to someone in the private sector?

Another factor came up – interprovincial and federal politics. During the summer the story surfaced in the press (*Financial Post*) that an offer was being made for DOSCO by a "syndicate of French-Canadian businessmen," and the price of the stock rose. Apparently Bob Stanfield, then Premier of Nova Scotia, was concerned that the proposed move might lead to the closing of DOSCO's Sydney mill, and asked Ottawa to intervene to stop the transaction. It was certainly true that DOSCO would have to dispose of its Sydney plant if a deal was to be consummated with Quebec.

Whatever the principal obstacle, the Desmarais discussions were called off; it was decided instead to try to follow through on the original plan and work out something with the management of the SGF. On August 20, Premier Lesage asked me to become part of a new study committee on steel, also to be chaired by Jean Deschamps, which would examine proposals put forward by Gérard Filion, then head of the SGF. I had met Filion several years before; publisher of *Le Devoir*, he was named vice-chairman of the Canada Council in 1962. I had found him to be intelligent and direct – a strong personality, but not particularly flexible.

Our committee included four members of the electricity nationalization team, Pigeon, Létourneau, Bélanger and me, plus Cyrille Dufresne and Jacques Boulanger. We met for the first time on August 28 in Montreal, at the Showmart building, just above the huge excavation for the Berri-Demontigny Métro Station then under construction. It was made clear to us by Pigeon that the government favoured the use of SGF as its chosen vehicle for launching the venture, although the Steel Committee had recommended the creation of an autonomous company. Our first task as a committee was to review Filion's financing proposals for the new venture, the forecast cost of which was about $200 million.

The discussion about form and methods of financing doesn't make for fascinating reading. However, we met four times within a month of our first meeting, and by the end of September had firm proposals to put in front of Premier Lesage and his cabinet. At our final meeting I recall our efforts to find a short and snappy name that signified both "Sidérurgie" and "Quebec." Sidque and Quesid were discarded before we settled on "Sidbec."

Sidbec was incorporated in November; Filion became president early in 1965. A board of directors was jointly selected by the SGF board and the government, to which were added that summer Jean Deschamps, who had replaced Filion as general manager of SGF, and Michel Bélanger. Their appointments arose from the desire of the government to have a more active voice in Sidbec's affairs – and represented a compromise between the cabinet's "nationalize it" wing (Kierans and Lévesque), and the group supporting the Filion concept of maximum independence from government.

Early in 1966 Filion resigned from Sidbec to become president of Marine Industries; informed circles said that the government had asked him to leave. But he made it clear that he felt there had been too much government interference, a *de facto* "nationalization," which conflicted with his own views and those of the SGF board that the company should be run – and appear to the investing public – as much like a private company as possible. Jean-Paul Gignac, a Hydro-Québec Commissioner whom I had met several times in our work with Hydro, was appointed to succeed him.

Just before the June 1966 election I wrote Kierans, observing that Sidbec's survival appeared in danger. Daniel Johnson had been attacking the Lesage government on the issue with some success, and to save the government's face I suggested that the DOSCO proposal be reactivated, but *via* Sidbec rather than through Desmarais (who in any event had other fish to fry by this time). I proposed that once DOSCO was acquired, the Sydney Steel Mill "could be sold to the Nova Scotia government at a bargain price." I learned later that negotiations with DOSCO had been continuing, and a settlement was close to being reached at the time of the 1966 election. In any event, in October 1967 Hawker closed down the Sydney mill. This opened the way for the implementing of the DOSCO deal, and Sidbec bought DOSCO's Quebec properties – and at a lower cost to the province than originally contemplated. But Sidbec has been losing money since ($36 million in fiscal 1976), despite expansion and a very substantial further injection of provincial funds. It has to be regarded as one of the least successful of government ventures.

The Quebec-Canada Pension Plan

As the Quebec study on pensions was being carried on, the federal government in its throne speech on May 16, 1963 announced its intention of bringing in a universal and contributory pension plan. On June 18, Judy LaMarsh, then Minister of National Health and Welfare, introduced legislation for an unfunded "pay-as-you-go" scheme. This was not at all what the Quebecers were working towards: they wanted an actuarial scheme, funded by individual and employer contributions, providing a large source of investment dollars for the Quebec government.

The federal government changed its formula into a partially funded plan, but this was not acceptable to Quebec, and at the federal-provincial conference in Quebec City, March 31 to April 2, 1964, the Quebec plan was tabled for consideration by all. It received considerable support from the other provinces, but Ottawa was not ready to compromise and the conference broke up in disagreement, over the plan but also over other shared-cost programs. A few days later Claude Morin, chief adviser to Jean Lesage on federal-provincial relations, phoned Maurice Sauvé, whom he knew well from Lesage's 1960 campaign, to tell him that Lesage was going to take a tough line in Ottawa in his forthcoming budget. "Couldn't something be done to sort this thing out?" Sauvé went to Pearson, and obtained permission to go to Quebec with Tom Kent, close adviser to Pearson, to see Morin. The pair went down, and a package deal was painfully worked out, which involved some concessions from Quebec but mainly a considerable giving of ground by the federal government.

The two important federal concessions were these: provincial control over the investment of the pension reserves, and an acceleration in the rate of federal withdrawal from the income tax field in favour of the provinces. The new proposals were approved by Ottawa and Quebec, and then by the other provincial governments; the Canada Pension Plan (for nine provinces), and the Quebec Pension Plan, came into being a year or so later. There were initially no differences between the benefits offered by the two plans and a person could switch without difficulty between them. Minor changes were introduced later but did not affect the interchangeability.

The agreement was hailed across Canada as having "saved Confederation," and as a splendid example of "co-operative federalism" – which indeed it was. Even Claude Morin had some good things to say about it in his 1972 book *Le Pouvoir Québécois. . . .en negociation,*[1] though by then he was committed to the péquistes. However, he qualified his approval by suggesting that it left Ottawa "bitter," and with a desire to "recapture" control.

For Quebec, this meant a significant and regular flow of savings into a central account. But how was it to be managed? The province's study committee on the pension plan had brought down its final report in April 1964. It had proposed two main organizations: the first an incorporated body, the Quebec Pension Board, to supervise the actuarial and administrative arrangements; the second, a completely separate body, a Deposit and Investment Fund, to invest the money. This latter Fund was based in concept on the French *"Caisse de dépôts et consignations,"* set up in Napoleonic times by the French government, but largely independent of it. Its function was to manage public monies collected for various purposes, including pensions. The French had found that the Caisse could and did play an important role in capital markets; their experience was not lost on Quebec.

On December 2, 1964, Premier Lesage asked me to become a member of a committee to draft the law establishing the new Caisse des Dépôts et Placements, and to examine its general objectives and functions. Other members include Roger Létourneau, Jacques Parizeau, Claude Castonguay, (who as consulting actuary to the Study Committee on the Pension Plan, had played a key role in the committee's deliberation; he was later Minister of Health in the Bourassa cabinet), and Ron Thomas, former treasurer and pension fund manager of Ontario Hydro. Roland Parenteau, director general of the province's Comite d'Orientation Economique, was to co-ordinate our work. We met for the first time on December 17; many meetings were held over the next four months. Several of our most interesting discussions were with Mr. Bloch-Lainé, head of France's equivalent "caisse."

A detailed review of the issues is not relevant to this book, but we were concerned about a number of contentious matters. The most central was to draw the fine line between allowing the Caisse enough independence to make investments on a sensible, "prudent man" basis, and giving the province enough power over it to keep the Caisse's overall policies in tune with the needs of the Quebec economy. On this I think we did a good job, with the board to be composed of about one-third civil servants, one-third drawn from the public or para-public, (e.g. Crown agencies such as Hydro-Québec) sector, and one-third from private business. The director general, appointed by the cabinet for a ten-year term, could not be dismissed during good conduct without a vote of the Assembly. We took a hard line on possible conflicts of interest, including prohibiting the Caisse from having financial transactions with directors, staff, members of the Assembly, or with companies which they or their relatives owned or controlled. Investment powers included the purchase of common stocks, but not to exceed a 30 per cent interest in any one company.

Our report was given to the government late in March, and on the evening of March 31 our Committee met with the cabinet – a discussion lasting until 1.00 A.M. Minor changes were made as a result of these and subsequent talks, Louis-Philippe Pigeon acting as intermediary. Bill 51, "Charter of the Quebec Deposit and Investment Fund" was presented by Mr. Lesage to the Assembly early in June, 1965.

Particularly effective speeches were made by Lesage and Kierans on June 9 and 10, on second reading of the bill. (Kierans had some kind things to say in his speech about my role, giving it special prominence in my mind!) Opposition was practically non-existent, and press reaction (at least the French press) was uniformly enthusiastic. In January 1966, the appointments of Claude Prieur, from Sun Life, as General Manager, and members of the board, were announced; in February the Caisse received its first deposit of pension funds. It quickly became a major factor in the Quebec capital market.

There is no doubt in my mind that the Quebec Pension Plan, and its investment offspring, the Caisse, represented a landmark in the province's history, on a par at least with the nationalization of the power companies. Some Quebecers, including Jacques Parizeau, argue that its long term effects will be greater, because it has served Quebec, and will continue to serve, as a powerful development instrument and economic lever. It has provided special support to the market for Quebec bond issues, giving the province considerable flexibility in its financing plans. However in recent years, with the extraordinary rise in Quebec borrowing, the Caisse can only provide a fraction, if an important one, of the province's capital needs.

Did the QPP, and its federal equivalent the CPP, lead to a profligate provincial attitude towards spending? A nice question, and one which probably has to be answered in the affirmative. The only rebuttal, I suspect, is how much worse off the provinces would be without these savings, and how totally dependent on the vicissitudes of capital markets. And the rise in provincial borrowing coincided with the great expansion of federal spending that became the hallmark of the Trudeau government – a government which must at least share in responsibility for the rise in provincial spending in the 'seventies.

Review of the Lesage era

Looking back at those first five years of the Lesage government – it had been elected in June 1960 – the record of accomplishment is an astonishing one, and it is a record of which Jean Lesage has every reason to be proud. My involvement, of course, had been almost exclusively restricted to the more practical and economic aspects of change, and with the twin achievements of power nationalization, and the pension fund. If Lesage, Kierans and some of us saw these moves more as good and desirable things to be done than part of a grand nationalistic design, those members of cabinet and the bureaucracy with separatist leanings viewed them as building a solid economic base for an independent Quebec of the future. Of the Quebecers in this latter group whom I knew best, René Lévesque, Jacques Parizeau and Claude Morin stand out; they made no particular secret of their feeling about the *"maîtres chez nous"* aspects of these and other major government projects such as the steel mill.

All through this period, however, developments were taking place in another area which may well have had even more implications for change for Quebec – education. Under the leadership of Paul Gérin-Lajoie, first as Minister of Youth and then, in 1964, as first Minister of Education, Quebec's church-dominated élitist system of schooling was taken apart, largely secularized, and put together again. Small parish and country schools were closed, huge centralized "polyvalent" secondary schools *(Cité des Jeunes)* built to which students were bused long distances. Control over the elementary and secondary schools passed from the bishops to the government. Plans were initiated for the CEGEP *(Collège d'enseignment général et professionel)* system of junior colleges, designed to replace the traditional and clerical *"collèges classiques,"* but were not implemented until 1967, under the Johnson government. The university system was heavily subsidized and rapidly expanded.

One beneficial result of this new régime was to allow a great many more Quebec students to obtain access to secondary and post-secondary education. The merits of other by-products of this system are more debatable. For one thing, the disruption in rural areas caused by the revolutionary changes in school location is widely regarded as being a major factor in Lesage's defeat by the Union Nationale in the 1966 election. The extraordinarily rapid decline since the early 'sixties in the authority of the Roman Catholic Church in Quebec may well have occurred on its own, but the freer and more open schools, the changes in curriculum, and the taking over of the schools by lay teachers, undoubtedly accelerated the pace of its slide. Finally, the new school system became a breeding ground for separatism; the teaching profession in Quebec today provides a focal point of péquiste strength. Allied to this has been the development of militant teacher unions, a Marxist infiltration, and the growth of a philosophy of education that seeks to give the teaching staff almost total control of the schools, CEGEP's and universities.

By 1965 Lesage was moving on still another front, health and welfare, parallelling the Ottawa activity in these fields during this decade. The appointments of Kierans as Minister of Health, and René Lévesque as Minister of Welfare, in October of 1965, served not only to revitalize both departments but gave each of Lesage's most dynamic ministers a new lease on life. Lévesque in particular had been restive under Lesage, seeking new outlets for his energy and his strongly nationalistic convictions. My own further involvement in Quebec did not touch on these new activities of Lévesque or Kierans, but occurred in a field with which I was more familiar – finance.

The Parizeau Commission

In December 1965 Premier Lesage asked me if I would serve as a member of a new committee to study Quebec's financial institutions, and I accepted. Jacques Parizeau was to be chairman; by this time he was economic adviser to the government. Other members were Michel Bélanger (we seemed always to be teamed up), who was now deputy minister of Industry and Commerce; Robert Després, who was deputy minister of National Revenue and whom I had met earlier through Eric Kierans; and Yves Pratte, who had just left the deanship of law at Laval and had become special legal adviser to Jean Lesage. Jacques Prémont, a government lawyer, was our secretary.

We had been created as the province's answer to the federal Porter Commission on Banking and Finance, which had reported a year earlier. The Quebec cabinet was concerned that the prospective changes in the Bank Act might have an effect on provincial financial institutions; they were particularly worried about the independence of the caisses populaires, the unique Quebec adaptation of the credit union movement. Our mandate however, was broad enough to cover every area of banking and credit under Quebec's jurisdiction (excluding of course the role of the federally chartered banks) – credit unions, trust companies, mortgage, loan and acceptance companies, mutual funds, the financial activities of notaries.

Our Committee was slow getting under way, Jacques Parizeau having to organize a research and study program, and all of us having to read or reread a variety of documents, including the Porter Commission Report. By the end of March we had met some half dozen times in Quebec and Montreal, and had set our course for the next six months to a year. But an event was coming up which was to preoccupy the attention of Quebecers, and to push our study into the background.

Three and one-half years having passed since the Liberal triumph at polls in November 1962, Jean Lesage decided to call a June 1966 election. One motive was the problems he was facing inside his own cabinet – his difficulty in riding his two wild horses, Lévesque and Kierans, the discontent of the conservative wing in the cabinet, and the growing clashes between ministers, as each tried to build and reinforce his own particular empire. There were also persistent rumours that Lesage had designs on succeeding Mike Pearson as Liberal leader and Prime Minister of Canada, and needed another victory in Quebec as his launching pad.

Certainly the dissatisfactions within the provincial cabinet were in some respects at least due to changes in Lesage's personality. The process of deification which affects most prime ministers or premiers after a period in office had worked its will on Lesage, and many ministers found it increasingly difficult to communicate with him. Kierans told me "You don't talk to Jean any more – he just talks to you." My own experience had been the same. In the early years Lesage had listened to me – some of the time. Later he listened briefly, and impatiently, if at all. I liked Jean Lesage (still do) – perhaps because I felt I understood the man behind the soaring ego, and knew what a tough job he had – but our contact in the year before the election was minimal and lacking the earlier give and take of opinion. Increasingly he gave the impression of knowing all the answers himself.

Although the polls in the spring were not all that promising, Lesage had enough people telling him he was not only God's gift to the party and the province, but that he could win an election in a walk. So the election was called, and Lesage decided to build it around himself. He ran it from Quebec City, and felt secure enough to carry on normal government business at the same time. The low-key campaign, dominated by the billboard pictures of Jean Lesage, and by his speeches, didn't work. Although the Liberal's won 47 per cent of the vote to the Union Nationale's 41 per cent, the lower-populated rural seats swung the victory to Daniel Johnson – fifty-five seats to fifty-one.

The Liberals had all kinds of explanations for the defeat, after the election, with a good proportion blaming Lesage, and his handling of the campaign. But there was no doubt that the school issue, the new education policy, had been an important factor. The rural voters who backed Daniel Johnson were angry seeing their children bused as many as fifty miles to the new "polyvalent" central schools, mixed in with children of all ages, and exposed to all kinds of hazards and bad habits while en route, in school, or waiting for the bus. They had also been swayed by the Union Nationale charge that the Liberals were going to "deconfessionalize" the schools.[2]

Daniel Johnson

To the surprise of most pundits – but not to Daniel himself, according to his family – he had become the new Prime Minister of Quebec. The question I thought of first was naturally how my own position would be affected. I had met and talked to Daniel Johnson some half dozen times since 1960, the latest when he spoke in February at a meeting of a discussion group organized by Rudy Casgrain. We had hit it off pretty well together, perhaps because of one memorable evening early in 1964. I had dined at Michel Bélanger's and consumed a fair amount of Scotch. I was staying at the Château Frontenac, and after eleven I rolled into the Place de la Fontaine and ordered scrambled eggs at the counter. Swivelling on the stool, I found Daniel beside me. He seemed friendly, and recognized me; perhaps because of my alcoholic state I said *"Comment çà va,* Danny Boy" (his popular nickname – used in every cartoon of him), and launched into a political discussion. He replied without offense, and I then proposed that we visit the Trépaniers, friends of both of us, who were noted for holding open house at all hours. He agreed, we went off to phone Victor and Ginette and were shortly in a taxi headed up the Grand-Allée.

We ended up at the Trépanier's kitchen table, eating spaghetti and drinking Chianti. Unfortunately, in my exuberance (I wave my hands more in speaking French) I tipped the bottle over, and spilled some of it on Daniel. He took it in good grace, but after I spilled a second glass, it was generally agreed that it was time to go; he got me back safely to the hotel where he himself lived.

This story certainly reveals the essential good nature of the man and why he was so widely liked. It also showed, I think, his loneliness at the time. I did have one concern, however, that I had spilled a few political secrets as well as wine! We had just started our talks on Hamilton Falls. I needn't have worried; at one time or another Daniel attacked on the floor of the Assembly almost every one of my francophone colleagues in the various task forces with which I was involved. He never had an unkind word for me, although as an *"Anglais"* I was a particularly vulnerable target. How could one *not* help being fond of a person like that!

I wrote him a congratulatory note on June 7 and added: "I hope that you will not interpret this letter as an attempt to climb on the Johnson bandwagon, with a view to continuing my role as an adviser to the Quebec government. One of my friends saluted me yesterday as the former adviser to the former government and I think that is the way things should rest. However, I am a member of the five-man Parizeau Committee studying the operations of financial institutions, and if you intend to keep that Committee functioning, I would be very glad to continue to serve on it."

He never replied (he was a notoriously bad correspondent except with political associates and supporters) but months later he dined our Committee, and teased me unmercifully all through the meal about my links with the Lesage government – quoting almost verbatim from my letter. He was to remain a good friend until his death in 1968.

Notes

1 Claude Morin, *Le Pouvoir Québécois ... en négociation* (Montréal: Les Editions du Boréal Express, 1972), pp. 19-30. Further discussions surrounding the agreement will be found in Peter Desbarats' *The State of Quebec,* pp. 125-135, and Peter Newman's *The Distemper of Our Times,* pp. 306-315, both published by McClelland and Stewart Limited.

2 See for example Dale Posgate and Kenneth McRoberts, *Quebec: Social Change and Political Crisis* (Toronto: McClelland and Stewart Limited, 1976), pp. 111 and 124.

VIII

Lévesque leaves the Liberals, and forms his own party (1966-1968)

I had not seen much of René Lévesque during the last year or so of the Lesage régime. Late in 1966 however, our paths crossed again under rather unusual circumstances. In September I began a weekly column on economic and financial affairs for the *Toronto Star;* for several years I had been doing occasional pieces for newspapers and magazines. Peter "Establishment" Newman, then columnist and later editor of the *Toronto Star,* and Martin Goodman, the Ottawa bureau chief, and also later *Star* editor, had both encouraged me to write on a regular basis. The *Star* syndicated my column, and I was particularly pleased that *Montreal La Presse* picked it up that fall, and did the translation. The column ran in eight to ten Canadian papers for the next three years, until I became chairman of the National Capital Commission in September 1969, and could not carry it on.

Lévesque's main career, of course, had been journalism. Although he had kept his seat in the 1966 election, the Assembly was not called into session until December 1. Naturally he turned to other things; one was his attempts to steer the Liberals towards a more nationalistic course; his activities in this direction are told in the books about him which have recently proliferated. I had not kept up to date on these activities, although I gathered from Kierans that he was worried about the direction of René's political thinking.

It was not surprising at all that René turned again to writing to compensate for the loss of his busy ministerial life and to provide a platform for his ideas. His first weekly opinion column for *Dimanche Matin,* "Point de Mire," (aiming point of target) appeared within days of the appearance of my first column. By coincidence, within a month or two we both began hammering the pharmaceutical industry for its high prices and profits, and for the methods it used to persuade doctors to prescribe its costly "brand name" drugs rather than much cheaper generic equivalents. We exchanged a few columns in November 1966, and on December 1 I wrote him a letter enclosing some further drug material – but taking issue with him on some of his views on capital investment in Quebec. My opening paragraph read:

> Cher René,
> . . . it seems to me that the proper posture at the moment for you and Eric, and for the Liberal Party (and for the government as well, I might say), is to water down both the nationalistic gestures and the attacks on Ottawa. I will agree that this is not a very palatable approach, for you particularly, but it seems to me to be the only one that makes sense at the moment. As the saying goes, 'More flies are caught with honey than with vinegar' and the province's goal now must be to try, with every means at its disposal, to keep outside capital flowing into both public and private investment in Quebec.

This led to a lengthy reply from him on December 6 – in longhand, presumably written while he sat (bored?) at his desk among the Opposition in the Assembly.

I quote his reply more or less in full for several reasons. One is to show Lévesque's very good grasp of colloquial English – and how persuasively he argues his points. The second and more important reason is that his views on the need to unshackle Quebec from the dependence on and domination of outside capital formed an integral part of his philosophy and that of the separatist movement:

> Dear Doug,
> Thanks a lot for your letter of December 1 – and also for the three articles. Yes, I did get the Report on Drugs, and have been digging through it assiduously for some time. And since you asked for it – enclosed please find a pretty complete file of Lévesque, the people's pundit in 'D.M.' – *(Dimanche Matin)*. I'll add a couple of other pieces on drugs as quickly as I feel the traffic can bear it! In the meantime, this should help you get the grasp of *colloquial* French!
>
> As for your kind advice about Quebec's capital investment needs, let me say how sorry I am to find you in the same corner with . . . G. Demers . . .
>
> But, seriously, I don't disagree so much with his position – as far as it goes. But I wonder why he and others (you too) never seem to find any other answer than just: Keep your heads down, be quiet and wait for the nice gentlemen with the dough to come and invest, when they feel good and sure that we're nice enough little boys.
>
> Now, as affects Quebec, which isn't exactly a champion foreign investment getter even at the best of times, this is even more of a cul-de-sac than for the rest of Canada – especially Ontario, with over 50

per cent of industry already. Geography, our present 'common market' and the rule that nothing succeeds like success, will keep Ontario growing anyway.

So – either Quebec bows to its own (Demers & al.) or other people's blackmail, friendly as all get out – and does it forever, from one 'crise' to another – or it starts, at least in a modest way, to generate and control its own capital requirements, looking – NOW – towards the day when outside capital will become a *useful but non-vital supplement.*

So – I've been saying Demers and guys like him are just 'Negro Kings' if all they can preach is: quiet boys, don't scare the money away – without giving a thought to our own indispensable investment effort.

Why shouldn't we think about insurance money, and keeping it here – and if need be, taking it over by stages? And, now it's rid of Filion . . . pushing as fast as possible for the build up of the Société Générale de Financement? (making it at least as big as – Power Corp as soon as possible! . . .)

Why not? Tell me – because, ok, I'd agree to our being quiet and 'hospitaliers,' as long as there's something else in the future (foreseeable, if possible) than just being more of a branch-plant every year.

Thanks again – and tell me!
Salut,
René Lévesque

P.S.
The Druggist's letter in my pieces was pretty much "in extenso" – except for a couple of irrelevant local bits.
P.P.S.
Enclosed: speech (in reply, as seconder, to Throne Speech) by another druggist – MLA (Nat. Union!) Martel from Sorel (Richelieu riding) which got Danny Johnson into a nice sulk when he heard it. The chief was not amused. . . .

On December 9, I did my best to reply to his challenge, not very successfully, I am afraid, if judged by Lévesque's later activities. I won't quote more than a paragraph – but I'm surprised how much they reflect the debate going on now about the cost of independence for Quebec.

Cher René: . . .
But the hard problem of scarcity of capital in the foreseeable future remains. Does it really not make sense to slow down a bit on nationalism at this time when the alternative might be a slowing down of investment and growth? I'm not talking about a supine reacceptance of the English capitalist feet on the back of your neck, because those days are gone forever. The quiet revolution has seen to that, and I can't imagine a resurgence of the roi nègre approach to Quebec by anyone. Sure,

> you must aim to free yourselves from excessive dependence on outside capital – but you don't make up twenty years' neglect of social capital in six years, finance a subway and Expo, and broaden education and welfare programs enormously, without heavy borrowing outside the province. Statements that frighten those who supply the capital you desperately need – whatever their domestic therapeutic value – do not seem to me to be either good economics or good politics. . . .

Well, the Johnson, Bertrand and Bourassa governments did cool the nationalism a bit – or push it more to the back burner. Money continued to flow in, and in rising quantities, but a good deal of it went to finance. Hydro-Québec and its giant James Bay power development. The flow has slowed markedly since November 15, 1976, and it remains to be seen how the government of Prime Minister Lévesque will fare in the search for the outside capital so desperately needed in the future.

Can I be accused of being overly pessimistic in my approach at the end of 1966? A péquiste would no doubt think so, and make the case that the province did continue to achieve substantial growth over the ensuing decade, and borrowed an amazing amount of money. The rebuttal is that such borrowing was possible only because the majority of investors assumed that with Mr. Trudeau in the saddle in Ottawa, and the péquistes in apparent retreat after the October 1970 crisis, the independence threat had effectively ceased.

Lévesque prepares to leave the Liberals

I had breakfast with Lévesque in the Château Laurier on February 7, 1967 as a result of the efforts of the CBC to organize a TV program critical of the drug industry. I've forgotten if we covered more ground than the prospective drug broadcast. Although our paths were to cross several times in the future, that meeting was the last at which we had any lengthy tête-à-tête discussion.

By then Lévesque was moving rapidly towards his departure from the Liberal party. Following the 1966 defeat, a cabal of the more left and nationalistic members of the Liberal party had been formed, and met frequently in Montreal at the St. Denis Club. That fall the group, which included Eric Kierans, had succeeded in electing Kierans president of the Liberal Federation. But the group was soon dividing again on the constitutional issue; Kierans was opposed strongly to independence on economic grounds – his line of argument being not far from my own.

In April 1967 a group of Liberals led by Lévesque met in Mont Tremblant to discuss the constitution; the group included Bob Bourassa, later to become Liberal premier. This work continued at meetings at Bourassa's home, but the federalists gradually withdrew. The debate, however, was severely damaging relations within the party, and Lesage tried to stop it. But on July 24 President de Gaulle made his famous speech from the balcony of Montreal's City Hall: "*Vive le Canada!*, *Vive Le Québec!*" and, finally, "*Vive le Québec libre!*" This gave the debate new life – and the separatist movement fresh vitality.

Late in the summer the group discussed Lévesque's plan, worked out over the holidays, of "sovereignty-association." What he proposed in essence was an independent Quebec, followed by a negotiated economic association with Canada. With the support of the remaining members of the group – Bourassa had left on grounds of the economic costs of independence – on September 18 Lévesque brought out his *Option-Québec*, reprinted in full in *Le Devoir*.

The annual meeting of the Liberal Federation was scheduled for mid-October. Efforts were made to reach a compromise between the Lévesque group and the others, notably by Bourassa, but not many Liberals believed it possible for Lévesque to remain in the party. On September 26 Kierans and Lévesque debated the issues in an hour-long CBC television program. Partly on the basis of that debate I decided to become involved publicly, and I wrote an open letter to Lévesque which appeared in the *Toronto Star* on October 6, and in *Le Devoir* on the same and the following day. The letter received wide publicity and is included as Appendix Three.

In the letter I used or rephrased some of the arguments I had put to René ten months earlier, but expanded it to emphasize the economic impact of the split, if it ever occurred, on the rest of Canada – and the impact on Québec of the inevitable backlash. Looking back at it from hindsight, I don't think there is much I would change in it. Some of the precise figures, of course, would be radically changed by the tremendous growth of government and the scale of federal transfer payments over this past ten years.

One of my statements had a curious result:

> . . . can one conceive of a (Quebec) monetary union with the rest of Canada, with one partner in a more serious deficit position than the other? I don't see how it could work, for a kind of Gresham's law would be at work – bad money replacing good. Without monetary union, the Quebec dollar would depreciate more than the (new) Canadian dollar. If you asked me to put a figure on it, I could see the Quebec dollar at .70, and the new Canadian dollar at .80 – both in terms of U.S. currency. A new equilibrium would eventually be reached at the lower rate, but the disruptive consequences in the transitional period would be severe.[1]

My .70/.80 figure was right off the top of my head, and had been based on no rigorous economic analysis of what would actually happen. How could one possibly make such a calculation? What I was simply trying to show was that Quebec would be hit harder, but that both new countries would be damaged. When *Option-Québec* was published in book form early in 1968, Lévesque referred to the .70/.80 cent guess in a footnote:

> At the beginning of last October, D.H. Fullerton, a prominent financial expert, who has acted on many occasions as financial adviser to the Quebec Government and to Hydro, wrote me an open letter . . . (Quoting the last three sentences from the last quotation above) . . . To the best of my knowledge, no other competent person has publicly risked calculating the probabilities on this issue. Mr. Fullerton's estimate illustrates simultaneously the mutual gain for the two countries of the formula we now propose, and the fact that by holding out despite our disadvantage for the first few years, an independent Quebec could if necessary live without our formula.[2]

The 70 cent Quebec dollar thus passed into separatist folklore; I get quite a charge every time I see it in print, used either to support or attack Quebec independence. The way the Canadian dollar has fallen since November 15, 1976, partly as a result of fears of Quebec separation, suggests that I may not have been far wrong, although as I write this .65/.85 would seem to be the more likely possibility for the two currencies that would result from *total* Quebec independence.

Finally, my last paragraph speaks for itself:

> . . . But what I think you must accept is that if the decision to separate or not is *largely* an internal one for Quebec – and I support this view – the matter of how much it will cost will be determined *largely* by those outside Quebec. I can only beg you to spend as much time on this difficult and awkward problem as you have on articulating '*indépendance et association*.'

At the October Liberal convention the battle was joined. According to reports, several attempts were made just before the opening session to bring the principal former ministers together to agree around a "special status" formula that Paul Gérin-Lajoie had put together, but it failed. That evening Lévesque made a final five-minute speech and then, to the cheers of a "small band" of supporters, walked out of the hall and out of the Liberal party.

The 1967 debate about sovereignty-association

Looking back over the clippings of that 1967 period leading up to Lévesque's departure from the Liberal party, and after it, the similarity is astonishing between the discussion then and the debate which has been going on in Canada since November 15, 1976. The issues have tended to be the same, on both sides, and many of the same people have been involved.

In *Option-Québec*, Lévesque made these basic points: "We are Québécois" he said. "That is to say first and foremost that we are attached to this one corner of the earth where we can be completely ourselves . . . be really at home . . . Being ourselves is essentially a matter of developing a personality that has survived for three and one-half centuries. At the core of this personality is the fact that we speak French."

He went on to examine the facts which had led him to take the plunge. He believed that, although Quebec had made some gains in "catching up" with the rest of the country, further gains in the fields of economics and culture would inevitably lead to conflict with the other provinces. This would be a waste of energy for both peoples, and more dangerous than a clean break now – "Two scorpions in a bottle" is one of his favourite phrases in describing this. Therefore Quebec should become independent – but renegotiate a new "association" with English Canada – a new partnership which might be called the "Canadian Union." He evoked the example of the European Common Market in support of his thesis.

Kierans attacked the proposal on a economic grounds. He cited a cost figure to a separate Quebec of $2.3 billions for five years, in lost federal transfer payments and other revenues, and said that Lévesque's approach "would lead our people down the road to poverty, heavy unemployment and misery." Head offices of many national corporations would leave – a calamity for Montreal.

Robert Bourassa, perhaps aspiring to pick up Lesage's leadership mantle when it fell from him, followed the same line in a speech on September 27. He saw many problems in Quebec creating its own money, particularly in the period of transition (although he noted that Quebec had with reason felt left out of discussions on Canadian monetary policy). He thought that Quebec would have to compromise on this issue, and accept some limits on its sovereignty rather than risk the hazards of its own currency. He raised a number of other problem areas, including the tariff question, the need for foreign capital, and its possible flight; independence would pose many problems in all of these areas. A good speech, revealing, one must conclude, why he himself had split with René a few months before.

The battle lines became drawn – the anglophones on one side, using the "costs of separation" argument, and supported by some francophone economists and businessmen. Against them were ranged the independence hard liners, who refused to acknowledge that economics is relevant to the great cause – or who argued that it was being exploited by opponents of independence as a form of "*matraquage*" or "*chantage*" (bludgeoning or blackmail), or "intellectual terrorism" (Lévesque's phrase) to beat the faithful into submission.

Formation of the Parti Québécois

Lévesque's *Option-Québec* led shortly to the formation of his *Mouvement Souveraineté-Association* (MSA), built around a group of his friends and ex-Liberals. The prestige of its leader, and the wide circulation given his book – really a manifesto – attracted to it separatist support from across Quebec. But it was far from being the only Quebec organization actively seeking independence. The largest, the *Rassemblement pour l'Independance Nationale* (RIN) had been functioning as a political party or movement since 1960; its initial goals were social democratic, with a left of centre orientation but with strong nationalist overtones. In 1964 Pierre Bourgault became its new activist leader, pulling the group towards a more aggressive nationalist posture. The group second in importance was the right wing *Ralliement Nationale* (RN) headed by Gilles Gregoire, former federal Social Credit M.P. Around these two parties were a profusion of others, some the products of schisms within the RIN or RN, such as the *Regroupement National,* a right wing, church-oriented, splinter group of the RIN. Others were Marxist oriented, revolutionary, like the FLQ, *Front de Libération du Québec*, which in 1963 blew up mailboxes and carried out other bomb attacks against federal symbols, and killed several innocent people in the process. There was also an RIN right wing splinter group, *Parti républicain du Québec*, headed by Marcel Chaput, former federal civil servant, but it did not survive long.

On the election front, the RIN and RN had between them amassed a respectable 9 per cent of the popular vote in the 1966 election, without, however, electing anyone. If independence was to get anywhere through political action, something clearly had to be done to pull these disparate forces together. René Lévesque and his MSA proved the catalyst. In August 1968 the MSA reached agreement with the RN, and at a congress in October, the Parti Québécois was founded. The RIN, which had held out against amalgamation because of its tougher stand for Quebec unilingualism, had no place to go; it disbanded several weeks later and adherents were urged to join the péquistes.

There were two obvious binding forces in this new aggregation of separatist factions, one the personality and moral influence of Lévesque, and the other the independence goal itself. But there was another powerful underlying force which has always been present in Quebec society – that of the clerical nationalist movement, whose patron saint in the twentieth century had become l'Abbé, later Canon, Lionel Groulx. Writer and historian, Groulx was prolific in his publications. The title of his most famous book was *Notre maître le passé* ; this became the slogan for the movement. Groulx preached that salvation lay in a return to the insular, inward-looking society that had developed under the church over two centuries. The problems of Quebec today could largely be traced back to anglophone domination since the Conquest, and to federalism. Groulx did not draw the line, however, at accepting federal recognition; I met him once at a Canada Council dinner at which he received an award for his historical work.

In 1967 the independence movement was given another push by the convoking in November of the assembly of the "Estates General of French Canada." In the corporate state tradition, it had been formed in 1961 to bring together representatives of the various groups in the society – unions, universities, cultural and historical societies, school boards and commissions, students, municipal councils, caisses populaire, Sociétés Saint-Jean-Baptiste, the professions. Most of the 2,500 delegates were from Quebec, but about 15 per cent came from French-Canadian areas outside the province.

The president of the Estates General was Jacques-Yvan Morin, now Minister of Education in the Lévesque government. His colleagues on the commission preparing for the assembly included some names which appear in this book: Arès, whom we quote below, Georges-Emile Lapalme, Jean-Marc Léger, François Albert Angers. At the opening of the first meeting, the assembly heard a voice from the grave, that of their honorary president, Canon Groulx, who had died in May. His recorded message rang with a sense of destiny; the time for decision had come, "to be or not to be" a nation. His generation had been compelled to play the role of Sisyphus, continually pushing the stone up the mountain, only to see it slip back down again. It was up to the new generation to seize the rock in their strong hands, and with the help of God, implant it firmly on the summit from which it would never again descend.[3] The assembly also heard, live, from René Lévesque; his independence goals were received with enthusiasm.[4]

Reading the accounts of the meeting, one has the impression that the delegates were in some respects more nationalistic than the péquistes. The proposals on the "Status of the French Language" are not very different from those in the Lévesque government's language white paper of April 1977 – official unilingualism, no English taught in primary French schools, francization of place names and signs, French schools for immigrants, legislation to enforce French as a working language, and so on.

Unanimity seems to go along with nationalism; most proposals put to the vote were endorsed by 90 to 100 per cent of the Quebec delegates – French Canadians outside Quebec were less enthusiastic. For example, the main policy statement: "The estates general of French Canada, reunited in assembly, affirm that (1) French Canadians constitute a nation; (2)

Quebec is the national territory and the fundamental political base of this nation; and (3) The French-Canadian nation has the right to choose the political system under which it intends to live" (my translation) was supported by Quebec delegates 783 for to 12 against; delegates from outside Quebec were 119 for to 129 against.

One of Groulx's disciples, the Jesuit priest Richard Arès, put the clerical isolationist philosophy succinctly in *Notre Question Nationale* in 1944. He spoke of four kinds of French Canadians:

(1) "the optimists," who believe that the BNA Act in 1967 protected their language, culture – supported by a belief in "le *fair play* brittanique." (Arès: "who are blind enough to think, when our history tells us the contrary, that even constitutional texts . . . are enough to protect us);

(2) "the resigned," who have given up (Arès: they develop the spirit of the vanquished and an inferiority complex);

(3) "the indifferent," who are above the battle (Arès: world citizens, only interested in international events and culture, the fate of their French-Canadian nation doesn't concern them);

(4) "the reactionaries" – ("guardian watchdogs," more than the current understanding of reactionaries, would be closer to what Arès meant). Clearly, these are his people. "Happily for the French, there are still the reactionaries."

> In their eyes, the French cannot maintain their rights, and the possibility of survival and growth . . . without opposing the growing menace of the unified and unremitting resistance to their particular ethnic existence. Their destiny is to react – not only against . . . the lion (presumably the English), but against the optimism, the defeatism, and the indifference of too many of their own kind.
>
> This situation imposes above all a state of alert . . . one must place on the ramparts and in the trenches vigilant and incorruptible sentries who . . . at the least suspect sound must cry 'qui-vive?'
>
> If in spite of all these outside attacks, and all these inner weaknesses, there remains a French-Canadian nation, it is to these reactionaries alone that we will owe everything . . . Given this healthy reaction by the French . . . psychological equality would soon develop between the two races, and the policy of association, instead of being more than simply vain phrases, would be established forever to the benefit of Canadian unity.[5]

In translating this, I may have missed a few nuances. But the interesting thing about it is the similarity these words bear to many péquiste statements today. Marc Lalonde said in May 1977, the péquistes are developing a "siege mentality . . . The enemy is at the gates." The "policy of association" phrase is fundamental to the Lévesque thesis. The tone of certainty, of religious conviction, about Quebec's problems is parallelled in Dr. Camille Laurin's language policy white paper and Bill One. Even the subtitle of Arès' book "The Facts" is misleading; it should be called "Beliefs"; present-day péquiste treatment of data is highly reminiscent of the rather loose way in which Father Arès dealt with alleged facts. If a "fact" serves the cause, highlight it; if not, attack it or bury it; if no facts fit, manufacture a few that do.

Anti-clerical many of today's péquistes certainly are, but numbered in their ranks is Father Arès, along with others from the same "reactionary" school, notably François Albert Angers, head of the right wing and nationalistic Sociétés Saint-Jean-Baptiste – recently rebaptized Société Nationale de Québec. The great historic triumph of this group, in waging its battle for French-Canadian survival, was the Quebec birth-rate – the "revenge of the cradle." French Canadians found out about the pill in the 'sixties, but there are a few signs that the péquistes will launch a modernized and secular version of the old approach, such as beefing up family allowances. Certainly, the Estates General provided more than a meeting place for the nationalists to get together and cheer each other on. Its religious origins brought an aura of respectability which the new – and for the most part irreligious – independence movement needed.

If these links with the past form an important element in the fabric of the new PQ party, another perhaps more important source of its strength was the rise of the new middle class in Quebec. The quiet revolution had brought with it a growing French-Canadian confidence in their ability to compete in the modern world of industry and business. For Quebecers, the building of the Hydro-Québec Manicouagan ("Manic") series of dams and power stations became the symbol of this new confidence. Many English Canadians hoped that this turning away from traditional pursuits of farming and church, the apparent acceptance of Anglo Saxon values and goals, would strengthen the attractiveness of Canadian federalism to Quebecers. Instead it seemed to generate a new form of nationalism.

Posgate and McRoberts discuss this phenomenon at some length in their *Quebec: Social Change and Political Crisis.*[6] They refer to the first emergence of the new bureaucratic middle class within the Church's educational, health and welfare institutions, with the Church becoming increasingly dependent on its lay administrators. This new élite developed a claim to power and status based on its specialized knowledge of the social sciences. With Duplessis gone, their next natural target was the provincial government; as its bureaucrats, they "could use the authority of the Quebec government to displace the clergy and bring these institutions directly under its control." But their professional training also constituted a claim to a larger role in the private sector. "Through nationalism, the new middle class could legitimize various government programs which would create new opportunities for Francophones to assume managerial positions within the economy."

Related to this middle class drive for power is the thesis that the group is searching for a new identity – French Canada being seen to be inferior in social and economic development. Charles Taylor is quoted by Posgate and McRoberts as saying that the "new middle class French Canadian could not feel comfortable defining himself as a French Canadian, nor could he adapt to the anglophone community because of wide differences in culture and language." Thus, the "modern" French Canadian turned to transforming French Canada so that it became more acceptable in terms of his values. Since the primary purpose of this was "to raise the status of the French-Canadian collectivity, it was critically important that these changes be undertaken by French Canadians themselves within exclusively French-Canadian institutions." Only the Quebec government could bring this about, by intervention if necessary in almost any area of the society.

Another aspect of this new nationalism was the inability, until recently, of French Canadians to penetrate the middle and upper management ranks in business in Quebec and in the federal government. As we shall see, the changes in this regard in the past decade have been immense, but it was in the 'fifties and 'sixties that this new nationalism developed, and most PQ leaders today grew up and formed their opinions and prejudices during that era.

The base of the Parti Québécois, however diverse the threads that were wound together to create the present movement, has clear roots in the ancient as well as the recent past. Its doctrine is associated with a narrow chauvinistic nationalism that depends for much of its support on reaction against the English in Quebec as well as against the federal government in Ottawa.

Notes

1 Lévesque, *op. cit.*
2 Lévesque, *op. cit.*, (English version), p. 40.
3 *Le Devoir,* supplement, November 25-28, 1967, p. A1.
4 *Le Devoir,* November 27, 1967, p.5.
5 Richard Arès, *Notre Question Nationale: (1) Les Faits* (Montréal: Editions de L'Action Nationale, 1944), pp. 30-33.
6 Posgate and McRoberts, *op. cit.*, pp. 96-110.

IX

Parizeau Committee – and a few digressions (1966-1969)

Early in 1966 our Committee on Financial Institutions had sent out a call for briefs. We received some twenty-seven of them, of surprisingly high quality, mainly from associations representing the trust companies, the caisses populaires, the credit unions, the sales finance companies and consumers, and, among the professional groups, the notaries, the lawyers, and the trade unions. Public hearings were set to begin in November 1966; altogether we heard testimony for fifteen days of such hearings, with the last taking place on April 14, 1967.

One problem we faced at the outset of the hearings was language. We all agreed that no simultaneous translation would be provided – we assumed that even anglophone associations or firms would put their best francophone face forward – but that since the five of us could cope with testimony in either language, any witness could speak English or French. The only weak link in the chain was me: I didn't feel I could carry on intelligent cross-examination in French – and the stuttering would further complicate matters. Thus, my colleagues agreed that if any witnesses appeared who didn't understand English, they would jump in and do any necessary translation.

Things worked out just fine. Most of the briefs were presented in French – but few witnesses could not understand English. I usually prefaced my first question to a francophone with a French phrase asking if they would mind if I posed my question in English. No one objected – if even on nationalistic grounds – and I fired away, occasionally putting some of my questions in French.

The sessions were all recorded. One of the transcribing secretaries spoke to Parizeau once, saying that they were "having a bit of trouble understanding one of the commissioners." Parizeau was a bit embarrassed, thinking my stuttering was the problem, but he assured them that I would fill in any gaps from memory. "Oh, not him," they said "it's that fellow who keeps his pipe clenched between his teeth when he's speaking." It was Yves Pratte – and he and Parizeau have told the tale often with great relish.

Most of our hearings were held in the Place Ville Marie, in the boardroom of the Montreal offices of the Quebec Department of Industry and Commerce, of which Michel Bélanger was then deputy minister. There was a fringe benefit – lunches in the Beaver Club in the Queen Elizabeth, and we soon became addicted to the Club's large martinis. We had thoughtfully scheduled most of the important hearings for the morning sessions, for I'm afraid that some of the people we saw in the afternoon didn't find us quite as probing as we might have been. But the lunches certainly did a great deal for our group morale and strengthened the co-operative spirit with which we attacked any and all problems.

I won't inflict upon you a detailed analysis of what we discussed at hearings, or in our own private sessions. Broadly, we attempted to analyse how the financial system functioned in Quebec, and how the federally incorporated companies (banks for example) and provincially incorporated companies (trust companies, caisse populaires), fitted into the system. The studies, done by our research group headed by Jean-Luc Migué, Laval University professor, were directed mainly to this end. Other topics of particular interest included:

- The safety of depositors in financial institutions. The Atlantic Acceptance failure of June 1965 was much on our minds.
- The protection of consumers: interest rates, repossession, unfair practices.
- The special role of the caisses populaires in Quebec society, and their relationship to the banking system.
- Investment regulation, including the adequacy of Quebec's administrative machinery for policing the investment business.
- Federal-provincial problems, including the question of the relationship between the Bank of Canada and Quebec financial institutions.

Events, however, were not standing still waiting for our deliberations to end. Several problems blew up demanding urgent action, and we had to make interim recommendations. The most important of these concerned the protection of depositors by new regulations, by tighter inspection, and by the setting up of a system for insuring deposits.

Proposals of the federal government to establish a national deposit insurance scheme had culminated in a bill respecting "The Canada Deposit Insurance Act," which was given first reading in Parliament on January 11, 1967. This bill proposed that deposit insurance be obligatory for chartered banks and other federally incorporated financial institutions. The bill raised immediate problems for us to consider. What about the position of Quebec-incorporated institutions? Deposit insurance would be an important competitive asset. What about the danger of double coverage if Quebec set up its own system? Was there potential conflict over federal-provincial and constitutional issues? Would acceptance by Quebec of the federal act force Quebec institutions to change their procedures to fit federal requirements? And so on. Ontario had set up its own scheme, similar to the federal proposal.

We met first on January 17 to discuss these and related questions, and had the help of Louis Bernard, then legal adviser to the Minister of Federal-Provincial affairs. Bernard worked with Claude Morin, and like Morin and Parizeau, was later to join the péquistes; until September, 1977, he was René Lévesque's *chef de cabinet* – head of his personal secretariat. We held subsequent meetings with trust company representatives, and produced a preliminary report in March.

Our report was devoted mainly to the establishment of a Quebec Deposit Insurance Board (QDIB). We proposed to dovetail the scheme with the federal plan, with the same $20,000 maximum guarantee per deposit; an agreement was eventually reached by negotiation with Ottawa that avoided most duplication of work. The agreement also satisfied two of the most important criteria we had set: (1) that the QDIB do the inspection of all insured institutions with Quebec-incorporation, and (2) that the QDIB have access to the backstop of federal funds, if needed in time of crisis. The QDIB was set up by act of the Quebec legislature, and deposit insurance came into effect in mid-1967.

We were required to consider several other emergency issues that came up in 1967. One was the financial difficulties of Alliance Credit, an acceptance and loan company, which led to its bankruptcy later in the year. Another was the case of the notary who had misused and lost substantial sums of money placed in his care. Notaries have a special place in Quebec society; they not only carry out legal work on wills and deeds, but often act as financial counsel and middlemen in financial dealings. In some instances, notaries had begun to function almost as private banks; conflicts of interest were inevitable.

We hired special consultants to examine these cases in detail, but felt that urgent action to tighten up supervision and inspection was essential. We therefore included recommentations to this effect in our March 1967 preliminary report. They were accepted by the government and shortly put into effect.

A few digressions - Le Devoir

As our study moved on at its rather unhurried pace, I became involved in several other activities which brought me into close contact with prominent French-Canadian personalities in Ottawa and Montreal. One of these was Claude Ryan, editor of *Le Devoir*, who in recent years has become widely known across Canada as an articulate spokesman on Quebec affairs. Lean, ascetic looking, with angular features and bushy eyebrows, Ryan came from a strongly religious background, and in fact had taught for a while at the Pontifical Gregorian University in Rome. He had also served for seventeen years as the general secretary of *L'Action Catholique Canadienne*, leaving to join *Le Devoir* as editorial writer in 1962.

Le Devoir did not have a large circulation, unlike the large and popular *La Presse*, but for many years it has been regarded as the intellectual's paper, a bit like *Le Monde* in Paris. Although it had its origins in ultra-nationalist, Quebec-first traditions, *Le Devoir* was very jealous of its independence, and had been in the forefront of the battle against the authoritarian rule of Maurice Duplessis. The paper's representative in Quebec during the later years of the Duplessis régime was Pierre Laporte. He was later to become a cabinet minister in the Lesage government, a losing candidate for the Quebec Liberal leadership after Lesage resigned, and to be killed by his kidnappers in the October 1970 FLQ crisis. Duplessis was so annoyed with Laporte and *Le Devoir* that he warned advertisers to avoid the paper, branding Laporte as a "pig," and ordering him to stay away from his press conferences.

Partly because of the paper's combative reputation, and also because I had become acquainted with Gérard Filion and with Ryan, I bought a few shares in the paper and became a regular reader. I regarded it more as a goodwill contribution than as an investment, because like many worthy causes *Le Devoir* was not a very profitable operation. I gathered that Eric Kierans and I were the only anglophone shareholders.

I had a long talk with Ryan about *Le Devoir's* problems at a conference at the Seigniory Club in 1965. The paper needed more advertising revenue, and I agreed to canvass some of the senior people I know among the larger Canadian firms. Those in Montreal were not very responsive, but an old friend from college days, Dick Murray, then managing director of the Winnipeg-based Hudson's Bay Company, came through with the placing of a few ads for Morgans, their Montreal department store subsidiary, and for Hudson's Bay whisky. Murray had wanted to meet Ryan for some time, and I arranged for them to get together.

In 1966 Ryan asked me for advice about the *Le Devoir's* finances and future plans. Their plant on Notre-Dame Street was run down and inadequate, they needed to expand and renovate, but lacked the funds to do it.

I had no ready answers for them, but counselled strongly against heavy capital expenditures; I thought rather that they should move to fairly modest editorial offices and contract out the printing operating to another paper or to commercial printers. My advice was followed – perhaps because no other course was open to the paper. Ryan and I have remained in close touch to this day; some of my columns, which he translated, appeared in the paper in early 1977. In September of that year he was being widely touted for the provincial Liberal leadership.

"Quebec Demain"

The Quebec Liberals, in an attempt to revive party enthusiasm, and perhaps to bring forward some fresh ideas and people, conceived the idea of a conference to be held in May 1969 at the Maison Montmorency, a kind of "think-in." Speakers were to be non-partisan, and presumably with something provocative to say. In January I was called by Pierre Laporte, then Liberal house leader, and asked if I would participate, and give a speech as a member of a panel discussion on "investments and full employment in Quebec." I agreed, and was asked down by Laporte in March to an organizing dinner in Montreal. At the dinner table I wound up seated between him and Bob Bourassa.

The Montmorency Conference was talked about all right, but what was on both their minds was the Liberal leadership succession. Jean Lesage had indicated he was going to step down soon. I swivelled back and forth between the two, sounding them out on their hopes and being sounded out in turn. Laporte was on my right; his concerns were practical and political. He did not appear overly intellectual, although his earthy approach masked a pretty good mind. Bourassa, thin, frail and ascetic looking, a bit like the boy on the beach who gets sand kicked in his face, was an intellectual with a good background in economics and tax law. He was more the kind of a person one could conceive as leader, even if his image was not exactly a strong one. However both men liked their own chances. Bourassa had the edge – with Ottawa support – and at the leadership convention a year later he defeated Claude Wagner and Laporte.

I gave my speech at the May conference, mostly in French – and I'm afraid, cut up badly by my stutter. Most of the comments I received after were for my "courage," rather than for the contents of the speech! My pitch was essentially this: capital is scarce and growing scarcer; it hates uncertainty; the goals of nationalism are in perpetual conflict with efforts to attract investment. On separatism, I expressed my concern that "those in the vanguard of the nationalist movement may be unaware that they are playing with a very special kind of dynamite, the explosion of which could ruin the province's external credit – and growth prospects – for a decade or more."

My colleagues on the panel were Henri Mhun, economic consultant and writer, and economist André Raynauld, later to head Canada's Economic Council, and, still later, to resign from it in the fall of 1976 to run in Quebec as a Liberal in the November 15 débacle – and win.

Did the conference help the Liberals or produce any worthwhile results? One rarely knows after such conferences. Anyway I received a nice *"Cher ami"* note from Jean Lesage later, thanking me for my participation in the conference which, he was sure, "would be an important landmark in the political history of Quebec." I think Lesage was pushing politeness a little far – but at least the Liberals, under Bourassa, were returned to power in the April 1970 election.

We wind up the Parizeau Commission - at last

One reason why our report had dragged on for so long – we had been appointed in December 1965 – was that we had to act as firemen, called upon by the government whenever a brush fire broke out in the field we were studying. Our preliminary report of March 1967, and the problems it touched on, was a case in point. But we also became involved as members of the Quebec government team at several federal-provincial conferences, including one in December 1966 on Consumer Credit and Interest Disclosure, and another in April 1967 on Financial Institutions and Securities Regulations.

We did keep the government posted on what we were doing, although things became a bit more difficult after Daniel Johnson's death of a heart attack on September 26, 1968. The new team was not so well briefed on the background as Johnson had been, and I can't blame them for thinking we were beginning to resemble a permanent fixture – a kind of a standing Royal Commission on financial issues. We also tried to keep the Opposition informed and met at least once with Jean Lesage. Claude Morin organized a lunch for us with René Lévesque as well, memorable more for its good fun than for any profound conclusions about our work.

By the beginning of 1969 we were fed up too, and resolved to close the report off as quickly as possible. Pratte had resigned in November 1968 to become chairman and chief executive officer of Air Canada. By March the report was largely completed. Our main recommendation had been implemented, the establishment of deposit insurance under the QDIC. The creation of a new Department of Financial Institutions, Companies and Co-operatives followed our recommendation to centralize the functions of inspection, supervision and control. In the final report we proposed a Consumer Bureau be set up to be attached to the new department, and laid out a series of recommendations calling for fuller disclosure of interest rates, clarification of terms of financing contracts, and limits on the seizure of merchandise.

Looking at our proposals as a whole, I cannot say that they were excessively nationalistic, particularly in the light of Parizeau's own views. We did recommend that more balances held by public or quasi-public bodies, or by trustees, be channelled through the Caisse de Dépôt, in order to build up the maximum flow of funds available to the Quebec government. But we proposed no changes of note in the financial institutional framework, nor did we suggest any attempt to strengthen the competitive position of Quebec institutions at the expense of their federal counterparts. Parizeau had the responsibility of editing the final report, and putting it in shape for printing; I edited the English translation.

Jacques Parizeau - our paths separate

On July 29 I visited Jacques and his wife Alice at their home in Outremont. It turned out to be quite a moving occasion; I told Jacques that I had just about decided to accept a federal position as chairman of the Crown agency, the National Capital Commission. He in turn told me that he had made up his mind to enter politics at the side of René Lévesque, although the decision had not yet been announced. Our paths were clearly and sharply diverging.

Knowing Jacques as well as I did, I was not surprised at his move. Parizeau's emotional and political transition had been taking place over the whole of the 'sixties. It had been in part a product of rebuffs from Ottawa, one of them certainly being the absence of any job offer from the federal economic establishment at a level that Parizeau felt was warranted by his intelligence, seniority, and training. On another occasion he had worked hard and long in Quebec to negotiate a tough 3 per cent wage settlement with medical workers in the hospitals, only to see Ottawa settle shortly after with its hospital workers for a much larger raise, making Quebec look niggardly.

His dislike of Ottawa was also unquestionably strengthened by the development of a solid provincial front against the federal government establishment, and by the provincial ties that he and Morin had forged, particularly with their opposite numbers in Ontario, such as Ian Macdonald and Don Stevenson. As a member of many provincial teams in this period and later, I can vouch for the depth of provincial dislike for the arrogant bureaucrats from Ottawa, a not inconsequential factor in developing feelings of separatism in every province, not just Quebec.

Parizeau had been a behind-the-scenes adviser to Lévesque in the preparation of the economic aspect of his *Souveraineté-Association* proposal in 1967. The story had come out in the papers, and Jacques, still a part-time economic adviser to the Quebec cabinet, as well as chairman of our Committee, was put on the spot. He acknowledged having had a "professional" role as an economist in advising Lévesque, but denied that he was politically committed to Lévesque's cause.

All through 1968 and early 1969 Jacques stayed on the fence, but kept agonizing about when to jump off, although the direction was becoming more obvious as the months went by. This in no way affected his efficiency as the key member of our Committee, because he was a damned good chairman, and a superb drafter. I was privy to some of his private thoughts on the choice he faced, and I may have done a bit to discourage him from premature commitment to Lévesque. But the ending of our Committee helped him make up his mind to jump, and he did. He was clearly a major catch for his old friend René, because of his background in economics, where the péquistes were weakest.

I told him that although I regretted his action, it would for my part make no difference to our friendship, and wished him (if not his party) well. Jacques, in turn, expressed *his* regret that I was going federalist, and would presumably no longer be able to continue working for Quebec task forces. He had some nice things to say about my understanding of and sympathy for Quebec, and Québécois, and said that when the day came that Quebec split with Canada, he could see me as one of the few people who would be acceptable to them as a mediator or bridge rebuilder. Very flattering to hear, of course, but I didn't tell him what was going through my mind: that neither he, Lévesque, nor I would probably be around when that particular independence day dawned.

Our press conference was held ten days later; Jacques fielded most of the questions. I gave an interview to several English reporters, and that was that.

A note on chronology

One problem I faced in this book was to keep the chronology straight for the reader. During most of the period from 1962 to 1969 I was involved in several parallel activities – Quebec consultant and task force member, bond adviser, associate of French-Canadian politicians in Ottawa, newspaper columnist, board member of a federal Crown agency. I decided that the best way to cope with this was to give priority to maintaining the continuity of my work and associations in Quebec. The past six chapters are therefore largely oriented towards my work at the Quebec provincial level. The next four chapters are more related to my other activities relating to Quebec, but mainly centred on Ottawa. In the chapter which follows I retrace my steps to discuss the role of French-Canadian politicians in Ottawa in the 1960s, with particular emphasis on two people, Maurice Sauvé and Pierre Trudeau.

PART III
Ottawa Scene

X

Ottawa: Maurice Sauvé and Pierre Trudeau (1963-1969)

From 1962 on the focus of my work switched to Montreal and Quebec. If the successive Quebec task forces had prior claim on my time, however, I continued to function as a bond consultant, and to work with my colleagues in Montreal. And I still had personal responsibility for the Canada Council portfolio, and maintained an office and lived in Ottawa.

Of my French-Canadian friends in Ottawa, the person I saw most frequently was Maurice Sauvé. He had been elected as Liberal member in the Iles de la Madeleine constituency in June 1962, when Diefenbaker was returned as Prime Minister with a minority of seats – 116 to the Liberals 99. In 1963, when Pearson became Prime Minister, Sauvé, himself re-elected, had high hopes of being appointed to the cabinet. It didn't work out. What galled Sauvé was not that Lamontagne, just elected but long-time associate of Pearson, had gone straight into the cabinet, but that Lamontagne's good friend, newly elected René Tremblay, former Quebec provincial civil servant, also was chosen.

Sauvé's relationship with Lamontagne, never very warm, chilled noticeably after that. He had never thought much of Lamontagne's capacity as a politician, but a further indignity was that after Lamontagne had failed twice in St. Laurent's old riding in Quebec, in 1963 he was given the safe Liberal seat of Outremont–St. Jean, the constituency in which Sauvé lived and which he naturally coveted. This Outremont seat was later to further embitter Sauvé in his relations with the Liberal hierarchy.

Sauvé's cause was certainly not helped by the fact that he was never a team man – always played a lone game – and he played it hard. Perhaps that was why I liked him. But few such mavericks last very long in politics, it being a team sport. When they do, they generally end up as leader – like Diefenbaker and Trudeau.

Pearson's memoirs make it clear that Sauvé was never one of his favourite French-Canadian ministers; the paucity of comment about Sauvé, in spite of warm praise for almost every other minister from Quebec, is revealing. One of the few references concerned Pearson's 1963 cabinet choices; after speaking of some of the prospects who "had never served in the House before, such as Maurice Lamontagne, Guy Favreau, René Tremblay and Jean-Luc Pepin," Pearson said "Another new man, Maurice Sauvé, was I think anxious to get into political life. He had a particular aptitude for the rough and tumble of politics."[1] Sauvé, who had been up to his ears in politics for years, and who had been first elected in 1962! It is not surprising that Sauvé felt neglected, and believed that Pearson was influenced too much by Lamontagne. With his background, Pearson appeared to prefer academic, bureaucratic or External Affairs types around him. However, he did finally appoint Sauvé to a cabinet post in February 1964, as Minister of Forestry.

Sauvé's role in the pension fund crisis with Quebec, related in an earlier chapter, may have raised his status a bit in Mr. Pearson's eyes. There was no doubt that Sauvé did have a better rapport with provincial politicians, and with the mood of Quebec, than did most of his French-Canadian colleagues. I found this out in my contacts in Quebec; a frequent comment at that time from Quebec ministers or officials was that "the only guy I can talk to down there is Sauvé."

Sauvé's relative position improved, too, as a result of the personal problems that seemed to afflict so many of Pearson's Quebec ministers: Lamontagne and Tremblay in the Sefkind furniture affair, Guy Favreau in the Dorion case, and Yvon Dupuis with the bribery charges against him. By the summer of 1965, however, it was clear to Mr. Pearson that he needed stronger representation from Quebec. A vigorous attempt was made to attract Pierre Trudeau, Jean Marchand and Gérard Pelletier into Liberal ranks. On September 7, Pearson called an election for November (on the advice of Walter Gordon, who later resigned because of the failure of Pearson to win a majority). The *trois colombes* (doves), or Quebec wise men, as they were variously called, proved willing, and a press conference had been called a few days after the election announcement to tell the world about the great coup. But for days a debate had been raging among the Quebec ministers, some of whom, including Favreau and Lamontagne, wanted Marchand only and not the other two. Marchand, with Sauvé's backing, said "All or none." The stories of the various participants in the drama differ – Marchand later was very critical of Sauvé[2] – but there was no doubt that Sauvé had been on the side of the three rather than the one, and used his weight effectively at the crucial moment.

Sauvé retained his seat, but ran into a problem which was to damage his political career: he was charged by his opponent with election irregularities. Shortly after the election on November 17, Sauvé flew to Rome to chair the 13th Conference of the Food and Agriculture Organization (FAO). On December 9, the story broke in the papers, leading to a *Globe and Mail* headline on page 1 (December 11) "Election Spells Shenanigans in Sauvé-land." John Diefenbaker called for his resignation.

Sauvé's office then was just downstairs from mine in the Victoria Building on Wellington Street, and I went down and had a council of war with Claude Frenette and Sonny Gordon, his two principal assistants. One problem was his chairmanship role at the FAO conference; he simply couldn't pack up and leave before its December 12 closing date. Still, I sent him off the following cable "Storm reaching gale proportions, urge return soonest or will lose by default." By this time his staff were busy, in Ottawa and in the Magdalen Islands, rounding up material to refute the charges.

Sauvé arrived home on Monday, December 13, and told the press he would reply publicly to the accusations on December 15. A meeting was called for the following evening at his Outremont home. On the afternoon of December 14, Sauvé, Frenette, Gordon and I, along with several secretaries, boarded one of the special private Pullmans used by cabinet ministers, and it was hooked on to the CN 4.55 train to Montreal. Our plan was to examine each separate charge in turn, and either rebut it or put the best face on it we could.

One important issue we had to get across was that elections on the Magdalen Islands are different than they are elsewhere in Canada – more like the situation a century ago. Everyone votes (the turnout was 94 per cent in 1965), the crowds are violently partisan, opposition gangs in cars follow candidates around trying to interfere with their electioneering, liquor flows freely.

As for the charges, they were mainly of the variety "221 people voted in a poll which listed only 219," "red stickers were placed improperly on cars taking voters to the polls." One charge was tough, that Sauvé had called Judge Duguay – who lived in New Carlisle over on the mainland (oddly enough, Sauvé's cousin, but a "blue," a UN supporter), and had asked him not to release two men who had been arrested as ringleaders of a mob the night before the election; Sauvé feared a riot. Our considered reply, replete with affidavits and detail, took up six legal length papers (they are big on affidavits in the Magdalen Islands); it's too complicated to go into here except to note that everyone calls the Judge by 'phone, there being no other approach possible except by boat, that Sauvé was indeed concerned about law and order, and that in fact the men had been allowed out to vote, but under guard.

Prospective answers to each of the twenty-three specific allegations were discussed that evening at Sauvé's home in Outremont; a big crowd turned out, twenty or twenty-five people – I remember Marchand, Pelletier, Jean-Pierre Goyer and Claude Ducharme among others – Trudeau arriving at 11.00 and not having said very much, leaving after midnight. By 4.00 AM we had the press *communiqué* more or less ready, in English and French, and headed back to the rail car to try to snatch a bit of sleep before and during the ride back on the morning train to Ottawa.

The typing was completed by noon – thirty-two pages long in English and thirty-five in French; Maurice turned up that afternoon to face 100 newsmen – some specially in from Toronto and Montreal – and to pass out his document and answer questions. He did a hell of a good job too; most press stories gave him a clean bill of health, commending him for the full detail and forthrightness of his reply. The incident quickly died down in the media as a "nine-day wonder." The press release achieved a certain enduring fame of its own, being used in several university political science courses, and finally being printed in the first issue of Trent University's *Journal of Canadian Studies.*

Unfortunately for Sauvé, if the incident didn't appear to hurt him in the press, it didn't do him much good politically. His "Mr. Clean" image had been tarnished, and no amount of washing could remove all the stain. Prime Minister Pearson's long heralded cabinet shuffle was due to be announced on December 17; Lamontagne and Tremblay had resigned, and Sauvé had been widely touted for a senior post. A *Globe and Mail* editorial on November 23 had said "Mr. Sauvé is ready for bigger things," and suggested he be given Trade and Commerce. Martin Goodman, in the *Toronto Star* of December 9, discussed the impact of the charges on Sauvé's prospects, saying "People invariably either like or dislike the strong minded, abrasive Sauvé – and Pearson is not one of his fervent admirers. . . . (he) might take the opportunity to bypass Sauvé for the senior post – probably an economic portfolio like Trade – he otherwise seems slated for."

The portfolio issue had in fact been settled before the election. I understand from Sauvé that he had gone to Mr. Pearson asking if he could have Trade and Commerce. He said "Pearson countered by offering me Agriculture. I replied that it should be saved for an M.P. from the west, where we were very thin, and then I asked Pearson if he had promised T & C to Bob Winters as an encouragement to run. Pearson refused to confirm or deny, and I told him I would just as soon stay put." In *Mike,* Pearson says "Trade and Commerce . . . remained a prestige portfolio. Marchand would have liked it, but I had promised it to Bob Winters

. . ."[3] Winters won York West, and was appointed immediately to the Trade and Commerce post. Marchand was appointed to Citizenship (later Manpower) and Immigration.

Sauvé's moment had passed, although I don't think it was fully realized at the time. Trudeau was coming along fast, and in January 1966 became parliamentary assistant to Mr. Pearson; he entered the cabinet, along with Jean Chrétien, in April 1967. Marchand had become head of the Quebec "reform group," as it was called, and Quebec leader. Sauvé, for a variety of reasons (many no doubt related to his personality and to his ambitions) had become an outsider. He saw further evidence of this at the time of Lamontagne's resignation from the Commons in 1967, in anticipation of his subsequent appointment to the Senate. Sauvé's own seat of Iles de la Madeleine was being abolished, to be incorporated into a mainland riding. He wanted to run in Outremont-St. Jean, but could hardly resign from his present seat in order to do so; it would look foolish and besides the government's minority position would be temporarily aggravated. What to do? Sauvé suggested that a seat-warming candidate be run, who would then not present himself at the next general election. He went to Mr. Pearson, and received a letter from him dated April 1967 which confirmed these arrangements. Sauvé was promised Liberal backing for Outremont, subject to one provision (which did not enter into subsequent decisions).

Mr. Aurelien Noel, age sixty-two, was picked, ran and won the by-election on May 29, 1967. Came the 1968 election, with Pierre Trudeau as Prime Minister but by this time Mr. Noel decided to run again. Sauvé tried for the nomination in the Montreal riding of Gamelin, but lost out to Arthur Portelance. He finally won the nomination in Ste. Hyacinthe, thirty miles from Montreal, a seat held by the Progressive Conservatives since 1957; in the election he lost, by 788 votes, to the incumbent. Mr. Noel won Outremont by 21,000 votes, but retired at next election in 1972 to make way for – guess who? – Marc Lalonde, Trudeau's right hand man!

Pierre Trudeau

I had met Pierre Trudeau several times before the encounter at Sauvé's home December 1965; one meeting had been over the poker table at a conference at Mont Tremblant. (He was a novice, but cool, and I think won a little money). However, for some reason which escapes me now, I arranged to see him in his office late in February 1966. Our meeting was rushed, and we agreed to lunch on March 30 in the Parliamentary restaurant.

The main discussion at our luncheon, if memory serves me right, was over some pretty fundamental questions – Quebec's role in Confederation and the language issue. I made the case for special status for Quebec on the grounds of its need to protect its language and culture – "la survivance." He argued, persuasively, that Quebec had a better chance for cultural survival in a pluralist society, in a Canada which under the right policies, could become more bilingual and receptive to a largely francophone Quebec. His feelings on this issue obviously ran deep. (See further discussion pp. 169-171).

We argued also over the nationalization of the power companies. Trudeau quoted his economist friend, Albert Breton, to the effect that the take-over had been unnecessary, and was merely a nationalistic springboard for Lévesque. Having tangled with Breton myself on this, I simply said that he didn't know what he was talking about, and that the nationalistic garb in which the package was wrapped by Lévesque in the 1962 election campaign did not diminish in any way the real economic need for amalgamation of the Quebec electric power companies.

My first impressions of Trudeau? Hard to say, except that I liked him, found him a tough customer in debate, and sensed something of the strength of both his intellect and his strong anti-nationalist feelings. I didn't see too much of him over the next couple of years, except the occasional brief talk at cocktail parties or receptions; I always found him very friendly. I was to see more of him after my 1967 appointment to the Cape Breton Development board, and still more after I became chairman of the National Capital Commission.

Cape Breton Development (Devco)

Devco had been set up in 1967 by the federal government in its efforts to try to do something about the problems of Cape Breton Island, and in particular the DOSCO coal mines which had been requiring progressively higher federal subsidies to survive. I had been interested in the coal issue for some time, and my concern for Cape Breton generally had been aroused by the unemployment problems we saw around us at our summer home near the northern tip of the island. I expressed an interest in going on to the board of directors of Devco, and my name was put forward by friends. Although the government took an unconscionable length of time to settle the matter, the appointment came through early in December.

Within a few weeks of my Devco appointment, I found myself board chairman; although not a salaried job, it took up much of my time in 1968. As Devco's contact man in Ottawa, I saw a fair amount of Jean-Luc Pepin, the minister responsible, and found him a very attractive personality. His Gallic mannerisms, which became so well known to Canadians when he became chairman of the Anti-Inflation Board in 1975, and his ready laugh, made it impossible to tangle with him. He was pretty talkative, mind you, but listened when it mattered.

Devco was shifted to Jean Marchand's department in July; he had taken over the Forestry and Rural Development portfolios which Maurice Sauvé had vacated after losing out in the 1968 general elections. The department was being renamed Regional Economic Expansion, and Devco fitted more comfortably into it than as a part of Energy, Mines and Resources. Jean Marchand was a different type from Pepin – not quite so boisterous, although volatile in temperament; less interested in detail, more political in his instincts and interests. Physically shorter and less voluble than Pepin, he still projected a strong image – and a warm one. I liked him on the spot, and we worked well together over the next few years.

The Liberal leadership race

The year 1968 proved to be one of the most exciting in Canadian political history. On December 14, 1967, Mike Pearson announced his intention to retire from politics and the Liberal leadership race was on.

The first candidate of any stature to come forward, to most people's surprise, was my old friend Eric Kierans. He made his announcement January 15, 1968, at a press conference. I gave him my support, such as it was, although I didn't think he had a hope in hell of getting very far. Still, I understood his need to make a federal splash, his only political experience having been at the Quebec provincial level.

Next in was Paul Hellyer, Minister of Transport, who while still in his twenties had become a minister in the closing days of the St. Laurent régime. Bob Winters had been expected to run, but on January 12 had said publicly he wouldn't. The next day Allan MacEachen announced, followed shortly by John Turner and Mitchell Sharp and then Agriculture Minister Joe Greene.

By this time no French Canadian had come forward, and into the breach stepped Paul Martin, whose candidacy was supported by my friend Maurice Sauvé. Many people thought Martin, then sixty-four, a bit too old to run; the trend was all towards youth. I have always been surprised both by his candidacy, and by Sauvé's support for him, and in this book I decided to get the story straight from Maurice. The conventional wisdom had him backing Martin out of pique with Trudeau and Marchand, and he was widely criticized for it.

This is what Sauvé told me:

> Paul came to me in January, and asked for my backing. He said Trudeau had told him he wasn't going to run, and Marchand had little Quebec caucus support. When Winters said no, Martin saw himself as beneficiary of the bulk of Quebec support – Jean Lesage was support-

> ing Winters, and had a solid block of Quebec delegates with him. Martin thought that his long service for the party, and connections across the country, would give him enough other support to come through as the best bilingual compromise, bridging French and English Canada.

Sauvé added that he had respect for Martin's skills in Parliament, and believed that with a minority government, this would be a great asset in a prime minister. He also thought that Martin could do a better job carrying on Pearson's work, and negotiating with Quebec, than the other candidates. So he promised Martin his support. He was to regret it later, because it did further damage to his already strained relationships with his Quebec colleagues.

Meanwhile a great many people were getting together to try to convince Trudeau to run. One draft-Trudeau group was co-ordinated by Sauvé's former executive assistant, Claude Frenette, who in January had become president of the Quebec wing of the Liberal Federation. In Frenette's Power Corporation office, periodic meetings were held involving Marc Lalonde, Jean-Pierre Goyer and several other key Quebecers. But Trudeau refused to commit himself – at least publicly.

I knew from my connections in Marchand's office that in early January he and Trudeau had frequent discussions, each promoting the other's candidacy, a kind of Alphonse-Gaston act. Marchand had ambitions himself, but perhaps because of his lack of clear Quebec support, or his weakness in English, he finally prevailed upon his friend that if either ran it would have to be Trudeau.

Public support was also building for Trudeau's candidacy. He had been seen to be doing an excellent job as Minister of Justice in the recent legislation on divorce, abortion and homosexuality. A quotation attributed to him, variously reported as "The Minister of Justice (or "The Government of Canada) has no place in the bedrooms of the nation" received wide publicity.

His televised confrontation with Daniel Johnson at the January Constitutional Conference had added to his charismatic image. The issue had been joined, as usual, on the question of special status for Quebec. Daniel Johnson had argued – as most Quebec Premiers had done before him – that Quebec must be recognized as a nation, not as a province like the others, and given commensurate powers. Trudeau's stand as a strong federalist won him support across the country, although it cost him some support in the Quebec parliamentary caucus.

Finally, on February 16, Trudeau threw his hat in the ring. Within two weeks, Bob Winters reconsidered and came in too. Winter's announcement really torpedoed the chances of three of the candidates: Mitchell Sharp, who had counted on support from the same group as Winters;

Allan MacEachen, who saw his Nova Scotia "favoured son" support eroding to his Lunenburg opponent; and finally Paul Martin, who had already been wounded, perhaps mortally, by Trudeau's entry into the race.

The convention was scheduled for April 4-6, 1968. A week before the *Toronto Star* came out in favour of Trudeau. In my own *Star* column on April 1, I led off with these sentences, which are not inappropriate to today's circumstances:

> Among the problems which will face the man chosen to be Canada's Prime Minister . . . two dominate all others: relations between French and English, and mounting economic difficulties, both domestic and international. I do not intend to touch on the French-English question except to say there is little place for a hard line on either side. Both must compromise some deeply held views. It is greatly to Prime Minister Pearson's credit that he understood the need for Ottawa to avoid strongly entrenched positions, and his approach should be a model for his successor.

I cited our economic problems, and our increasing bias towards inflationary spending policies, and wrote, "Only two candidates, Mitchell Sharp and Eric Kierans, have clearly shown a grasp of the scale of our economic difficulties . . . Both are trained economists, and both have the experience, toughness and intellectual capacity to be the kind of economic prime minister that this country will so need in the coming time of trial." I lost my vote for Mitchell Sharp even before the convention opened. Sensing defeat, he withdrew and threw his support to Trudeau. He had no love for Winters.

In the first ballot on Saturday Trudeau led with 752, Hellyer was second with 330, Winters third with 293; Martin and Turner were tied at 277; Greene was at 169, MacEachen 165 and Kierans 103. Kierans and Martin quickly withdrew, Sauvé, and his wife Jeanne making their agonizing way over to Trudeau's box. MacEachen also withdrew.

In the second ballot Trudeau climbed to 964, Winters to 473, Hellyer to 465, and Turner to 347. It was at that time that Judy LaMarsh, who up to then had supported Hellyer, made her loud and overheard comment about Trudeau. She urged Hellyer to switch to Winters, to keep "that bastard" from winning. Hellyer procrastinated until the next ballot – Trudeau 1051, Winters 621, Hellyer 377, Turner 279 – but it was too late to set a Winter's bandwagon rolling. On the final ballot, Trudeau received 1203 votes to Winters 954, and to Turner's loyal 195. Trudeau had become Liberal leader, and Canada's fifteenth Prime Minister. The day of the next House sitting, he called an election for June 25. He won it big, too, with 155 of the 265 seats, sweeping both Ontario and Quebec.

As for Maurice Sauvé, Trudeau did not come through with any acceptable offers of a government post, nor was a seat opened for him, and he became a vice-president of Consolidated Bathurst Corporation in Montreal. Sauvé's active political career appeared over, but there was one curious aftermath. His wife Jeanne had always been as interested in politics as Maurice, had done political commentary on her TV program, and was well-regarded in Liberal circles. She ran in 1972 in the Montreal riding of Ahuntsic; won, and entered the Trudeau cabinet in November, 1972. Now it was her turn to do the commuting between Ottawa and Montreal! I can't recall any parallel of a husband and wife simultaneously carrying the "honourable" designation, earned for life by appointment to the federal cabinet.

And how has Prime Minister Trudeau measured up to the two criteria I set out in my pre-convention column? Not very well, if mid-1977 is to be the basis for judging his performance. The French-English problem has never been more serious, unemployment at its highest levels in decades, our balance of payments is in worsening deficit, our dollar down 10 per cent in eight months, our economy floundering. People's expectations, fed by years of double-digit wage increases and expanded welfare programs, remain high, threatening further inflation. It would be presumptuous in the compass of a paragraph or two to try to render a balanced judgment on Trudeau's nine-year reign as Prime Minister, or to apportion blame for all our troubles. I must report, however, that in recent years I have found myself increasingly critical of the Trudeau government. My weekly columns reflect my disenchantment, as did a long article I wrote for the May 1976 edition of *Saturday Night*.

Notes

1 Lester B. Pearson, *Mike: The Memoirs of the Rt. Hon. Lester B. Pearson* (Toronto: Signet, 1976), p. 92. Reprint of University of Toronto Press hardcover edition, 1975).

2 See for example Martin Sullivan, *Mandate '68* (Toronto: Doubleday Canada, 1968), pp. 93-108.

3 Pearson, *op. cit.*, p. 235.

XI

The National Capital and the French Fact

The federal capital was given considerable attention in the Report of the Royal Commission on Bilingualism and Biculturalism; a volume was devoted to it, Book V.[1] While its main recommendations were concerned with giving equal status to both English and French languages in the capital, the Commission proposed changes in the governing of the region – the setting up of a tripartite advisory agency – and it noted the overwhelming imbalance in federal buildings between the Ontario and Quebec sides of the Ottawa River. This led to its specific recommendation number 16 that ". . . any future planning for investment in federally owned or leased buildings in the capital area include a programme specifically aimed at correcting the present imbalance . . ."

The extent of the differences between Ottawa and Hull had indeed been a cause of considerable comment for many years. Before the war neither city was very large. Since Hull's industrial vocation was taken for granted, as was Ottawa's as a civil service town, the disparities were not of wide general concern. But the post-war boom in government buildings, particularly during the 'sixties, changed all that. With the exception of the Printing Bureau, every single new federal office building, government built or leased, was on the Ontario side. While the aesthetic appearance of Ottawa was not improved by the forest of new towers, the gap between Ottawa and Hull, in physical and economic terms, became highly visible and much remarked on, not least by French-Canadian M.P.s and ministers.

With the spur of the B. and B. Report, the Pearson government began to move on the bilingual front – language training instituted, the hiring of French Canadians increased, signs made bilingual, more documents issued in both languages. On the building front, however, nothing much happened until Pierre Trudeau became Prime Minister. The Public Works department, under George McIlraith, made some tentative efforts to get something going in Hull. However, on grounds of economy, it had switched earlier to a policy of renting offices from speculative builders on the basis of competitive bidding, and was not doing much office construction itself. The private builders, unaware of the Hull issue, did their building on the Ottawa side of the river, much of it on land they had assembled, hopefully, or confidently, some time before.

Marcel d'Amour was Mayor of Hull in the last half of the 'sixties, and he tells me how difficult it was to get federal politicians to listen to his plea for "at least one" building. Ottawa anglophone members took a pretty selfish line, he said, more or less, "what we have we hold." But things started to change under Trudeau, and two men in particular hastened the process of change. One was Marc Lalonde, then principal secretary to Mr. Trudeau; the other was Jean Marchand. The National Capital Commission (NCC), the federal agency charged with responsibility for "the development, conservation and improvement of the National Capital Region," was told to get cracking on a plan for offices in Hull. It did, and picked a fifteen acre site in the centre of Hull. In May 1969, cabinet approved the expropriation of this land and, with appropriate publicity, the decision was announced.

It was about the time of the expropriation that I had lunch with Jacques Pigeon, son of Louis-Philippe Pigeon. Jacques was executive assistant to Marchand, then minister of Regional Economic Expansion, under whose aegis the NCC had been put a year earlier. The government was looking for someone to run the agency who was a bit more bilingual than the incumbent chairman – "did I know of any one who fitted, and who might be interested?" I thought immediately of Jacques Gagnon, a colleague on the Cape Breton Development (Devco) board and a person for whom I had considerable respect. I knew also that he was a friend of Marchand. I sounded Gagnon out, but he was earning more as a vice-president of Alcan, and was not too keen to move out of Montreal.

I had made it clear earlier to both Pigeon and Marchand that I wasn't going to be hanging around Devco much longer, for reasons about which I had fully – even tiresomely – briefed them, and I suspected that Pigeon's approach might have been more to test my own interest in the NCC chairmanship than to find a candidate for them. I confirmed this with him in June, said I was indeed interested, but that I would prefer to postpone discussion until I left Devco. After my resignation from Devco was accepted by Mr. Trudeau on July 9, I met Jean Marchand and agreed to take the NCC job on, and I began work as NCC chairman on September 4, 1969.

In the first month or two I was exposed to most of the kinds of problems I was to face during my nearly four years as chairman. Within days, in fact, I had to attend a meeting of the preparatory committee studying a proposed "tripartite" – the federal government, Ontario and Quebec – approach to the governing of the capital. Discussions about this new approach had been launched in 1967 by Prime Minister Pearson in letters to Premiers Robarts of Ontario and Johnson of Quebec. The proposed governing body would be a kind of "troika" arrangement, with representation from the three governments. This was favourably received by Robarts; Johnson was less enthusiastic but was willing to talk about it. This initiative led to the declaration by the eleven first ministers at the January 1968 Constitution Conference that "the cities of Ottawa and Hull and their surrounding areas shall be the Canadian Capital Area." The National Capital Act of 1958 had established a National Capital Region, about 1,800 square miles of terrain, situated in a rough square surrounding Ottawa and Hull; about 60 per cent of it is in Ontario and 40 per cent in Quebec (see map). However it had no juridical significance, apart from defining the boundaries in which NCC could function.

I needed some francophone help immediately; luckily Paul Pelletier was available. He had been involved in the initial tripartite discussions, and I brought him in as a special consultant. Our paths had crossed many times since I had first met him during the war at the artillery training camp in Petawawa; latterly I had seen him regularly as a colleague on the board of Le Cours Claudel, the French lycée in Ottawa.

At the September 17 tripartite meeting, I found it an odd sensation to be sitting as a member of the federal team, across from my old friend Claude Morin, leader of the Quebec delegation. For the previous seven years Quebec had claimed most of my time as well as my allegiance; yet here I was, very much in an adversary position. Morin, then Quebec's deputy minister of intergovernmental affairs, had first been hired by Jean Lesage as a speechwriter, on the recommendation of Father Lévesque, with whom he had studied and worked. He had specialized on federal provincial relations, and had served Lesage and Johnson in this capacity, as well as the then Premier, Bertrand. Most Ottawa politicians and officials viewed him as a kind of Talleyrand, weaving a web of intrigue which often frustrated federal constitutional objectives. They saw him as devious and a strong nationalist, not one of their favourite sons of Quebec.

In 1971 Morin left government to return to university teaching. Shortly thereafter he joined René Lévesque and the péquistes as a senior member of the team. In the 1976 provincial election he beat Jean Marchand in the Quebec City Louis-Hébert riding, and on November 26 he became Minister of Intergovernmental Affairs. Oddly enough, he is regarded by some

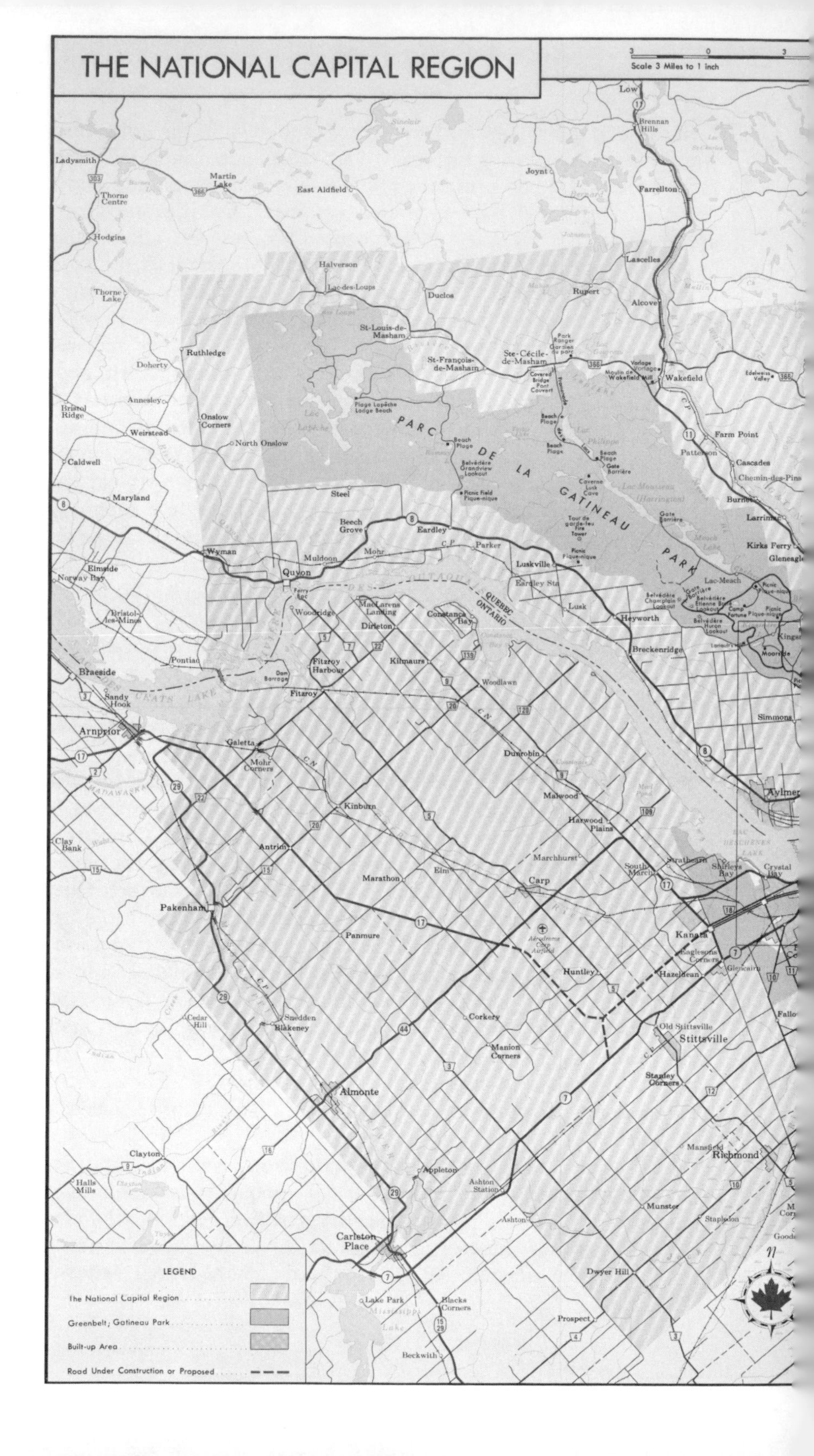
THE NATIONAL CAPITAL REGION
Scale 3 Miles to 1 inch
PARC DE LA GATINEAU PARK
Low
Brennan Hills
Ladysmith
Martin Lake
East Aldfield
Joynt
Farrellton
Thorne Centre
Hodgins
Halverson
Lac-des-Loups
Lascelles
Thorne Lake
Duclos
Rupert
Alcove
St-Louis-de-Masham
Ruthledge
St-François-de-Masham
Ste-Cécile-de-Masham
Wakefield
Doherty
Annesley
Bristol Ridge
Onslow Corners
Weirstead
North Onslow
Farm Point
Caldwell
Pattemson
Cascades
Chemin-des-Pins
Maryland
Steel
Beech Grove
Eardley
Parker
Wyman
Muldoon
Mohr
Luskville
Kirks Ferry
Gleneagle
Elmside
Norway Bay
Quyon
Eardley Sta
Lac-Meach
Woodridge
MacLarens Landing
Dirleton
Constance Bay
Lusk
Heyworth
Bristol-les-Mines
QUEBEC
ONTARIO
Breckenridge
Pontiac
Kilmaurs
Fitzroy Harbour
Braeside
Woodlawn
Sandy Hook
Fitzroy
Simmons
Arnprior
Galetta
Mohr Corners
Dunrobin
Malwood
Aylmer
Kinburn
Harwood Plains
Clay Bank
Antrim
Marchhurst
South March
Strathcona
Shirleys Bay
Crystal Bay
Marathon
Elm
Carp
Pakenham
Panmure
Kanata
Huntley
Hazeldean
Glencairn
Cedar Hill
Snedden
Blakeney
Corkery
Old Stittsville
Stittsville
Manion Corners
Stanley Corners
Almonte
Clayton
Mansfield
Richmond
Appleton
Halls Mills
Ashton Station
Munster
Ashton
Stapledon
Carleton Place
Dwyer Hill
Lake Park
Blacks Corners
Prospect
Beckwith
Mississippi Lake
LEGEND
The National Capital Region
Greenbelt; Gatineau Park
Built-up Area
Road Under Construction or Proposed

Map reproduced with the permission of the National Capital Commission.

péquiste extremists as too conservative – too much of a "gradualist" – not committed enough to independence!

Quebec's attitude towards the NCC had always been cool, and at times downright hostile; Maurice Duplessis barely acknowledged the existence of the predecessor commission, the Federal District Commission (FDC). Its land acquisition on the Quebec side, mainly to create Gatineau Park, was generally through quiet open-market purchase rather than expropriation. Many Quebecers, however, had resented these "encroachments" on Quebec territory, and had said so in briefs to the Quebec Tremblay Commission in 1954.

The growing NCC land accumulation in the 1960s led to a study of the issue in 1966 by the Quebec Dorion Commission, which had been set up to investigate problems relating to the boundary of Quebec, notably that with Labrador. Its main responsibility was to make recommendations to ensure Quebec's territorial integrity *(L'integrité du Territoire Québécois"),* but it was given a special mandate to examine the problems "posed by the existence of the National Capital Commission," and, incidentally, posed by the presence of a large body of anglophones just across the river. In its May 1968 report, Dorion argued predictably that the federal government, and particularly the NCC, did indeed threaten Quebec's territorial integrity.[2]

Among its recommendations, the Dorion Commission, presumably with some guidance from Quebec, proposed that the NCC be replaced by a "Tripartite Commission" with equal Quebec, Ontario and federal representation; that NCC be dissolved and all its lands in Quebec, including Gatineau Park, be transferred, free, to the Quebec government; and that each of the two provinces have a veto on any decision affecting its territory. The role of the new Commission would be largely restricted to overall planning, pollution control, and designation of transportation corridors; all "doing" would be carried out by the two provincial governments, or their municipal creatures; on the Quebec side, a new "Western Quebec Development Commission" was proposed.

At the outset of our September meeting, Morin tabled a document which was a revised Quebec version of a draft agreement setting up the new tripartite body. He made it clear to the meeting that it had been based on the conclusions of the Dorion Report. Carl Goldenberg (now Senator), a prominent political scientist, labour negotiator, and a friend of long standing of Pierre Trudeau as well as of mine, was our short, pipesmoking chairman. He asked Morin if the Quebec document conflicted with the statement of the federal position given by Marc Lalonde at the previous tripartite meeting, "that the federal government was anxious to ensure that it would not place itself in a position, as a result of the constitution of a Tripartite Commission, where it could not do in the

Capital Region what it had been doing very successfully for a number of years through the NCC." Morin allowed as how there was a conflict, and that Quebec, through the new Commission, wanted the NCC taken over. Morin was to suggest in 1972 that Quebec favoured giving the new body "vast powers" – not at all the way in which we had interpreted his document.[3]

For all practical purposes, that marked the end of the tripartite talks. Ontario had clearly been having separate discussions with Quebec, but the extreme line of the Quebec proposals was a surprise to its representative too. The federal team met a few weeks later and agreed that the direction of the tripartite approach was all one way; the feds giving up power to the two provinces, and paying the bills, in return for a new body of uncertain authority, subject to a provincial veto. We recommended to cabinet that we pull out of further discussions or alternatively switch the form of the proposed Commission to that of an advisory body; cabinet agreed.

My purpose in recounting this tale is to emphasize how strongly Quebecers feel about the "territorial" question. Quebec's boundaries are regarded as sacred, not even (or perhaps most of all) to be breached by the intrusion of a federal capital. Yet Dorion had proposed that the Quebec side of the Region should obtain a larger share of federal investments, but those investments should be made under Quebec direction and without strings. The Quebec approach was not without its humorous aspects; in effect they said: "We want the benefits of proximity to the federal capital, and of the economic fall-out, without recognizing that the federal authorities have any right to exercise the same powers on the Quebec side of the river that they do in Ontario!"

Federal initiatives in Hull

The end of tripartite had little effect on our plans to get things going in Hull, and to end the "100 years of injustice" which with justification had become the cry of the Hullois. A federal office building was about to go up in the expropriated Hull terrain; the site was that of a private builder who had made the excavation but was on the verge of bankruptcy. It was to be the first of many buildings, designed to accommodate eventually some 36,000 public service employees. At NCC we saw our role as two-fold; to help out with the costs of the water, sewers and roads needed to service the new planned developments and expected growth on the Quebec side; and to develop plans for linking the new buildings to Parliament Hill and the centre of Ottawa.

In October I made it a point to give my first public speech as NCC chairman in Hull, and in French, to the Richelieu Club. Televised too, stutter and all. Three weeks later I was a guest of the same club to hear the Hon.

Robert Lussier, Quebec Minister of Municipal Affairs in the Union Nationale government. Lussier and I met before lunch in the office of Mayor Marcel d'Amour, and arranged for an early meeting in Quebec to discuss how to work together on the growth problems in the Outaouais region. Dr. Lussier was a heavy and rather formidable doctor from L'Assomption, and, I found out later, a strong nationalist. Just before our planned Quebec meeting, I heard that there had been a breakdown in the arrangements to build a badly needed filtration plant in Hull, to cost over $5 million. The problems were in part jurisdictional, but they also involved the perennial problem of "who pays."

Lussier and I went out to dinner in Quebec City, and we soon established our mutual fondness for red Bordeaux. By the third bottle we were buddies. I decided to fly a kite, and brought up the Hull filtration plant. I asked him (without any authority) "If we at the NCC can persuade the federal cabinet to kick in one-third of the cost, could he get his government to match it?" Although he was worried about the precedent, he agreed to try. I went back and persuaded Marchand to go along, Lussier got *his* colleagues to approve, and the municipal authorities, on the strength of our agreed grants, lined up the remaining one-third. This cost-sharing pattern, sometimes 1/3 – 1/3 – 1/3, sometimes 50 – 50 between Quebec and NCC only, was to form the basis of other agreements on sewers and roads in the future.

The Portage Bridge affair

An important element in our plans for Hull was a proposed road and new bridge crossing the Ottawa River. It would link the Portage building complex directly with Ottawa, extending Maisonneuve Street (later Boulevard) in Hull in a sweeping curve to join Wellington Street in Ottawa (see picture). This $14 million Portage Bridge project was approved in principle by the federal Treasury Board in February 1970, with the considerable support of my bureaucratic friends Simon Reisman and Sylvain Cloutier. I was instructed to discuss it with Ontario and with the new Regional Municipality, and hopefully get some contribution from them. I set up talks, but the government plans were leaked to the press by the late Arthur Laing, then Minister of Public Works. All hell broke loose, and both the bridge and I came under attack from both Ontario and local politicians. I was charged with unwillingness to consult, the bridge itself damned as going nowhere, and involving municipalities in millions of unplanned expenditures for connecting roads. Ontario and Ottawa opposition was understandable, if only because the project was serving specific federal goals in Hull that clashed with their own interests; the complaints of local Liberal members were a different kettle of fish.

Photo reproduced with permission of the National Capital Commission.

The Liberal caucus in the capital area included two ministers, John Turner and George McIlraith. George had had the responsibility for NCC when he had been Minister of Public Works; he was the dean of Liberal politicians in the area, having been elected first in 1940 and re-elected nine times. With this background he naturally saw himself as an expert on NCC, and he was not happy with the new emphasis on Hull, nor with my independent style. The Quebec members of the caucus had never found it congenial; one of them, Dr. Gaston Isabelle of Hull told me that he had ceased turning up at caucus meetings because of its pronounced "anti-Hull, anti-French" biases.

In any event, some caucus members, headed by McIlraith, took their complaints to Marchand and to the Prime Minister; some (but not Turner) had complained to the press. I was upset by this because I had briefed them at several caucus meetings about the bridge, and in the first few months of my being in office had got the government to accept the building of a new Airport Parkway. This new limited access road would link the airport to Bronson Avenue, and was to be built largely on NCC land which had been bought as part of the parkway network, proposed in the 1950 report of planner Jacques Gréber, brought from Paris by Mackenzie King. My main selling point, in making the presentation to the cabinet committee, was not just that it was needed (anyone flying in or out of Ottawa, as all ministers had, would testify to that) but that it would balance some of the expenditures on the Quebec side, and "pacify the Ontario residents and M.P.s." But on the Portage Bridge, the M.P.s apparently preferred to believe Ottawa council members they had talked to than accept our arguments.

John Turner, an old friend, had made few if any public comments. He

The bridge builders

The Citizen, Ottawa

did 'phone on April 24, however, and lectured me about the bridge and about my lack of "co-operation" with local politicians and officials, and even suggested that the whole project should be reconsidered or withdrawn. He gave me the straight (or rather twisted) Ottawa City Hall line and – it was the last straw – I blew my stack. Perhaps because of our friendship, or possibly because I had had a good lunch, I let him have it across the chops. "Fuck you, Turner" I said "it's bad enough being given hell by the Ontario Tories, and Ottawa municipal spokesmen, but to get it from another colleague of Art Laing's, whose premature press leak had compromised my negotiating position on the bridge, is just too much. If you don't believe my side of the story, take it up with the prime minister." And hung up.

I decided I'd gone a little far, and 'phoned the next day to touch base with him. Got through, too. "No sweat, Doug, just wanted to see what you'd say. Forget it," he said. But a few days later he did write to Mr. Trudeau, with copies to Jean Marchand, Laing, McIlraith and Drury, raising the issues he had put to me. I had the exquisite pleasure of drafting a reply to him from Marchand (copy to Trudeau), that picked apart the arguments that he had been fed by his Ottawa municipal friends. John never raised the issue again.

There was some further flak in May, mainly from local parliamentarians, about a speech I had made to a large group of young Canadians from across Canada, the annual Rotary "Adventures in Citizenship" event, which was well attended by M.P.s. I had commented on the gross disparity between Hull and Ottawa, and on the need to make francophones feel more at home in the national capital. By now, every time I opened my mouth it was front page, and the adjective "abrasive" was normally coupled with my name. In mid-May, my wife and I took off for a trip to Scandinavia and London; when we got back and I looked at some of the clippings, I thought it time I went and had a chat with the prime minister.

The *Ottawa Journal* on May 23, 1970 (six days after we left) had a front page banner headline "FULLERTON MAY HAVE TO GO." It went on to say "Unless Chairman Douglas Fullerton quickly sweetens his sour National Capital Relations with the provincial, regional and municipal governments, he may have to go." Mr. McIlraith was reported as saying that "responsible and substantial people in the Capital, many of them community leaders" had been "greatly alarmed by Mr. Fullerton's abrasive manner and aggressive action in NCC relations with other governments." The press stories had considerably upset our sixteen-year old daughter, Kate, who took a ribbing from her schoolmates.

Mr. Trudeau, who himself had been away when that story appeared, was agreeable to seeing me and we met alone in his office on July 17; we talked for nearly an hour. I told him I was upset by these attacks from within his own party and government, and wanted to know "where I stood with him." He said that he and Marchand had picked me for my "toughness," and that as far as they were concerned, I was doing the job they wanted me to do. He said he was a bit disturbed by some stories he had heard about my readiness to take things into my own hands, without adequate consultation. He cited his own experience of the vegetable garden at Harrington Lake, which had been eliminated by NCC as part of the austerity program his government had launched earlier in the year. He said he would have gone along had he been asked, but did not care much to be presented with a *fait accompli*. I agreed with his view on this, and apologized.

I then filled him in on the background of the Portage Bridge affair, and on several other contentious issues which had come up, saying I wanted him to get things first hand rather than second or third. As for the bridge, Trudeau said that Marchand's letter to Turner had cleared up most of the points puzzling him. I told him I was prepared to stay on, because of the importance of the plans for the Quebec side (and because I would find it difficult to resign from the post of chairman of two different Crown corporations within one year!). He seemed pleased, and we parted on good terms.

I look back now on the Portage Bridge affair as a crucial testing time for me, a baptism of fire. Had I quit, which I had certainly thought of doing, I would probably have been remembered most for the failure to consult; resignation would be construed as an admission of guilt. By surviving, I gained confidence in my ability to take on anything, or anyone. And I had learned several hard lessons.

One was that no head of a government agency can find much comfort in the theory that he will be protected by the politicians against attacks made on him, that as a public official he should keep silent and let his political "masters" defend him. Hell, I had been attacked as much as supported by members of the Liberal government, to say nothing of having to shoulder the blame for one minister's press leak. Clearly it was to be *sauve qui peut*, and from that point on I would defend myself. The weapon I was learning to use was the press, and that meant being used by them as much as I was using them.

They wanted stories and headlines? Give it to them. It meant being provocative; it meant being frank, saying one's piece, getting the story to the people directly; above all it meant being ready to leave the job at any time if the government didn't like what you were saying. I said as much to a parliamentary committee. When asked if I was supported by the government, I replied that "if the government doesn't like it, it can tell me to get the hell out."[4] I meant it, too, and also that I would pack it up on the same basis if I felt too hard done by.

This approach came to be recognized as "my style"; it was not universally admired, and the "abrasive" adjective stuck to me fairly closely over my NCC years. For my opponents, of course, I became a "mouthy son of a bitch"; their opinions were countered by the many people cheering me on. People like controversy: that's why the media play it up so much. It was also good for NCC staff morale; they liked reading about NCC in the papers, and found that the many battles made good party conversation.

Well, the Portage Bridge and road were built, and linked to the newly widened Maisonneuve Street at the Hull end (the Quebec authorities had co-operated fully), and to the NCC Parkway at the Ottawa end. Years later there are no signs that our project had forced either Ottawa municipalities or Ontario to lay out any substantial sums for connecting roads, or to cope with new traffic problems. In fact, without the Portage Bridge, the crossing between Ottawa and Hull would have become a traffic nightmare. Certainly without it the new Portage office building complex would have become an orphan, badly isolated, without direct and rapid access to Ottawa.

At the beginning of 1969 Ontario had set up the Regional Municipality of Ottawa-Carleton (RMOC), under which Ottawa, Nepean, Gloucester and other local Ontario municipalities were grouped. Up to this time, NCC had dealt with individual municipalities, and mainly with the City of Ottawa, in which the majority of the people of the area lived. The Portage episode did not improve our liaison with the Ontario municipalities. Events had made conflict almost inevitable; RMOC's arrival on the scene had challenged the City of Ottawa's position as main NCC contact, and chief beneficiary of federal largesse. The government's plans for Hull threatened both the regional government and the City. In addition most of the population growth on the Ontario side was occurring in the rapidly growing suburban townships of Nepean and Gloucester, and the reeves of each started to throw their weight around. In the space of five years the NCC's tidy municipal arrangements with a willing, if occasionally obstreperous partner, the City of Ottawa, had developed into a free-for-all.

Still, we did manage to work together with the Ontario municipalities on some developments of common interest, including an expansion of the region's sewer system. The municipalities had been pleased by the Airport Parkway, but had tried to subvert its use. We had built it as a two-lane road, discouraging local traffic by making access possible only in the direction of the airport, and providing exits only in the direction *away* from the airport. The municipalities wanted it to become four-lane, (at our expense) and to be used by everyone; we pointed out that local traffic had ruined the previous airport road. It remains as we planned it, for which most airport users are truly grateful.

Changing the NCC's programs and image

If the main change at NCC was in the new emphasis on Hull, I sought to bring about other changes in it of a fundamental nature. All through the 'sixties the NCC's main preoccupation had been the acquisition of land by purchase or expropriation, for the greenbelt around Ottawa, and for the expansion of its justly famed parkway system. I brought the parkways program (except for the road to the airport) to an abrupt halt, and no land was expropriated by NCC while I was chairman.

Some major changes in our expenditure patterns were clearly necessary because of the money needed for the essential Quebec program. But I was thinking of something more basic – a turn away from the parkways, which encouraged automobile use and the expansion of suburbia, to projects which would make downtown Ottawa more lively and a more attractive place to live. I had a particular hostility for the car – and attacked its use in a number of speeches (see cartoon below). I was also looking for relatively low cost proposals that would be popular, and

Reprinted with the permission of Duncan Macpherson and the Toronto Star.

help offset any animosity generated by the switching of so much of our infrastructure spending – roads and services – to the Quebec side.

I can hardly say we began with a clear, coherent program; it was more trial and error. But the following list shows some of the things we tried to do on both sides of the river:

- Blocked or watered down some municipal or regional arterial roads projects (the NCC land holdings proved a handy weapon).
- Shifted the emphasis in Gatineau Park away from active recreation towards wilderness preservation; banned snowmobiles on NCC lands and in the Park, and encouraged cross-country skiing rather than downhill. The enraged snowmobilers once organized a march or parade to my Ottawa home, but we brought in the Mounties and it fizzled out. I also got a personal note from Pierre Trudeau: "I congratulate you on your decision to ban the use of snowmobiles on NCC land. They are a threat to plant and animal life and a nuisance to all who value the tranquility of the woods."
- Developed a network of bicycle paths and cross-country ski trails across the whole region.
- Exploited the Rideau Canal for skating and boating. The five and one-half mile skating rink was unquestionably the most successful of all the projects, and it helped me considerably in defusing the criticisms I referred to earlier in this chapter. I saw John Turner out skating the day after the rink opened. He said "Doug, you've hit the jackpot. This is the greatest." I even had ministers pass me notes in cabinet committees, saying how much they and their families were enjoying "the rink."
- Made available open NCC land in urban areas for vegetable gardens – at last report over 4,000 of these, 25' by 50', were being leased by the public at a nominal cost of $10 a year.
- Tried to persuade the government to charge its employees for downtown parking, thereby encouraging public transit (a modest policy was finally adopted in 1974).
- Assisted public transit with grants, and the making of parkways available for bus express routes (or buses-only at rush hours).
- Encouraged citizen's groups by provision of technical assistance.

Our efforts to improve the capacity of NCC to function in French, consistent with the aims of government bilingualism policy, and the consequences, good and bad, of our experience on the Quebec side of the region, is recounted in the next two chapters.

Notes

1 Report of the Royal Commission on Bilingualism and Biculturalism, *Volume 5: Book V The Federal Capital* (Ottawa: Queen's Printer, 1970), p. 98.
2 Rapport de la Commission d'étude sur l'intégrité du territoire du Québec, *Les problèmes de la région de la capitale canadienne* (Quebec: Dorion Report, 1968).
3 Claude Morin, *op. cit.,* p. 174.
4 House of Commons, Public Accounts Committee, February 17, 1970.

XII

NCC – the Quebec program and backlash

Putting a more bilingual face on the NCC was not the easiest of tasks. It had always been overwhelmingly an anglophone organization, with few French Canadians among the senior staff. Some changes would have to take place, if only to service adequately the new demands from the expansion in Hull. And government policies were placing greater emphasis on the use of French and in serving the francophone public in its own language.

I had been a guest at a meeting of the Commission in late August 1969, the last at which the retiring chairman, Jack Frost, presided. I made a short speech, saying among other things that I observed that all discussion had been in English, and that "I hoped the day would come soon when both languages would be in common use around the Commission table." It took longer than I thought, but a little more than a year later simultaneous translation was in place and functioning at Commission meetings.

Jean-Claude La Haye, slight, intense, a respected architect and urban planner from Montreal, and a friend of Marchand, had been appointed a year earlier as NCC vice-chairman. Only the chairman served full time, however; other Commissioners, including the vice-chairman, were paid for service on the various committees, but not for attendance at Commission meetings. I had lunch with Jean-Claude my second day on the job, and found him seething with resentment about the neglect of the French fact at NCC, and about his frustration at his inability to improve the situation.

I liked La Haye, and wanted to give him a more important role at NCC; we could certainly use his planning knowledge. However, he had his own business in Montreal, which was dependent on him, and he could at best serve part time. What I did was increase the scope and importance of the planning committee and put him in charge of it, with some funds and a specific mandate.

So far as senior staff were concerned, I noted earlier that Paul Pelletier had been hired on a contract basis. His help was invaluable, not only in relation to the tripartite talks, but later in dealings with the government and the various cabinet committees. The number two job at NCC was that of general manager; like the chairman he was appointed by the cabinet. I felt that with an anglophone chairman, and our move into Hull, it was essential that the general manager be French-speaking, and Pelletier became an obvious candidate. The position was opened (not without some awkwardness) and I nominated Pelletier for it. On September 10, 1970, his appointment was to go before cabinet; that morning I was called by his wife to say that he had just died of a massive heart attack. He had made many friends around the Commission during his year there, and his death was a blow to us all.

The NCC secretary was Alex Morin, a French Canadian in his thirties, who had come from Kirkland Lake years earlier to study and later to work as a writer with the *Ottawa Journal* and Canadian Press. He also had had some political experience as an executive assistant to Public Works Minister George McIlraith. I found him not only personally *sympathique,* but bright, tough, and loaded with good judgment. He had come along fast during the year, and despite his youth I was able to persuade the powers in the cabinet to appoint him general manager. It couldn't have worked out better; his style was totally different from my rather noisy aggressiveness, and we complemented each other. He spoke softly, which disarmed his listeners, and he dealt easily with abstract ideas. The Cartesian twist to his argument sometimes led people up the garden path before they even knew they were in the garden, a quality which was useful in the dense underbrush of political and professional intrigue that characterized local municipal affairs. Through it all, he kept me and the Commission on an even keel. He remained my right hand man during my remaining years with NCC.

Several other changes strengthened our capacity to cope with our added responsibilities on the Quebec side. A separate Quebec planning division was established, and expanded; all members on it were francophone or bilingual, and French was the working language. The director of finance, Marcel Couture, became my special adviser, and he was actively involved in the extensive negotiations with Quebec. In 1971, the government gave NCC the further duty of co-ordinating federal activity in improving bilingual capacity and services in the National Capital Region. A completely bilingual former foreign service officer, Jim Weld, was brought in to handle these new responsibilities; he was to work closely with me in the study of Capital government which I took on in 1973 following my resignation.

Hon. Oswald Parent and the NCC role in Quebec

When the Bourassa government came into power in April 1970, Oswald Parent was appointed a Minister of State and given the responsibility for liaison with NCC. An accountant, forty-five years old, he had been the deputy for the Hull constituency since 1956, and remained the member until he was defeated by two votes, on recount, in the péquiste sweep of 1976.

I always got along well with Oswald, as everyone called him. I found him direct and straightforward, a man of his word, and certainly one of the best organized ministers I ever met in my life. He had a file on every topic that might come up at our meetings, and knew the complete contents of each. Yet Oswald was not exactly a popular fellow in the area, despite the very large voting majorities he had managed to build up.

For one thing Parent *looked* raffish; swarthy, with long sideburns. He was also a politician of the old school; he ran the Hull region almost as a personal fiefdom, had a hand in all provincial or municipal appointments, and sometimes even selected candidates in municipal elections, and used his influence to get them elected.

When Parent arrived on the scene, the Outaouais Regional Community – the area's regional government – was just getting under way. We at NCC faced somewhat the same problem we had on the Ontario side, to talk to the region or to the municipal governments. That problem was resolved quickly by Parent; he stood on the solid constitutional position that a federal government agency should deal with the province *only*; henceforth we dealt with municipal politicians through him, except for exchanges at lower-level technical committees. The Outaouais municipal people resented this, and frequently attacked me publicly for refusing to consult, when they knew damned well the reasons behind it. But attacking NCC was always fair game on both sides of the river, and it did give us a chance to fire back, and make some points publicly which needed saying.

When I was doing my study, in 1974, I raised this question of excessive provincial intervention with Parent. He replied as follows:

> The federal government's move to expand its offices in the Quebec side in 1969 caught us unprepared – a relatively backward municipal structure, a severe lack of the basic municipal needs such as water, sewers and roads, and a group of municipalities that had been fighting each other rather than working together. The only way we could get things going, and persuade the municipalities to think and act regionally, was

to apply a degree of centralized control that admittedly could be regarded as authoritarian or dictatorial. However, we have now progressed to the state of being able to relax the provincial control and begin to hand the powers back; in fact this relaxation began last fall.

In the three years I worked with Parent, we managed to reach agreement on almost everything we tackled. Naturally we federal representatives came bearing welcome gifts in the forms of new federal office buildings, the Portage Bridge, and many millions of dollars for shared cost spending on water, roads and sewers. Yet the Quebec government made some significant compromises in its own plans, notably on its road program. Most of the local politicians wanted a big four-lane expressway, close to the river and across the Island of Hull. We persuaded them to push it farther north, limiting the potential impact on the urban area.

Specific agreements were reached on a $100 million roads program and a $45 million sewer program, both later to cost much more. Quebec approval for substantial changes in the road structure at the Hull end of the Portage Bridge was quickly obtained, and the province paid most of the costs for them and for the substantial expropriation that the new Maisonneuve Boulevard entailed. I even obtained Quebec government approval for the transfer to NCC administration of some 10,000 acres of provincial property in the north-western sector of Gatineau Park – land NCC has been trying to obtain for twenty years – in exchange for a small but more valuable parcel of land in the outskirts of Hull. One important issue which arose concerned the E. B. Eddy Company.

Eddy's

For a century the Eddy pulp and paper complex, situated astride and along the river boundary between Ottawa and Hull, and across and upstream from the Parliament Buildings, had been a highly visible source of air and water pollution. Parliamentarians for at least fifty years had denounced it. Prime Minister Mackenzie King tried to buy it after the war from Garfield Weston, who controlled it, but balked at the price. Further efforts over the next twenty-five years were stalled by the political difficulties which would be created by the closing of the various plants, and the loss of some 2,000 jobs.

In the spring of 1969 a proposal to buy or expropriate Eddy's 110 acre site (most of it on the Quebec side) had been put forward by NCC, at the time of the fifteen acre Hull expropriation for federal office construction. The cabinet turned the Eddy expropriation down, but authorized NCC to continue discussions with the Weston interests which still controlled Eddy's. When I saw the file a few days after my appointment, I was delighted that the expropriation had not taken place; my Quebec experience had convinced me that there couldn't be a worse way to acquire the property, in terms both of politics and of the expenditure of dollars. A month later I asked G. E. (Ted) Creber, Weston president, to drop in when he was next in Ottawa and we met for the first time on October 21, 1969. Our talks began, and our first decision was to agree to share in a feasibility study of the cost of moving Eddy's to a nearby location, presumably to Weston land downstream at Gatineau.

Discussions intensified with the Portage Bridge announcement; we needed Eddy's co-operation, because rail and power access to their main plant was affected by the bridge, and we had to pass over some of their land. This new issue put the feasibility study in abeyance, but by then I had established a good rapport with Creber, and with Ray Jones, Eddy president. In the course of the discussions one interesting idea surfaced. The sulphite mill, directly across from Parliament Hill, was not only ancient and inefficient, but was the main source of the visual, air, and water pollution emanating from the Eddy complex, and of their operating losses. Why shouldn't they close it, sell the land on which it sat to us at NCC, and buy the pulp they needed from the Pontiac mill of Consolidated Bathurst, seventy miles up river? Pulp was everywhere in surplus supply at that time.

Why not, indeed? It was agreed that I would take the initiative, possibly through my friend Paul Desmarais, head of Power Corporation which controlled Consolidated. This issue arose just at the time of the FLQ *(Front de libération du Québec)* terrorist activity in Montreal. James Cross, senior British Trade Commissioner in Montreal, and Quebec minister, Pierre Laporte, had been kidnapped; on October 17, Laporte was murdered. Desmarais, as a prominent Quebec "capitalist," had received a threat to the lives of himself and his family, and they were advised by the police to leave Montreal. Through a mutual friend, Pierre Genest, I tracked Paul down at the Royal York in Toronto on October 22; although he was registered under an assumed name, I had the room number, and he was expecting me. He was a bit embarrassed, but in those days no one knew how strong – or how weak – the FLQ forces were, and everyone had been shocked by Laporte's death. The armed forces had been called out, and Quebec and federal ministers were guarded by soldiers for some months.

The bizarre atmosphere did not affect our talks. Paul thought the pulp proposal worth pursuing, and discussions between Eddy's and Consolidated were initiated shortly after, and a tentative agreement eventually reached. The proposed closing of the pulp mill making available some forty-four acres of desirable riverfront land for federal use made sense to me. What we had going for us was the depressed state of the pulp and paper business at the time, Eddy's current operating losses, and its (and Weston's) need for cash. It was a case of a willing seller and willing buyer, and by the spring of 1971 I could see the possibility of a deal emerging;

we figured from an independent appraisal we had made of land values that the settlement should be in the area of $25 million.

Our main concern was the employment problem. Things got a bit complicated when Jack Davis, Minister of Fisheries, suggested publicly that the whole of Eddy's would be gone by 1975 (politicians will do anything to get a headline!). The story aroused great concern in Hull and was raised in the Quebec legislature, and we had to damp down the fire. To cut a long story short, our talks with Eddy's and Westons continued, but the major emphasis was placed on how to cope with the 450 employees who would be affected by the closing of the pulp mill.

More than half a dozen meetings were held that fall in the NCC boardroom, involving at times as many as thirty union representatives, along with Creber's people and our own. We began with the premise that no one would be "laid-off." A program of early retirement, substantial separation allowances, and seniority guarantees on other jobs in the remaining Eddy complex, was hammered out with the unions, and agreed to by them. These added significantly to the costs of the settlement, which was finally negotiated at $29,500,000.

I went to cabinet with the proposal, and they accepted it subject to a written agreement by Eddy's to give the federal government a right of first refusal on the remaining Eddy property, at a comparable price per acre, and containing a similar "no lay-off" clause. Eddy's agreed in writing, and the deal was closed. On February 21, 1972 Ron Basford, recently appointed Minister of State for Urban Affairs, read in the House of Commons the statement I had prepared. I sat in the gallery, feeling rather proud of myself; we had solved most of the Eddy pollution problem, we had done it by negotiation, not compulsion, the thorny employment issue had been settled, and the price was fair by any standards.

Creber described the transaction later as constituting a unique example of co-operation between government, business and labour, where the interest of all parties and the community had been recognized, and all parties have been given an opportunity to see that their interest was protected.[1]

Oswald Parent, Hull municipal leaders and the unions had been advised of the closing well in advance, and they endorsed the transaction publicly, if with varying degrees of enthusiasm. The only really sour note came from the separatists in the area, assisted by some of their friends in the media. It was part of the growing opposition that the NCC, and Oswald Parent, were experiencing with the developments that were taking place in the capital on the Quebec side of the Ottawa River.

Backlash in Quebec

The changes that were being wrought in Hull and its environs by the development program were massive, and it was not surprising that resistance developed. Some of it was justified. The new office complexes and the new road system had caused the demolition of many hundreds of homes in the central area, notably on the Island of Hull. Neighbourhoods had been disrupted or destroyed; new housing was not always available, and when it was, it usually proved to be more expensive than the old. Many more jobs were available, of course, and the economy of Hull region prospered, but "man does not live by bread alone." Our combined planning had not paid enough attention to the social dislocation, perhaps because the preservation of neighbourhoods only began to become an urban concern in Canada in the 'seventies.

Another problem we faced was the fear in the Hull region, not unjustifiable, that the new federal office buildings would flood the region with anglophone public servants. Hull itself was still over 90 per cent francophone, and could see itself becoming anglicized. Efforts could be made to choose departments for the move that had a higher than average concentration of francophones, but even so there was bound to be some significant impact on the restaurants, stores, and residential character of Hull and of adjoining municipalities. Fear of assimilation has always been strong in Quebec; any diminution of the "Frenchness" of a city or region reduces its capacity for cultural survival, given the overwhelming dominance of English in North America.

Related to the survival issue was the opposition on nationalistic grounds, some of it taken straight from the Dorion Report, some of it built into separatist doctrine. Hull was the focal point – the presumed growth pole – of western Quebec; therefore it should try to keep its industrial character and not become integrated into the big federal machine. The Eddy transaction was attacked by the péquistes as damaging Hull's industrial "character." Moreover the NCC shouldn't be allowed to own land on the Quebec side; it was an affront to "territorial integrity." The NCC swap of urban land for a large acreage of Quebec government land at the far end of Gatineau Park with a $1 million net benefit to Quebec on the exchange, was called the exchange of "a horse for a rabbit."

I could accept these attacks as having some base in doctrine or theory. What I found very distasteful was the distortion of news – the mis-statement of facts – to build up anti-federal sentiment in the region. The technique was that of Dr. Goebbel's; "Tell a big enough lie, and tell it often enough, and it will supersede the truth." The bulk of the French media was pro-separatist, and although my personal relations with most reporters were good, we at NCC became accustomed to the most outrageous anti-federal anti-NCC propaganda on the air, and in the Ottawa French newspaper *Le Droit.* Let me give a few examples.

The Eddy transaction had been an arms length deal, without pressure from us. The company had its own plans for removing the sulphite mill, and had fully intended to sell the land for development if we hadn't come through as buyers. Our action had in fact *prevented* the loss of jobs, rather than as the péquistes saw it, *caused* the loss of jobs. Yet week after week the stories would come out "The NCC expropriated Eddy's" – destroying industrial jobs. I wrote *Le Droit* several times but still editorials and news stories kept using the word "expropriation," drumming into the public consciousness its association with NCC. It had its planned effect: few persons in Quebec today will believe the true facts about Eddy's.

Another ludicrous example occurred at the time the federal Department of Public Works bought the Metropolitan Life's head office on Wellington Street in Ottawa for $15 million. The story was correctly reported, but the heading read "The NCC expropriates the Metropolitan!"[2] Things at *Le Droit* became so bad that the editor, Marcel Gingras, resigned in November 1973 on the grounds that "Being a federalist is now a crime at *Le Droit* . . . Separatists only can express themselves – freedom exists only for separatists and anarchists."[3]

This had been, of course, only a very minor skirmish in the battle for Quebec. It does illustrate, however, the lengths to which some péquiste zealots in the media will go in support of their religion. "Any stick to beat the feds" takes precedence over accuracy, although it must be admitted that the dazzling light of the revealed Lévesque gospel may blind disciples to truth. Of course, all journalists have biases, as do the newspapers and broadcasting companies for which they work. What is relatively uncommon in the Canadian media, thank God, is the systematic exploitation of lies and half truths to sell a political doctrine. I don't think the long run interests of René Lévesque or his Parti Québécois will be well served by followers who surrender their journalistic integrity in the hope of furthering party goals.

Whether fair or not, separatist attacks on the NCC and on joint NCC-provincial programs were hurting; the pro-federalist support on the Quebec side certainly outnumbered the nationalists, but it was incoherent and unfocused. Parent's obvious role as "Mr. Big" in the region hadn't helped either, because he was blamed for many things that went wrong, and was seen to be working too closely with us, the despised federal government.

In 1972 the Hull Chamber of Commerce decided to try to do something positive to show support for the initiatives we had taken to improve the economics of the Outaouais region and to counter separatist propaganda. I was sounded out. Would I be their "Man of the Year"? "Sure, why not," I said. A little later the word came back that it had been discussed with Oswald, and "would I object if we were jointly made 'Men of the Year'"? I went along – I liked Oswald – and the big night was set for April 21, complete with dinner, speeches and presentations. Tickets were printed and sold, but a strike was on which affected the school where the function was scheduled and it was decided to postpone it a week.

Meanwhile the word got through to us that the separatists were organizing to disrupt the meeting. They had even printed false tickets. Oswald countered by calling out the provincial police, who set up a cordon around the school and parking lots on the evening of April 28. The fake tickets had a discernible flaw, and the separatists were screened out.

Some 700 people turned up, and there Oswald and I were, perched up on the stage like stuffed birds in front of all those people, listening to lengthy introductions extolling our great contribution to the growth and prosperity of the Hull region. A presentation of plaques followed, each of us getting two; one with both our pictures, the other with our own picture only. Inscribed on them was *L'outaouais ça Marche* – ("the Outaouais is booming," or "on the march") – "Gratefully presented on April 21, 1972 by the Hull Chamber of Commerce" – mine in English, Oswald's in French. As late as 1975 I noted that Oswald still had his plaque on his wall, beside Bourassa's picture.

Our speeches followed, mine two-thirds in English – then we mingled with guests. About 100 people came up to say hello, and express appreciation. Not a bad show altogether, although as we drove out the gate we wondered if we might be the object of attack by the frustrated separatists. We weren't, and got home safely.

During the next year or two, my friends Lévesque, Parizeau and Claude Morin made several forays into the region in search of votes, and it came back to me that some of the local separatists had been surprised to hear from them that "Fullerton wasn't a bad guy at all" – just that I had fallen into bad company!* This endorsation, and my own reasonably good press relations, may have kept them from hammering me very hard personally – not that I cared particularly.

One thing they didn't like was my noting several times in speeches that if Quebec separated the whole national capital would be a disaster area, with the Hull side hardest hit. My arguments were based on the likelihood of Canada's capital being moved in a westerly direction, and on the Anglo Saxon backlash which would be directed at francophones in government. I made one such speech during the October 1973 election campaign, when the péquiste candidate Jean-Baptiste Bouchard, who had been an unremitting opponent of NCC for years, went after me. I had left NCC by this time, but he trotted out the old anti-NCC arguments – no consultation, destruction of jobs at Eddy's – and he went on to cite

*Lévesque is quoted in the *Ottawa Journal* on October 17, 1973 as saying "even . . . Fullerton, whom he called 'an honest man,' would thank him for the break-up (of Quebec and Canada)."

Lévesque's promise that Hull would become the regional capital of a free Quebec, the centre of the administrative relations with the residual country of Canada, saying no jobs would be lost. I had no overt political goal in mind, but Parent won his seat (15,325 votes to Bouchard's 8,218) in the Liberal sweep.

Still, Bouchard's vote total had risen from the 3,814 the péquiste candidate had received in 1970. There was no denying that the separatists were growing in strength in the region and across the province. The Liberals won 102 of the 110 seats, but their gains had come from splitting their opponents support. The péquistes, however, had received 30 per cent of the total votes, compared to 24 per cent in 1970; although they only elected six members in 1973 to seven in 1970, the near wipe out of the Union Nationale put the PQ party into the new role of official opposition.

Notes

1 Letter from G. E. Creber to chairman of National Capital Commission, October 5, 1973.
2 *Le Droit*, January 25, 1973.
3 *Ottawa Citizen*, November 8, 1973.

XIII

Bilingualism – the impossible Canadian dream?

Few issues in recent Canadian history have been more agonized over than bilingualism, the role and use of the two official or "founding" languages in our society. The Royal Commission on Bilingualism and Biculturalism, set up by the Pearson government in 1963, had studied the question exhaustively, and had brought forth a series of reports beginning in 1965. The government acceptance of some of the Commission's recommendations on the use of English and French languages in the federal administration resulted in the Official Languages Act, which entered into force in September 1969.

In 1970 the post of Commissioner of Official Languages was created, and Keith Spicer appointed to it, responsible to Parliament for "ensuring recognition of the status of each of the official languages and compliance with the spirit and intent of this Act in the administration of the affairs of the institutions of the Parliament and Government of Canada."[1] In 1970 and 1971 the government clarified the application of the Official Languages Act to the public service, and provided for bilingual services being made available by all federal departments and agencies in the National Capital Region. A target date for 1975 was set, by which time specified percentages of bilingual staff at various levels of government were to be achieved.

Out of all this official activity, two basic government policies emerged: (1) Canadians should be able to communicate with their federal government, and receive service from it, in either French or English, whichever is their preferred language; and (2) federal public servants should be able, as a general rule, to work in either language.

I had always sympathized with these goals, and indeed in 1966 had staked out my own position on bilingualism in a friendly exchange of correspondence with the Hon. Dick Bell, who was the member for the local Carleton riding, and a former minister in the Diefenbaker cabinet. Bell had suggested in Parliament that the merit system in the public service was being jeopardized by government efforts to hire more francophones, by the device of providing a 10 per cent "points" bonus for bilingual capacity. My reply was essentially that the ability to use both languages is "meritorious" – a person with both languages is better equipped than someone who has only one – and that the system up to then had been stacked against French Canadians and positive corrective measures were needed.

I went on this vein:

> So far as I am concerned, bilingualism in the civil service means essentially that ultimately any French-speaking civil servant in a government department *in Ottawa* will, as a matter of right, be able to speak and write in his own language if he so chooses. It follows from this that civil servants, particularly those in intermediate and senior positions, must eventually be required to read and understand the other main language . . .
>
> Even people who join the civil service from parts of Canada where no French is taught or spoken must accept the fact that to achieve promotion they will have to learn enough French to permit their French-speaking confrères to function in their own language. I am not saying that recruits from English Canada should be forced to learn French on their own; certainly the provinces have been very backward in providing adequate instruction in the French language. Training in French should be given by the government, on government time, in much the same way as the American State Department and Armed Forces give people going to foreign lands intensive training in the language of the country. It is surprising how much can be learned in a short time, given the proper training and incentives.
>
> No one expects bilingualism to be achieved overnight, and it would be unfair to expect civil servants above a certain age to comply. However, unless the government publicly accepts a policy along the lines I describe above as an objective, and puts forward concrete measures for achieving it, then it will be increasingly difficult to attract people from Quebec to work in the government, and the cause of the separatists will be given enormous impetus. This issue is seen in Quebec as a fundamental one in their attempt to work out a new relationship with English Canada, and it will be regarded by them as a crucial test of the willingness of English Canadians to accept French Canada as an equal partner in Confederation.

At NCC we had made considerable progress by 1972 towards the first goal of communicating with citizens in either language. We had also increased the proportion of francophones on the staff, particularly at the senior level, and were close to the 1975 target. French was heard frequently in most departments. We had set up several "French language units," but had clearly a long way to go in ensuring that francophones could, "as a general rule" work in French; given the historically anglophone nature of NCC (as of most branches of the federal government) this was going to be a long uphill battle. Flexibility in moving people around, or hiring more francophones, was limited by budgetary constraints or simply by the job protection afforded to employees under the Public Service Act, or by union agreement.

I had made several public statements about these difficulties, and in addressing a group of French and English high school students in October 1972, I incautiously suggested that I didn't think the government's 1975 percentage targets would be reached. Nothing startling about the statement, except that a federal election was on; the result was headlines coast-to-coast: "senior bureaucrat attacks government's bilingual policy."

I spoke again on November 29 to a conference on education in the offical languages, discussing some of the problems in government language training, particularly for older people; the failure rate of "graduates" through inability to use the new language on the job; the cost in terms of time lost; the backlash; the failure of the government to sell bilingualism on a cultural rather than a political basis; above all the failure of the provincial governments – Quebec included – to give priority to the teaching of the second language in the schools.

The government had become aware of the backlash problem in the 1972 election. Ottawa constituencies have a heavy concentration of public servants, and in the English sections of the capital all Liberal candidates lost ground, and one lost his seat. Yet the existing pace of progress toward the government's goals was still not regarded by federal politicians and senior officials as fast enough

On the same day I gave the speech to the conference, the government launched a new bilingual policy offensive. The essence of it was that every position in the federal public service was to be designated as bilingual or not. A "SECRET" (eyes only of addressee) paper was circulated to heads of departments, containing specific rules and regulations as to how this new policy was to be implemented, and how exceptions were to be handled, such as a job-protecting grandfather clause for older employees, and language training for unilingual employees. Pages and pages of bureaucratic jargon, all complete with a whole new bureaucratic superstructure to enforce the new rules.

As soon as I saw it I thought that the authors of this new policy were out of their collective minds. As one of my colleagues noted: "This paper would set back the cause of bilingualism by twenty years! It is incomprehensibly labyrinthine and bureaucratic. Most of all it is politically insensitive – indeed, cruel and arrogant . . . I am so flabbergasted that I cannot exclude the possibility that it might be intended to put the kiss of death on bilingualism – perhaps even national unity." In summary, all flexibility was to be removed from the system; no longer could departmental heads exercise judgment in coping with government objectives; everything had to be done by the book; and what a book it has turned out to be. No provision was made for a group approach, such as having certain members of an office designated to cover off calls or requests in the minority language. No provision for the frequent changes in the language requirements for any job; simply fix every position in perpetuity.

A meeting of deputy ministers and agency heads had been called for December 4 by Al Johnson, Treasury Board Secretary, (Al later became head of the CBC), to discuss the proposed policy. Some forty of us turned up. I figured I had nothing to lose – I had made up my mind to leave NCC soon – and I let my friend Al and the other top bureaucrats present have it. I denounced the policy for its rigidities, for its impracticality, for its centralizing effects on language policy, for its bureaucratic language and philosophy. I said that arguments about bilingual designation would be tailor-made for union negotiators, and a source of endless argument; that the policy would be divisive and a cause of backlash, and that it wouldn't achieve the government's objectives. I forgot what else I said, but there was no mistaking where I stood. I had some support from a few colleagues, notably the late Jean Boucher, and Pierre Juneau, then head of CRTC, and in 1976 to become NCC chairman, but most for one reason or another, felt compelled to go along with the government.

I asked a friend close to the seat of power why they hadn't left some flexibility in the system. "We no longer trust department heads to carry out the government's bilingual policies," he said. Jesus wept.

Well, the policy was adopted and announced on December 14 by the Hon. Charles (Bud) Drury, President of the Treasury Board, and the public service and government have been trying to live with it ever since. The number of bilingual positions was grossly understated and the need for language training facilities underestimated. Anglophones clutching their diplomas went back after training to their bilingual posts, seldom to use the French they had so painfully acquired. Hundreds of millions of dollars spent, and what have we got for it?

Some progress certainly – more francophones in senior positions; in the "officer" category, for example, up from 16 per cent in 1971 to 22 per cent in 1976; for "senior executives" the current francophone proportion is 20 per cent; for the service generally it is 26 per cent. More French is used at work, more anglophones are able to understand French. In my judgment most or all of these gains would have come about anyway if the earlier, or gradual, decentralized policy had been followed instead of the bureaucratic nightmare we got, and much less painfully, perhaps more effectively, and certainly more cheaply. I look around Ottawa now and see a public service so alienated that the government delayed a long time in calling a by-election in John Turner's old seat, and then lost it in 1976 to the Progressive Conservatives. I see Quebec, indifferent and uncaring about the federal bilingual initiatives, electing the separatists to power.

I note that even Keith Spicer, Commissioner of Official Languages, that zealous scourge of violators of the Official Languages Act, that great apostle of bilingualism, finally concluded in his 1975 Report that the bilingual policies in the public service hadn't worked out very well: too many positions had been identified as bilingual; and many of the anglophones trained never used their newly acquired French at work. He concluded that basic language learning should be left to the "elementary and secondary schools, from which we must come to expect a far richer linguistic harvest." In his 1976 Report he backed off a bit, complimenting the government on progress, "80 per cent of Ottawa's initiatives have turned to a decent measure of success . . . the Official Languages Act is working." Francophones in the public service "have held, since 1975, nearly their 'fair' share of federal jobs (with 27 per cent of Canada's population) – about one in four."

Yet I wish that Spicer had paid a bit more attention to the backlash generated by his efforts to follow up complaints. He has made a mark for himself as a francophile, fighting for the language rights of the French minority. I give him credit for it, but he could perhaps have benefited from some of our experience at NCC, having to placate staff who, doing their best to follow the rules, had been ticked off by Spicer's watchdogs for some trivial slip which had been reported, often, we discovered, by some separatist with an axe to grind, seeking to discredit the NCC.

Partly as a result of Quebec's Bill One in the spring of 1977, the federal government reviewed its bilingualism and language policies, and the first part of a new or revised policy appeared on June 21. It viewed the bilingual issue in a balanced historical perspective, and set out some basic principles: the right of Canadians to have their children educated in the official language of their choice; the right to communicate with federal institutions in either language; the equality of status of the two languages; encouragement and support for minority language groups; and the right to work in either language, as a general rule, in the federal government.

These principles appeared to challenge Bill One, but the impact was largely undercut by an accompanying statement by Secretary of State John Roberts. Mr. Roberts suggested that Quebec "apprehensions" about its language and culture might justify deferment of "full freedom" of educational choice in that province. The ineptness of the statement led to considerable confusion in the press about what the federal authorities really meant, and led to a good deal of criticism of the government's incoherence in the most fundamental of its policies. As for bilingualism in the public service, the announcement of changes in policies was deferred pending discussions with the public service unions.

Whatever revisions are made in bilingualism policies in the federal public service, I am convinced that the rules, regulations, and penalties type of approach simply will not work well. If true bilingualism is to be achieved at all it can only be done over a long period of time, through the hiring of more French-speaking and bilingual recruits, by providing the kind of incentives that would induce the provinces to place greater emphasis on language training in the schools and universities, the best incentive being the insistent demands of parents seeking greater job opportunities for their children in the federal government. It can even be argued that the government's present policy, that unilinguals can be hired if they study the other language at government expense, has in fact damaged incentive for language training at the provincial school and university levels. Why couldn't the government bring out a ten-year policy which provides that a rising annual proportion of jobs be for bilinguals only – regardless of job requirements – and so stimulate second language training in the schools in both English and French?

The provinces, of course, must accept a large measure of blame for the appalling state of second language training in Canada. Anyone who knows what is being done in Europe has to hang his head in shame. As Spicer noted in his 1975 Report, the provincial education departments (except for some experimentation in immersion courses at elementary levels) seem to be moving in the wrong direction. In Ontario the Hall-Dennis philosophy of a cafeteria style approach to education – pick what you like – has produced a declining enrolment in French in secondary schools in favour of Mickey Mouse courses. It is not very comforting to know that English and mathematical skills of high school graduates appear to be deteriorating for the same reasons. It is to be hoped that there will be more interest in French when today's immersed children reach the higher grades; by that time even our professional educators may have grasped that the road to knowledge does not lie through complete freedom of choice in the secondary school system.

Quebec – Péquistes oppose bilingualism

If second-language training is in relatively poor shape in English Canada, it is in deeper trouble in Quebec, despite all the continuing economic incentives to learn English. The rising tide of separatism has engulfed the francophone teaching profession, so much so that many teachers have been indoctrinating their students with the notion that the learning of English as a second language is unpatriotic, a threat to the survival of the French language in Quebec. Although any foreign language is best taught by someone brought up in it, there are few anglophone teachers in the French Catholic school system, and the likelihood of any new ones being hired is remote, given declining enrolments and the power of the unions. This latter power even extends to giving teachers the right to choose what courses they will teach on the basis of seniority. English, being lowest in popularity, gets the least experienced teachers, many with little knowledge of or training in the language.

Reinforcing this direct impact of nationalistic bias is the theory, enunciated by many péquistes, that studying two languages in the early school years damages a child's ability to learn his own well. I first saw this view put forward in an editorial by Marcel Turgeon, a lawyer, in *Ici-Québec,*[2] a péquiste journal that sprang into being following the November 15 election. Listen to this: "If Mr. Trudeau studies history he will find that bilingualism is a bad thing for everyone . . . It is only after studying one's own language in depth that one can later, with extreme prudence, begin to study a second language . . . How can a student learn easily two languages when he can't even master his own?" He quotes Rémy de Gourmont (possibly out of context?) "Bilingual peoples are almost always inferior peoples." He went on, "The intellectual élite can afford the luxury of bilingualism, but only because they already know their own language. As for the bulk of the populace, bilingualism can only impoverish them . . . For Quebec, bilingualism is a dangerous menace. Only traitors and utopians wish to ignore this."

There are unpleasant élitist overtones in this protectionist view of language training. Behind the piously expressed need to preserve the French language and culture is the implication that only a few francophone Quebecers need to, or can, learn English. The masses will be denied the chance. Ironically, at least ten members of the Lévesque cabinet have chosen to send their children to private schools, notably to the Montreal French lycées, Stanislas, or Marie de France, where the English training is excellent. One is reminded of the Soviet system where priority in access to university is (or was) given to sons and daughters of Communist party members.

Does the theory stand up that second-language training damages young minds, prevents them mastering their own? All the myriad studies in Ontario of the children going through French immersion point to just one conclusion, that they do better in *all* their work, including their English studies. I can vouch for this personally; all three of my children went to French schools and then went back, after a varying number of years, into the English school system. They all did well, particularly in English.

Mr. Turgeon may not be totally reflective of the mainstream of péquiste thinking, but I suspect he isn't far from it. Echoes of his stand appeared on April 1, 1977, in the Quebec government's language white paper, the brainchild of psychiatrist, and Minister of Cultural Development, Dr. Camille Laurin. From Chapter II:

> We do not deny that it is essential for certain French-speaking Quebeckers to speak English. This is irrefutable. There are two main conditions, however: the learning of English must not be imposed so early in that it constitutes a danger to the required basic technical and cultural training which in any country must remain a fundamental human concern, and the learning of another language must not be inconsistent with the need to play a full part in one's own culture.
>
> The political and cultural environment of Quebec and the constant threat which it represents for French-speaking Quebeckers puts the whole question of the teaching of a second language in a false light. In any society, learning a language other than his own is an important acquisition for an individual; no one would dream of considering this a threat to the native tongue. The education system of any modern state should provide citizens with the opportunity of acquiring a good knowledge of a second and even a third language. Such a situation already exists in several industrialized nations of Europe. In a world which is shrinking daily, multilingualism is always an advantage and is becoming more and more of a necessity. However, the fact remains that in the Quebec context, as in many others, it is necessary to reconcile the teaching of a second language with the destiny of the first. Improvement in the teaching of a language other than French is a necessity for Quebec and must not be considered an impediment to the increased use of French.
>
> Only when the survival of the French language is assured, however, will second language teaching programs be seen in their proper light and become truly effective. . .
>
> It is equally hoped that, the day the English language ceases to be, in the eyes of many, the pervasive symbol of perpetual economic and cultural domination, the lack of interest in and even downright aversion toward the learning of that language on the part of the Quebec student body will give way to a much more constructive attitude.

The experiments of famed Dr. Wilder Penfield at the Montreal Neurological Institute showed that the early years of childhood are the best time to learn a foreign language, when brain cells are more receptive. If francophones in Quebec have to wait until their later years to study English their learning capacity, and their desire to learn, will be diminished.

Maybe that conforms to the overall péquiste objectives.

As for Mr. Turgeon's implication that bilingual people are inferior, I commented on this in an article I wrote for the Quebec Liberal Party *L'Electeur,* published April 28, 1977.

> What bloody nonsense! Look around you among the most learned of your acquaintances. Look at the Swedes, who speak three or more languages by the time they leave school. Look at the educated Europeans you meet . . . The essence of my argument is that a policy that tries to prevent any group, such as Italian immigrants, from learning the language of their choice is coercive and doomed to failure . . . and to a backlash that cannot help but hurt Quebec economically.

I proposed instead a complete departure from the archaic 100-year-old system which separated the schools into four groups: French Catholic, English Catholic, Protestants and non-denominational. I suggested three main groups of primary and secondary schools: (1) French only, with a minimum of language training, (for dedicated péquiste parents or those frightened of English "contamination"); (2) French mainly, with good English training, leading to reasonable knowledge of that language; and (3) English basically, but with instruction in French obligatory, with an acceptable fluency in French necessary for graduation from high school.

In summary, I did not quarrel with the basic péquiste objective that every student in Quebec, whatever his origins, should be able to function in French by the time he leaves school, but suggested that this can be achieved simply by making French as much a part of the English school curriculum as reading, writing, and arithmetic.

Learning French outside the schools

But what about all those who have not been provided with adequate training in the second language seeking federal employment?

So long as a bilingual public service continues to be an objective of the federal government, a better approach will have to be found than part-time language instruction. Even accepting the fact that government language training may inhibit corrective action at the provincial level, there may be some virtue, as a short term expedient, in giving intensive training to all new entrants to the public service who are weak in one of the two languages. Governor-General Léger, when he was a deputy minister, told me that he supported this approach. If nothing else, the enormous language training facilities which have been put in place in the federal capital should be devoted almost exclusively to younger public servants; for most older employees – define them how you will – such training is very costly and largely a waste of time.

The intensive language course on entry to public service has merit, but if the new language is going to "stick," the graduate must have a chance to use it frequently. This is a main reason why existing public service courses have failed; English is still the common language of work. The concept of French language units (FLU's) has been helping to provide an ambience where francophones can use their language at work, but it cannot absorb many anglophones who are not completely fluent in French – and few reach that state in language courses – without damaging the purpose for which the FLU's were established. "Ambience" is not solely language, but shared history, common ideas and traditions, jokes and slang, all the things one learns last about a foreign language or culture.

My own experience in working in French is that perhaps we have been aiming too high in seeking to train anglophones to speak French. Maybe the primary goal of government language training should be to give the public servant a "passive" knowledge of the second language, that is the ability to read it and to understand it when it is spoken at conversational speeds. Time and again I have been told in francophone groups that all they want is to be able to present their arguments in their own language, and that they vastly prefer the anglophone to talk English rather than to garble his own arguments by being forced to use his own indifferent French. But the often-heard anglophone refrain "I don't understand French," which forces the francophone to speak English, is what the latter finds hard to take as a steady diet. I also think that the teaching of languages in the public service may have focused too much attention on speaking and writing at the expense of improvement in comprehension; I agree that they all go together, but for many anglophones at least, their real hang-up is fear of appearing a fool in oral expression.

My colleagues on the various Quebec task forces, usually fluent in English, invariably had just one requirement of me, that I comprehend enough French to allow *them* to use the language. I would venture into French, but they were inclined to be impatient – "For Christ's sake, Doug, speak English" – or, to kid me, "speak white."

Nevertheless, I felt guilty enough to want to do better. In 1966 "total immersion" courses were just coming into vogue, and in April I decided to try a Berlitz one-week immersion course at Morin Heights in the Laurentians. Of the intensity of the course there was no doubt; from breakfast until the time we went to bed it was French all the way. The teaching was one-on-one, question and response, with each reply requiring a reformulation of the question. Corrections were drawn out of us by a rephrased or repeated question. This took up to seven or eight hours daily, together with a group session each evening for speeches and discussion, and written essays.

It was an exhausting process – as much for the staff as for us – and given the ratio of one teacher to a student, a very expensive one. I found it effective and it improved my French, but I had the usual experience of slipping back into the rut after I went home to my family and the Ottawa environment. I attended one more weekly session in November, but decided after it that I had obtained about all I could from immersion.

Conclusion

It is difficult to be optimistic these days about the future of bilingualism and language training in this country. The trend in Quebec, whether the péquistes win their referendum or not, is clearly against the use of English and instruction in it. The Quebec approach is not likely to encourage other provinces to move very far or fast in French use or instruction; their record in secondary schools in recent years, no doubt partly the product of the voluntary approach to courses, has been dismal.

Is bilingualism, then, to become the impossible dream in Canada? Are we to be forced back into our two solitudes? That appears to be the goal of the péquiste government of Quebec, which hopes to use the language issue to build voting strength for independence. It will take extraordinary tolerance on the part of Canadians outside Quebec, a demonstrated willingness to treat francophone minorities in other provinces better than the Quebec government proposes to treat its anglophones, an acceptance of the teaching of French as much for its cultural merits as for its political imperatives, if we are to counter successfully the linguistic arguments of the Quebec nationalists. The separatist battle may well be lost on economic grounds, but if we are to hope to be united afterwards, then it will only be if we are ready to recommit ourselves to the bilingual challenge we Canadians so bravely accepted a decade ago, and to use a good deal more common sense and patience in going about the task than we have shown in recent years.

Notes

1 *Official Languages Act,* 17-18 Elizabeth II, Chapter 54 para. 25.
2 *Ici-Québec,* Vol. 1 No. 1.

XIV

Return to Montreal – following study of the Capital (1974-1977)

By the end of 1972 I had made up my mind to leave the National Capital Commission. Up to that point I had managed to tolerate the frustrations of working in the federal government through a combination of personal job satisfaction, public recognition, and the help of a network of friends inside the big machine who made it possible to get a few things done. My network was recognized as a good one, since it included many of the top civil servants, most of them whom I had known a long time. Certainly the two most powerful were Gordon Robertson, cabinet secretary, and Marc Lalonde, principal secretary to Prime Minister Trudeau, until he went directly into politics himself in the fall of 1972. Both were interested in the capital, and backed me up.

What disturbed me, however, was that the federal system itself was so creaky and ponderous that it was necessary to have influence to accomplish anything. In my judgment, an important source of its growing inefficiency has been the increasing concentration of power in the prime minister and his office, all allegedly in the name of a more democratic, collegial form of government. Delegation is out; every decision is presumed to be made around the cabinet table. But trying to involve everyone in everything leaves no one really responsible for anything, and not much decided or done. Since decisions are needed, the power to make them inevitably gravitates to the centre. Centralization has been reinforced by the constant shifting around of ministers and deputy ministers. ("Keeps 'em dumb," said one senior aide cynically).

I have watched this process go on with a certain wry sense of amusement. Mr. Trudeau is an apostle of Lord Acton, that brilliant Catholic scholar, philosopher and historian of the last half of the nineteenth century. Trudeau venerates Acton because of his strong opposition to nationalism. Yet Acton's most memorable battle was over the manner in which Pope Pius IX had concentrated power in the Vatican by destroying the independence of the Roman Catholic bishops.[1] Mr. Trudeau, in centralizing power in his office at the expense of his ministers, has behaved very much like Pius IX. All we lack is the propagation of a new doctrine of prime ministerial infallibility, along the lines of the decree of papal infallibility, which Pius IX pushed through by packing the 1870 Vatican Council with his supporters.

Not that I have ever had anything against Pierre Trudeau personally. At his invitation I lunched with him, alone, several times at 24 Sussex, and always found him appreciative, receptive, and about as gracious a host as one could find. He went out of his way to make a guest feel at home, perhaps because he sensed that the aura of his office makes people uneasy – ("Geez, this is not old friend Pierre I'm talking to, it's the PRIME MINISTER"). He used one little gimmick which helped me and presumably other guests to relax. I would turn up a few minutes before he arrived in his car from his office; as soon as he came in he would take off his jacket, loosen his tie, unbutton his collar, and say "Let's have a drink."

My talks with him were always very frank and direct; my language was about as profane as it usually is, and my views expressed in uninhibited fashion, even when it came to giving unflattering opinions on his policies or his colleagues. He didn't always agree, but he was a good listener; one problem, however, was that it wasn't wise to be too offhand, as one often is in casual conversation with a friend. His mind worked so quickly that he would pick you up on a loose statement. For all that, I found I could talk to him more easily than with many people I knew a good deal better. His questions were probing: the only time I saw him uncertain was on economic matters, where I sensed that he had no solid base or philosophy, but rather had absorbed somewhat superficial impressions of the problems of the day and the latest theory of how to cope with them.

In early January 1973 I talked with Mr. Trudeau briefly at a Speaker's reception, saying I would like to discuss some things with him. He agreed, asking me to clear it with his appointments secretary. I did, and a meeting was set up for January 15. I had two things on my mind: to tell him I was leaving, and why, and to raise with him an idea about a study on the governing of the national capital. One important "why" behind my departure was that I was fed up with the increasingly confused and tangled web of jurisdictions operating in the capital, not only those of the three levels of government (the regional municipalities were in fact a fourth), but also the lack of any good mechanism within the federal government itself for co-ordinating the activities of the various departments that had an impact on the capital.

I saw the prime minister as scheduled and gave him a memo I had prepared about the capital's jurisdictional problems, and said that they would likely get worse, not better. I told him I'd had enough of trying to function inside a system that was doomed to fail, and offered my resignation. I suggested, however, that the government undertake a study of these problems, and offered my services. He was sympathetic, and said he would discuss it with his colleagues. After a delay of several months, the cabinet gave its approval for me to do the study as a one-man task force, and I resigned from NCC at the end of May, 1973.

The study

The terms of reference of the study were given in the prime minister's May 17 press release:

> to undertake a study of the most effective arrangements for the future administration of matters directly affecting the National Capital and its development, including the role of the National Capital Commission and its relation to other bodies concerned with the governing of the Capital Region and the co-ordination of those federal activities which bear upon the development of the Region as a national capital.

I don't propose to go into detail about my Report, except to suggest that those interested obtain a copy and read it.[2] It was finished by mid-May 1974, with the printed version available to the public, in English and French, in November. I would like to say that its publication received wide acclaim from a waiting world, but like many such studies it proved to be a nine-day wonder and dropped quietly from sight.

However, the government did appoint the following year a special Joint Committee of the Senate and House of Commons to study the National Capital Region. I appeared before it four times, and was cross-examined about my Report. The Committee, at time of writing, had not met for a year, and it does not appear that its deliberations will be very fruitful.

As for the Report, in looking back I don't think there is much I would add or subtract, except to observe that the importance of the capital as an issue has been overtaken by events, the problems of the economy, regional discontent, Quebec-Canada relations. Parliament, the press and the people have become bored with the problem of trying to build a capital "worthy of this great nation," and have turned to other things, such as how to keep this great nation from falling apart.

But let me try to put what I said in a nutshell – even at some considerable sacrifice in the flow of the argument:

(1) The federal government is overwhelmingly dominant in the capital as an employer, and has turned the region around Ottawa-Hull almost into a one-industry metropolitan area; in practical terms, this fact has overridden municipal boundaries, and to a lesser extent the provincial boundary.

(2) The federal government has a right to a say in the governing of its own capital, by virtue of its economic impact, its past record as planner and creator of the capital as we know it today, its legal and constitutional rights, and because it is the *only* government to have based its approach on the essential unity of the whole region.
(3) The capital has suffered over the years by being part of Ontario, rather than a separate district on both sides of the river, carved out of Ontario and Quebec. It may be too late now to create such a district, because of entrenched positions, powers and emotions.
(4) Any form of municipal government that does not recognize that the capital lies *on both sides of the Ottawa River,* and does not provide a voice for the federal government as well as for the residents, and for the two provinces, will repeat the mistakes of the past.

My suggestion for meeting this latter dilemma was the creation of a "Supra-regional Council," straddling the Ottawa River, composed of representatives as follows: 50 per cent elected by residents, 25 per cent federal appointees, and 25 per cent Ontario and Quebec appointees. Predictably, it did not arouse much enthusiasm from local politicians, who saw their powers diminished, and who fired hard at the Report (see cartoon).

What now for the capital? In the face of péquiste statements and actions, it is difficult to be very optimistic that further progress can be made towards achieving the program, so courageously launched by the Trudeau government in 1969, to build up the federal presence on the Hull side and make the capital of Canada a bilingual and bicultural example

The Citizen, Ottawa.

for the country. The new Assembly member for Hull, Jocelyn Ouellette, who defeated Oswald Parent by a couple of votes on recount and who became a member of the Lévesque cabinet in July 1977, has in fact called for an end to the NCC presence on the Quebec side of the National Capital Region. Federal spokesmen, like Urban Affairs Minister André Ouellet, countered with references to the hundreds of millions of federal dollars spent on the Quebec side, and to the fact that problems are those of excessive growth and prosperity in contrast to the depressed conditions of the 'fifties and 'sixties. Yet on November 15 this enormous expenditure of federal funds was more than offset by the emotional appeal of independence, and the poor image of the Bourassa government.

Does the federal government's policy for the capital, like its bilingual policy, need substantial change? Should it turn now instead to *decentralization,* giving the poorer regions the benefits of the federal presence and federal spending, rather than continuing to pour vast amounts of federal money into Ottawa-Hull? It may be too early to fly the white flag, but I am afraid that the capital, as a symbol of the nation, has come to be regarded across the country more as a symbol of waste, of bad government, of overpaid and underworked bureaucrats, than, as one 1969 cabinet document suggested it should become: "the true reflection of Canada, the major element contributing to national pride."

Back to Quebec – Montreal suburban transit

My study on the governing of the capital was just about completed by early May 1974, when I received a call from Oswald Parent, from Quebec. He said, "I think we've got a job for you that you'll find challenging." The proposal was that I take charge of a new project for Quebec, the building of a suburban rail connection from downtown Montreal to Mirabel Airport. My reaction was "Why me?", saying I had little experience with rail transit. He said that he and Claude Rouleau, deputy minister of Transport, had figured that anyone who cared so much about slowing down the depredations of the car in our cities, and encouraging public transit in its place, was clearly the man for them. He reminded me about our battle over Leamy Park on the Hull side, when I had taken the two of them on over the building of an expressway through the Park – in spite of having approved the plans earlier – using the stopping of the Spadina Expressway as my precedent. They didn't win their point, either, until I had resigned.

I saw Rouleau in Quebec on May 21. He was an engineer and a close friend of Paul Desrochers, the *éminence grise* behind Robert Bourassa. Rouleau was one of the four or five most powerful bureaucrats in Quebec. A big man, he had a quick mind and a quicker tongue; he spoke French so fast that even his close associates had trouble some time understanding him. It was even tougher for me, but he had a cheerful, boisterous nature, and believed more in using the telephone – it seldom left his hand – than in writing memos. He replied to his 'phone calls quickly, too, a virtue I have learned to cherish in people.

Rouleau gave me a report on the project that had been prepared, and then we had drinks and dinner with Parent and Paul Berthiaume, Minister of State for Transport. In the course of the discussion, it became clear that the ministry was earnest about changing its priorities. It had been on an autoroute jag for a decade or more, and was finding that road building often creates more problems than it solves. Some four hours and several bottles of red wine later, it was pretty well agreed that I would take on the transit job that fall. I promised to give it half my time, and would be paid a *per diem* and expenses rather than a salary. Technically I would be reporting to the Minister (Raymond Mailloux) but I recognized that faster action would result if I dealt through Rouleau.

I did need a good number two, preferably someone who was well plugged in to the bureaucratic machine in Quebec. A few weeks later I went to Quebec again, and Rouleau suggested Denis de Belleval as the man for me. He said "He's a péquiste, mind you – and not too popular with some Liberal ministers because of it – but he's bright and well trained." I met de Belleval and liked him on the spot. He was a tall, good-looking fellow, about thirty-five, radiating self-confidence, who expressed himself clearly and who had a good grasp of English.

I heard his story later. He had been accepted at Royal Military College at Kingston, but had come down with Menières disease, which deafened him in one ear. He went instead to Laval, and then to London School of Economics, and had worked for the Quebec government since, mainly in fields of economic and urban planning. Of his dedication to the péquiste cause there was little doubt, but it never interfered with his work in any way, that is, until September 1976. His friends persuaded him to contest the péquiste nomination in his home riding of Charlesbourg, in Quebec City; he won on the third ballot, ran, and was elected on November 15. On November 26 he made it into Lévesque's cabinet as Minister of the Public Service and vice chairman of the Treasury Board – the post just vacated by my old friend, Oswald Parent!

In mid-September 1974, de Belleval and I started work in Montreal on our two-man BAREM task force – *Bureau d'aménagement du réseau express de Montréal* – loosely translated as "headquarters of planning for the Montreal rapid transit network." We set out to learn all we could about the project from the existing studies, and began discussions with the railways, with the various municipal planning authorities, and with politicians of all levels of government in the areas likely to be affected.

To head up the technical side of our operations, at the end of 1974, we were lucky to find André Gravelle, a civil engineering graduate of McGill, ex CNR employee, and who was then second-in-command of the task force building Mirabel Airport. He was a great addition to the team, beefing up the side of the business where the two of us were weakest. The three of us were to work together more or less as a management committee, until de Belleval left for politics.

As our studies continued, a number of conclusions emerged which differed somewhat from those in earlier studies, or which took account of factors not previously considered adequately:

(1) A new rail line to Mirabel, even if built largely along existing rail rights-of-way, could not be justified economically unless its principal function was to serve commuters in the area north-west of Montreal.

(2) the new line could serve as a major instrument of development, if properly planned. Studies carried out by the provincial "Office of Planning and Development of Quebec" had shown this north-west area as the best place for Montreal to grow (the region south of Montreal, then building up rapidly, was eating up valuable farm land, and a new bridge or tunnel over the St. Lawrence would now cost $500 million or more).

(3) there was, however, no official plan for the Greater Montreal region, nor was there any instrument for co-ordinating transit in the region. The main transit system, composed of the subway (Métro) and buses, was run by the Montreal Urban Community (CUM), a grouping of the municipalities on Montreal Island. However, it was dominated by the City of Montreal and by its powerful and colourful mayor, Jean Drapeau. The province had never been able to exercise much effective control over Montreal in either planning or transit.

(4) Montreal was well endowed with train tracks running into the downtown area, providing a basis for a first class commuter rail network. There were several commuter train services in operation, including the CNR's old (World War I) line through a tunnel under the mountain to Mount Royal, St. Laurent and ultimately in a westerly direction to Deux Montagnes. In spite of run down equipment, these CN trains carried up to 25,000 passengers a day, the largest such service in Canada. The CP service along the Lakeshore also provided an important commuter service (but the French Canadians viewed it as the "English" line, serving the predominantly English West Island).

(5) All the commuter trains were losing money, at an annually rising clip. No subsidies were forthcoming from the federal government, and the railways kept complaining and raising fares. The province was reluctant to pick up the tab (they regarded the trains as a federal responsibility), so the service deteriorated. Few public transit services are profitable anywhere; we believed that although a new system would cut manpower and maintenance expenditures, – the major source of the CN and CP losses –

subsidies would have to be provided for both existing systems, and for new or upgraded services such as our proposed Mirabel line.

Our work progressed on two main fronts. One was the planning aspects of the new line, including the areas around stations, and the necessary integration with municipal and rail plans. Paul St. Jacques, formerly with Jean-Claude La Haye's firm, headed this work. To help us with the engineering studies we brought in a consortium of consultants, who provided us with technical and office help. To buttress our own studies, de Belleval, Gravelle, and I, and at different times other staff members, visited suburban rail systems in Paris, London, Stockholm, Munich and Frankfurt, as well as several U.S. systems. Nothing proved more instructive than a first hand look at the efficient modern electric commuter trains that are common in Europe but rare in North America. Everyone was very helpful – some obviously were hoping for orders for their country's equipment producers – and it was quite an education.

As a result of this experience we had come to several conclusions. The first was that Canadians were silly trying to "reinvent the wheel" by starting from scratch, seeking to design our own trains; unfortunately this latter approach appeared favoured by both the Ontario and federal governments. The Europeans had made great strides in recent years in the design of attractive and efficient modern trains. The second was that almost every suburban system in Europe was electrified, with high voltage service; all used roughly the same kind of equipment, large cars, side door openings, steel wheels, with self-propelled traction. The third conclusion was that the Europeans were finding costs of digging subway tunnels almost prohibitive, except in built up urban core areas where surface congestion and land costs were very high. As a result they were doing all they could to put their urban and commuter lines above ground.

This latter discovery brought us into conflict with the Montreal transit authorities. The Montreal Métro was attractive, but distinctive. Early in the 1960s Jean Drapeau had opted for the original Paris Métro type of cars, with rubber tires; the cars were as small as the Paris cars, partly to reduce tunnel excavation costs. Unlike the Paris trains, however, the Montreal Métro trains could not surface because of the problems of snow, and the lack of winterizing. This meant that new Métro extensions would continue to require expensive tunnelling. Another factor was cost; Montreal cars cost nearly twice as much per square foot as longer and more conventional subway cars, such as those used in Toronto, and operating costs per passenger were thus much higher.

The battle was joined over the projected extension of the Métro to Cartierville, a line which had been planned in 1970. From our point of view this would tap an area already partially served by the CN Deux Montagnes' service; we argued the CN line could be fixed up and turned

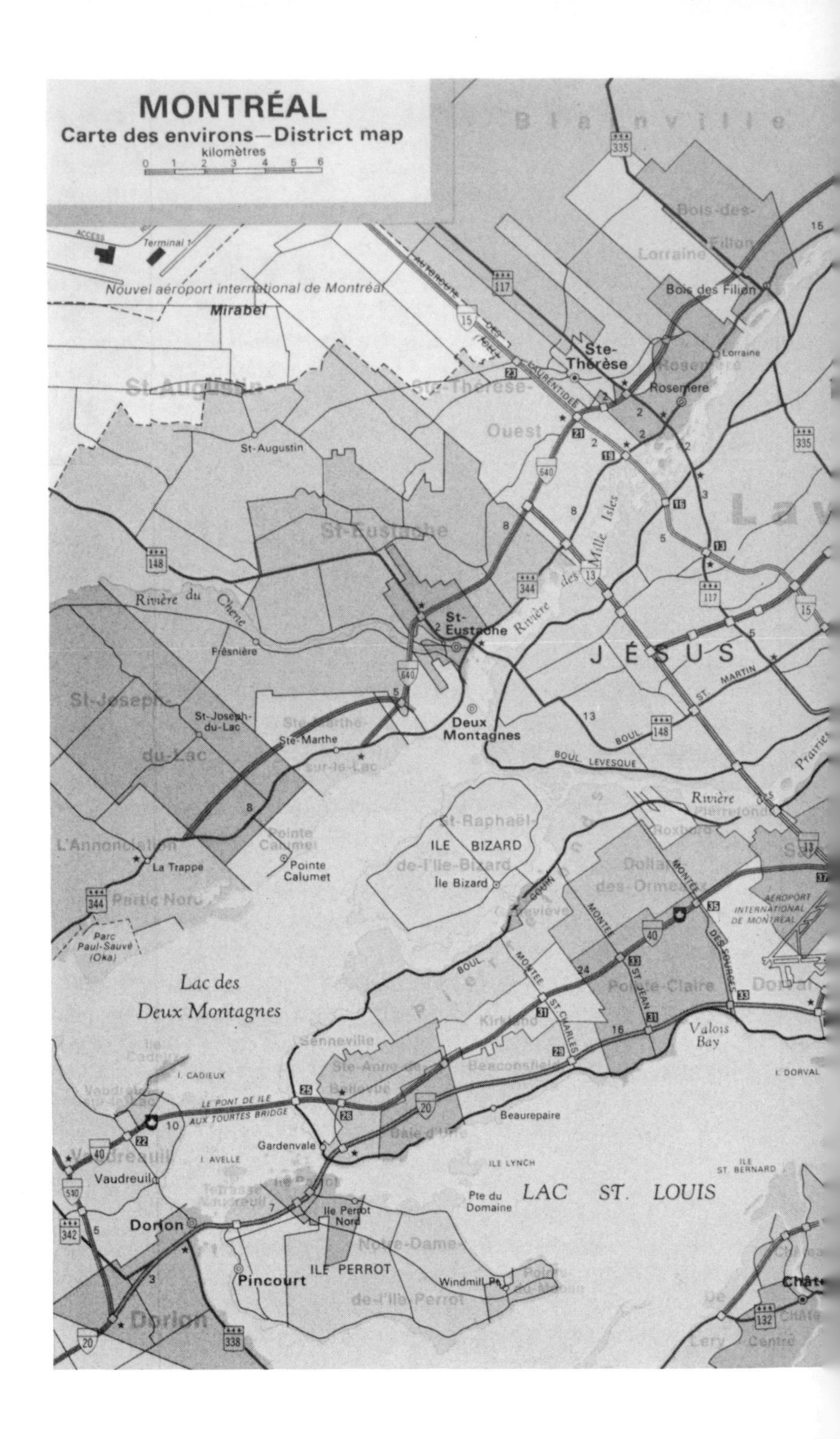
MONTRÉAL
Carte des environs—District map
kilomètres
0 1 2 3 4 5 6
Nouvel aéroport international de Montréal
Mirabel
Terminal 1
Blainville
Bois-des-Filion
Lorraine
Ste-Thérèse
Rosemère
Ste-Thérèse-Ouest
St-Augustin
St-Eustache
Deux Montagnes
Rivière du Chêne
Rivière des Mille Isles
JÉSUS
Fresnière
St-Joseph-du-Lac
Ste-Marthe-sur-le-Lac
Ste-Marthe
L'Annonciation
La Trappe
Pointe Calumet
Parc Paul-Sauvé (Oka)
St-Raphaël-de-l'Ile-Bizard
ILE BIZARD
Ile Bizard
Rivière
Roxboro
Dollard-des-Ormeaux
AÉROPORT INTERNATIONAL DE MONTRÉAL
Lac des Deux Montagnes
Pointe-Claire
Valois Bay
Kirkland
Senneville
Ste-Anne-de-Bellevue
Beaconsfield
Beaurepaire
I. CADIEUX
I. DORVAL
LE PONT DE ILE AUX TOURTES BRIDGE
Gardenvale
Vaudreuil
I. AVELLE
ILE LYNCH
ILE ST. BERNARD
LAC ST. LOUIS
Pte du Domaine
Dorion
Ile Perrot Nord
ILE PERROT
Notre-Dame-de-l'Ile-Perrot
Pincourt
Windmill Pt.
BOUL. LEVESQUE
BOUL. ST. MARTIN
MONTÉE ST. JEAN
MONTÉE DES SOURCES
MONTÉE ST. CHARLES
BOUL. GOUIN
AUTOROUTE DES LAURENTIDES

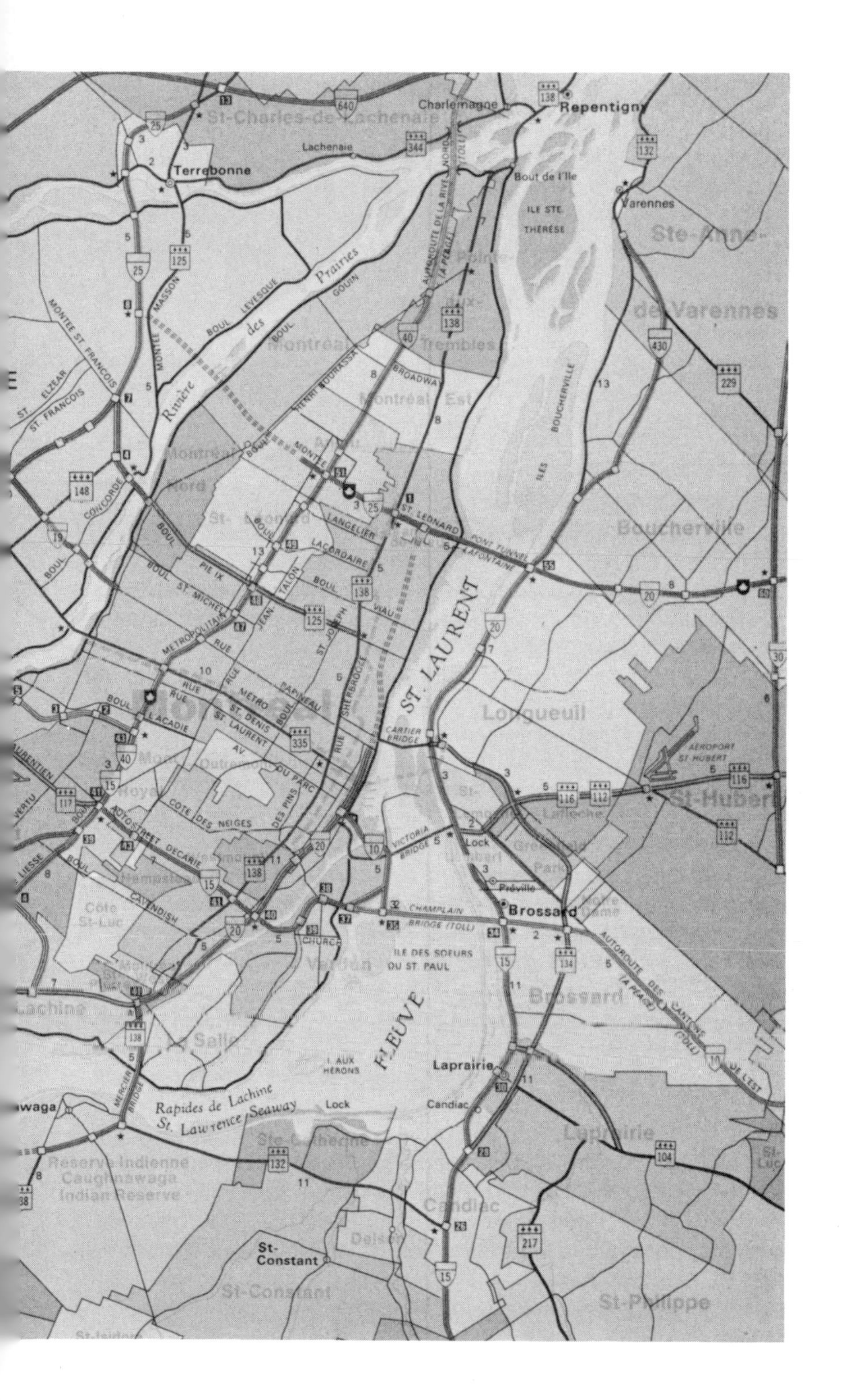

Charlemagne
Repentigny
St-Charles-de-Lachenaie
Lachenaie
Terrebonne
Bout de l'Ile
ILE STE. THÉRÈSE
Varennes
Ste-Anne-de-Varennes
Pointe-aux-Trembles
Rivière des Prairies
BOUL LEVESQUE
BOUL GOUIN
MONTEE MASSON
MONTEE ST FRANCOIS
ST. ELZEAR
ST. FRANCOIS
Montréal Est
BROADWAY
HENRI BOURASSA
AUTOROUTE DE LA RIVE NORD (A PEAGE)
BOUCHERVILLE
ILES
Montréal Nord
CONCORDE
BOUL
St-Léonard
ST. LEONARD
LANGELIER
LACORDAIRE
PONT TUNNEL L. H. LAFONTAINE
Boucherville
BOUL PIE IX
BOUL ST. MICHEL
JEAN TALON
VIAU
ST. JOSEPH
METROPOLITAIN
RUE PAPINEAU
RUE METRO
ST. DENIS
ST. LAURENT
SHERBROOKE
ST. LAURENT
Longueuil
CARTIER BRIDGE
L'ACADIE
DU PARC
DES PINS
AÉROPORT ST-HUBERT
St-Hubert
Laflèche
LAURENTIEN
AUTOSTREET DECARIE
COTE DES NEIGES
VICTORIA BRIDGE
Lock
Préville
Greenfield Park
BOUL CAVENDISH
Côte St-Luc
Brossard
Notre Dame
CHAMPLAIN BRIDGE (TOLL)
CHURCH
ILE DES SOEURS OU ST. PAUL
Verdun
AUTOROUTE DES CANTONS DE L'EST (A PEAGE) (TOLL)
Lachine
FLEUVE
La Salle
I. AUX HERONS
Laprairie
MERCIER BRIDGE
Rapides de Lachine
St. Lawrence Seaway
Lock
Candiac
Ste-Catherine
Réserve Indienne Caughnawaga Indian Reserve
Candiac
Delson
St-Constant
St-Constant
St-Philippe

into a first-class surface rail operation at one-fifth the cost or less of the Métro extension, then running (1976) at close to $50 million dollars a mile, equipment included. And in many ways the CN line would give better and faster service to the downtown; fewer stations, higher speeds. The Métro – any subway – suffers in comparison, because the stations are closer together, making for much slower trips over intermediate and long distances.

We had been keeping the Quebec Ministry of Transport informed of our conclusions. In February 1976 it became clear to us that the Métro people really didn't give a damn about our views, and were going ahead with their extension to Cartierville. I kept raising the issue with the province, and they were beginning to listen, if in part because of their own financial problems arising out of the colossal expenditures on the Olympic games; Quebec subsidizes urban transit capital costs by 60 per cent, and operational deficits by an average of about 50 per cent. I helped things along a bit by filling in Ryan at *Le Devoir* about our concerns; one of their reporters checked things out with the minister in Quebec, who confirmed that they were indeed thinking of preferring our CN alternative to the Métro. On February 25, *Le Devoir* came out with a big front page story, "Quebec veut stopper le Métro."

I had met Lawrence Hanigan, chairman of the Montreal Transit Authority, (CTCUM), and also chairman of the CUM executive committee, some months earlier; he was rather a cold fish, but seemed decent enough. The story, however, sent him post haste down to Quebec to try to fix things up. He did not meet with much success, but made some defiant statements about going ahead anyway. In April, the CTCUM called for tenders for the excavation of about four miles of Métro tunnel at the Cartierville end of the proposed extension. I wrote Mr. Mailloux, suggesting that he was about to be faced with a *fait accompli* by Mr. Hanigan, when obviously a comparative study was needed. The minister came through with an order to Montreal to suspend further construction tenders, until the matter had been thoroughly studied by the province. On the basis of our recommendation, a new study group called the Transport Committee for the Montreal Region (CTRM) was set up to do the studying; it was to be chaired by Claude Rouleau, with Hanigan as one of the four members (BAREM was not then represented on it, except in an advisory role).

Hanigan by this time had acquired a certain aversion for me and for my ideas, and told me publicly to mind my own business. I reciprocated, having seen some of the superficial calculations on which their original 1970 decision on the Cartierville line had been based, and which, despite their inadequacies and outdated figures, he had supplied to Quebec in defending his position. I felt that Hanigan was not well advised, and I attacked his "tunnel vision" attitude in the press.

By the summer of 1976, however, it was clear that the money shortage caused by the Olympic disaster would slow every Montreal capital project – the badly needed sewer system, the Métro, road building, and our own proposals. It was puzzling how Mayor Jean Drapeau retained public support; his colossal waste of public funds in the pursuit of the building of monuments, his preference for "circuses" to "bread," his lack of concern about the planning of Montreal, and the mess that demolition has made of the city, all these in most places would have brought about his impeachment. Still, he's a very persuasive fellow, a great salesman, and I suspect many Montrealers believe that he was clever enough to get his great ventures for Montreal, and have someone else pay for them.

Our BAREM operation was slowing down, and de Belleval's departure in September convinced me that it was time I left too. However, the election was called in October, and I felt I should stick around until after the dust had settled. With Denis installed in the Lévesque cabinet, I decided to give the new Minister of Transport, Lucien Lessard, time to catch his breath. Just before the election, I had given Mr. Mailloux a letter containing both a progress report, and some recommendations to help us cope with some of the problems we were facing. The election intervened, and I then passed the same documentation to Lessard via de Belleval. Having heard no answer from him for two months, however, I decided to send in my letter of resignation on February 11.

My reasons for leaving were quite straightforward; I'd made my contribution over the thirty-month period, and nothing concrete about the project was likely to be accomplished in the near future. I also told Lessard that I had started this book, and was continuing my weekly column, and it was quite impossible to do either without expressing some views on Quebec and the Lévesque government; this would inevitably cause me problems if I were still working for Quebec. I said also that I would welcome the chance to speak out freely and openly on the question of transit in Montreal.

I had a speech scheduled before the Women's Canadian Club of Montreal, on March 7, 1977, and wrote an article to appear in *Le Devoir* about the same time. In both speech and article I set out all the questions and doubts I had about the Métro – the article was in fact entitled "The Montreal Métro – Olympics on Wheels?" In it I said "The Métro is in danger of becoming, like the Olympics, a monument to the uncontrolled and extravagant decisions of the rulers of Montreal." I called for a fast study by outside experts, mainly from Europe.

Hanigan and Drapeau both replied. Drapeau said, in dismissing my criticism of his Métro, that it came from "an expert on everything and a doer of nothing." Hanigan accused me of being "anti-Québécois" for proposing an independent study and attacked some figures I had given.

The newspapers liked the continuing exchanges and they provided the public forum which I had been seeking all along. Yet at the time the issue had first surfaced, a year earlier, I had concluded that my days at BAREM were probably numbered. As an anglophone I was particularly vulnerable, but what was worse I had crossed the Montreal municipal establishment; neither Drapeau nor Hanigan were good losers.

Informing the public was one goal; educating the province had been another important objective right from the start. The department in Quebec had had little expertise in rail transit; the creation of the BAREM organization gave them a valuable tool for exercising some control over the Montreal civic establishment, not only in transit but in planning as well. I don't think they've made enough use of BAREM, but at least we kept pushing them on the issues we felt they should be concerned about.

And our train project? We were certainly optimistic at the beginning, perhaps too optimistic, given the wide range of conflicting jurisdictions and government levels involved. I think we gave it as good a shot as we could, and if any easing in Quebec's financial stringency occurs, our planning by the summer of 1977 had brought the Mirabel project to the stage where enough facts were known on which a well-informed decision could be taken. The work we had done on other proposals had also given the government a base on which to form judgments on the best way to meet Montreal's emerging transit problems, and a base from which to appraise the relative merits of the Métro extensions.

On April 1, I received a nice note from Mr. Lessard, thanking me for my services, and saying they were in favour of many of my proposals, including the global approach to Montreal regional transit. André Gravelle was appointed to succeed me, which pleased me very much. Mr. Lessard wished me "good luck" in my writing career (he couldn't have seen some of my columns critical of the péquistes), and that – again – was that.

Although I was involved in some other activities during and since my work with BAREM, from November 15, 1976, the focus of my interests and writings became increasingly the new péquiste government, the statements and the actions of its members, and the threat that the Lévesque government poses to the Canadian Confederation, and to the future of Quebec itself.

Notes

1 For the full story, see Gertrude Himmelfarb, *Lord Acton: A Study in Conscience and Politics* (Chicago: University of Chicago Press, 1952).

2 Douglas Fullerton, *The Capital of Canada: How Should it be Governed?* (Ottawa: Government of Canada, 1974).

PART IV
November 15, 1976
– and after

XV

The péquistes come to power

Whatever one's view of the triumph of René Lévesque on November 15, 1976, there was no gainsaying the atmosphere of celebration in Montreal the day after. People had wanted a new deal, and they got one. Friends stopped each other in the streets, and chatted excitedly about the scale of the victory; the péquistes, with 41 per cent of the popular vote, had won 69 of the 110 seats, compared to the Liberal's 28 and Union Nationale's 11.

In a little Stanley Street restaurant the BAREM people frequent, La Rapière, (Louis Naud, its short, bouncy and cheerful French owner, sets a good table), we noted one threesome lunching on champagne. They were still there at the same table at 7.00 that night, not drunk, but just happily revelling in the heady aftermath of the victory at last of "their own government"; there was in fact an extraordinary sense of pride in almost every French Canadian I talked to that day. For the péquistes, of course, it was like the second coming of Christ. Reservations were expressed by skeptics about how far and how fast the new team would move towards independence, but that was more than offset by the belief that René and his scholarly crew would deliver infinitely better government than had Bob Bourassa. Even some anglophone friends I spoke to were caught up in the euphoria of the moment.

We at BAREM had our own particular moment of reflected glory ten days later when de Belleval was appointed to the Lévesque cabinet. Some of us had thought that with his experience in the Ministry of Transport he might have had a chance at that portfolio even if, like Paul Berthiaume in the previous government, it was in a secondary role; it would certainly simplify BAREM problems to have a minister who knew our background and objectives. René had also taken into his cabinet, in a senior role, two other of my old colleagues from the 'sixties, Jacques Parizeau, as Minister of Finance and Revenue, and Claude Morin, as Minister of Intergovernmental Affairs. I had met several of the other new ministers in the course of my BAREM work – Jacques-Yvan Morin (Education), and Marcel Léger (Environment).

Election post-mortem

There was little doubt that the vote had been much more against the performance of the Bourassa government than in support of Quebec independence. In my one conversation with de Belleval during the course of the campaign, he had told me that he found it best to stay away from the independence issue in his house calls and speeches, and instead to play the "new broom" angle, the need to sweep the old corrupt gang out of office. Bourassa himself with his weak image was certainly a liability to his party, and the péquistes took full advantage of it. Even many of the non-French voters were inclined to give Lévesque a chance, risking the separation possibility; most had found the Liberals' language policies, in Bill 22, repugnant. Indeed it was only the prospects of a péquiste sweep, revealed by polls shortly before the election which swung some of them back into the Liberal camp.

Lévesque kept Bourassa on the defensive during the campaign, with his charges about waste and corruption, and particularly with allegations about the secret corporate sources of the Liberal campaign funds. Four days before the election, the Parti Québécois published a full statement of the funds it had received between October 18 and November 11, $640,000 – reflecting an average donation of $21.22 – and reiterating its $250 limit on political donations from "companies, associations or unions."

Bourassa was thus left with only one real argument, invoking the spectre of the costs and risks of separation. Yet this had been largely defused by the "referendum" policy adopted at the 1974 péquiste convention. Claude Morin, its author, had argued "Let's do one thing at a time: first elect a government, then put the independence question to the people in the form of a referendum." The formula worked, and even one of the Liberal leaders had called it "the lucky windfall of the century."

But if one gives full credit to Mr. Lévesque and his party for running an intelligent campaign, part of their success was unquestionably due to the powerful emotion appeal of the péquiste message, essentially the logical extension of the *"maîtres chez nous"* pitch which had been so effective for the Liberals in 1962. English Canada had made its own contributions to the emotional appeal of the péquistes: the strike of the air traffic controllers and pilots over the use of French in ground-to-air communications at Quebec airports; and the booing of French announcements at Toronto's Maple Leaf Gardens during the Canada Cup Series. The "French in the Air" question particularly aroused nationalistic feelings in Quebec, and contributed to Lévesque's victory.

We anglophone Canadians have some difficulty in fully understanding the French-Canadians' passionate attachment to Quebec as "homeland" – to quote Lévesque again– "this Quebec, the only place where we have the unmistakeable feeling that 'here we can be really at home'." Most Canadians have their own particular territorial attachments, be it a house, a neighbourhood, a cottage, a city, a province, or a region like the Prairies or the Maritimes, but except perhaps for Newfoundlanders and Cape Bretoners, our loyalties tend to be more diffuse and subject to change. We can move almost anywhere in the country and as Canadians eventually feel reasonably at home. Not so with most Quebecers, for whom the péquiste territorial message has a gut appeal.

Pierre Dupont reflected these feelings in "15 November 76 . . ."

> The evening of November 15, when René Lévesque, new Prime Minister of Quebec, said 'I never thought that I could be so proud of being a Québécois,' an enormous thrill of excitement (frisson) ran through the crowd assembled in the Paul Sauvé arena, and probably through the majority of television spectators of the event. It was a moment doubly historic, because not only had the people of Quebec just defeated an age-old fear, but above all, had just affirmed themselves as a nation.[1]

Pierre Trudeau and Quebec nationalism

Unquestionably, in the months that lie ahead, this emotional homeland issue will provide good fighting ground for the péquistes; their claim to it is well staked out. One problem facing Prime Minister Trudeau, in attempting to combat it, lies in the very strength of his own profoundly held anti-nationalist convictions. For a long time he has seen Quebec nationalism as an evil, a cancer, something to be attacked and rooted out. In *Cité Libre,* in April 1962, his views on this question appeared in his article *"La Nouvelle Trahison des Clercs"* (The new treason of the intellectuals) – "this self-deluding passion of a large segment of our thinking population for throwing themselves headlong – intellectually and spiritually – into purely escapest pursuits."

In this article Trudeau described his discussions with a number of separatists, and was struck by the amount of totalitarianism and anti-Semitism he found, and particularly by the general lack of understanding of basic economics.

> The nationalists – even those of the left – are politically reactionary because in attaching such a high importance to the idea of a nation in

> their scale of political values, they are infallibly led to define the common good as a function more of the ethnic group than of all citizens . . . It is for this reason that a nationalist government is in its essence intolerant, discriminatory, and, when all is said and done, totalitarian. [2]

He quotes his hero, Lord Acton, on this point:

> The nation is here an ideal unit founded on the race . . . It overrules the rights and wishes of the inhabitants, absorbing their divergent interests in a fictitious unity; sacrifices their several inclinations and duties to the higher claim of nationality, and crushes all natural rights and all established liberties for the purpose of vindicating itself. Whenever a single definite object is made the supreme end of the State . . . the State becomes for the time being inevitably absolute.[3]

Finally, Trudeau argued that the interaction of our two strongly-entrenched cultures is healthy for the Canadian society, not damaging. If the two will collaborate within a truly pluralistic state, Canada can become a privileged land, where the federalist form of government, the choice of the world of tomorrow, will be perfected. Better than the American melting pot, the Canadian federal example could show the way to the countries newly created in the post-war world. Again he quotes Acton:

> A great democracy must either sacrifice self-government to unity or preserve it by federalism . . . The co-existence of several nations under the same State is a test, as well as the best security of its freedom. It is also one of the chief instruments of civilisation . . . The combination of different nations in one State is as necessary a condition of civilised life as the combination of men in society . . . Where political and national boundaries coincide, society ceases to advance, and nations relapse into a condition corresponding to that of men who renounce intercourse with their fellow-men . . . A State which is incompetent to satisfy different races condemns itself; a State which labours to neutralize, to absorb, or to expel them, destroys its own vitality; a State which does not include them is destitute of the chief basis of self-government. The theory of nationality, therefore, is a retrograde step in history.[4]

If Trudeau can be faulted for his stance it can only be that he assumed too readily that logic and reason would automatically triumph over the more visceral appeal of Quebec nationalism. And by nailing his flag so firmly to the mast, he made it more difficult for himself and his government to undertake the compromises that may be necessary to hold the country together. Certainly the current wave of nationalism in Quebec has many unpleasant aspects: strong elements of ethnocentricity and racism, excessive fears about "threatened" language and culture, envy and resentment of the Anglo Saxon presence, the desire for revenge for the "Conquest," and the perennial hunt for scapegoats; but underlying it all is the essential, historic and deeply felt love of French Canadians for Quebec. Differentiating between these basic emotions, and the excesses of the nationalist zealots, will not be the easiest of tasks for Trudeau or anyone else.

The difficulty is compounded by the special appeal of the independence movement for the young. It provides an exciting cause around which they can, and do, rally. With most teachers in the péquiste camp, one can begin to understand why so many young people in Quebec are solidly behind Lévesque.

Another dimension of the emotional appeal is the revision of opinion in Quebec about the FLQ terrorist activity in the autumn of 1970. There is a fairly broad consensus now that the calling out of the army under the War Measures Act had been "overkill," although at the time it had certainly the wide support of the public in Quebec and across Canada. In Parliament only the NDP opposed the action; René Lévesque had been very critical, calling it "fascist manipulation" by Trudeau, to "take over" the Bourassa government.

The péquistes had been unfairly associated in the public mind with the FLQ; many Quebecers found it difficult to distinguish between change by persuasion and by revolutionary activity. This may have hurt the péquistes in the 1973 election. But by 1975 and 1976, the critics of the government's 1970 action were well in the ascendant, and they were helped by a film of Michel Brault, *"Les ordres,"* which was a realistic if fictionalized version of the police arrest of over 400 presumed revolutionary sympathizers. Most of course were not, but rather a mixed bag of left wing unionists, péquistes, hippies and activists. In reviving the injustices of the arrests, the film made a great impression on Quebec society and particularly the young. It had its own special impact on the 1976 election.

First moves toward independence

The first few months after the election were regarded by everyone as a kind of honeymoon period, with the new ministers and government settling in and finding out some of the hazards as well as the joys of office. However, it was not very long before the péquistes, elected to office mainly on a "good government" platform, gradually began to talk and act as if independence had already been achieved. They withdrew without notice from the federal prices and incomes control program, freeing nearly 500,000 public servants and construction workers from the expected Anti-Inflation Board rollback of the settlement that had been made by the Bourassa government in its dying days in office. Communications Minister Louis O'Neill called the federal government a "foreign power." There was controversy about a sewer contract in Hull, where the winning bid by an Ottawa firm was rejected, although the federal government was putting up most of the money; and increased inspection activity on trucks entering Quebec to ensure that gasoline taxes were paid on mileage within Quebec. These moves appeared part of a systematic "muscle-flexing" campaign, rather than isolated incidents.

The direction of my own thinking during this period was reflected in my weekly columns. In my first comment on the election, I spoke of the sick economy that the péquistes had inherited, and suggested that the prospects of separation would worsen the economic situation. I qualified this by acknowledging that the PQ government is a substantial cut above the former government in the intellectual quality of its membership, and said of Lévesque "of the honesty and integrity of its leader there can be no doubt." However I argued that even a magician would have problems in steering a safe course through the rapids ahead, but "if Lévesque and his colleagues fail to solve the most pressing economic problems . . . the province will then be in danger of slipping into chaos." I went on

> It is at that time that the separatist risk becomes the strongest alternative. A disillusioned people searching for scapegoats will be susceptible to the argument that 'they' did it to 'us,' and more ready to accept radical and perhaps authoritarian solutions that cut Quebec off politically from the rest of the country.
>
> This is not pleasant to contemplate. Still there is some cause for optimism about Quebec's future role within Canada and those with the power to bring about the second scenario above – whether they be in private business or in government, in Canada or outside it – should pause, stay calm and give the new Quebec government a fighting chance, along with the help it needs to cope with the real and intractable economic problems that lie ahead of it. That is the best way to fight separatism.

In the next few weeks I discussed a possible compromise approach to the separatist option, arguing that events are pushing us towards a looser Confederation, one with a greater provincial say and special status for Quebec. I went on in my December 27 column

> But would the PQ government accept anything short of full independence? Party dogma suggests not, but it will have a tough enough time as it is selling its case to Quebecers. How much more difficult it would be if a substantial part of its program were already available within a looser Confederation.
>
> It may be that the emotional tide now running in Quebec is too strong for any compromise. Maybe we are again faced with 'too little and too late.' After all, we English Canadians were arguing about bilingual stamps when we should have been giving serious thought to

Quebec's demands for special status. And maybe all the problems that even a modest compromise would generate – including the role of Quebec members in the federal Parliament – would be too wrenching for us to contemplate.

Early in January, however, I raised some questions about the cavalier way in which the péquistes were brushing aside their economic problems, as if they could all be resolved by independence. I suggested that

> It is surprising that a movement so philosophically and emotionally tuned to the attachment of Quebecers for their province should deny that feeling to other Canadians. The stereotyped Quebec image of the anglophone as a businessman, with no other interest than making money, apparently dies hard. This misjudgment of the attitudes of English Canada was further evidenced recently when Premier Lévesque banned the phrase 'separatism' from his government's vocabulary.
>
> Well, 'one man's meat is another man's poison,' and to English Canadians the *independence* of Quebec would *separate* Canada into two parts. No semantic fiddling will change that fact, and the emotional impact is potentially enormous.
>
> Lévesque and his colleagues are being very naive if they assume that Quebec independence could be followed by a relatively harmonious renegotiation with a truncated but co-operative Canada. As Pierre Trudeau suggested in his year-end interview, it might indeed be difficult to prevent the aftermath from turning into a shooting war . . .

However, I concluded, hopefully perhaps,

> My own guess is that a Quebec within the present Confederation, but with enough special status to protect its culture and language, will prove far more attractive to Quebecers than the emotional allure of a leaky independence barque, sailing forth on an uncertain course over uncharted seas.

Lévesque's New York speech

On January 25, 1977, René Lévesque was scheduled to speak to a very prestigious audience, the Economic Club of New York. I was invited by an old acquaintance from bond market days, and finally persuaded myself to go, thinking it would make an interesting story for this book. Although I did not realize it at the time, it was to be a turning point in my attitude towards the péquiste government.

There were some 1,500 men and women in the grand ballroom of the New York Hilton, most of the men dressed, like the guests on the dais, in dinner jackets. At my table were some eight or so American investment men, and a couple of Canadians from the same business. We Canadians were a bit startled to see only three flags hung behind the podium – the Stars and Stripes, and the flags of Quebec and New York State (Governor Carey was also speaking); the Canadian flag was conspiciously missing, at the insistence of the Lévesque party, we heard later.

The content of the lengthy Lévesque speech was well covered in the Canadian press and was broadcast in Canada (in English), and I won't attempt to summarize it here. The main thing about it was its extraordinary misjudgment of both the audience and American opinion at large. Apparently assuming that his U.S. listeners would be sympathetic to the concept of an independent Quebec – and the implicit division of Canada – he drew an analogy between the Quebec of today and the Thirteen Colonies in 1776. He followed it up with a ringing affirmation of the "inevitability" of Quebec's independence from Canada.

His audience sat on its hands. Expecting to be reassured about the Quebec economy by its new leader, they heard instead an emotional appeal from the leader of a movement dedicated to causing more uncertainty. They didn't like the message they heard and, for many, René himself – as charming and persuasive as only he can be – sounded like a dangerous man. I canvassed American opinion all that evening, and the next day on Wall Street, and a phrase that came up often, in the discussion of Lévesque's speech and personality, was "a potential Hitler."

I wrote an article on what I had heard – a straight job of reportage. It appeared in *Le Devoir* as well as the usual English papers; Ryan, who did the translation, had been at the dinner, and agreed with the main thrust of my remarks. Unfortunately, my comment that the speech was a "disaster" clashed with the péquiste conviction that it had been a "great triumph." I found this out first in discussing the speech with some péquiste friends in Montreal. Sorrowfully, they asked me, "why I had turned against them," and accused me of "overreacting emotionally." Several letters to *Le Devoir* about my column were more virulent; one, from a novelist and critic, Claude Jasmin, said "The genius of the speech was that . . . Lévesque, with an intelligence or sure instinct, defused the fear of the Americans." Jasmin spoke of my references to the American view of Lévesque as a potential dictator. "Now you are removing your mask! You are projecting your own Anglo wish to see a Canadian dictator put the French Canadians again in their subservient place!"

I found a bit curious this use of a psychological term, (Projection: "A defense mechanism involving the attribution to other people of impulses and traits that the person has but cannot accept"[5]), until the language white paper came along in April. In defending the paper, psychiatrist Camille Laurin, Minister of Cultural Development and sponsor of the paper frequently employed the word "projecting" to attack critics. He appears to have impregnated his thinking solidly into the collective péquiste consciousness.

The Lévesque New York speech certainly changed the climate in English Canada towards him and his party, much as it affected my own. By his emphasis on independence he was in effect telling us all that no compromise short of political sovereignty was possible. No longer should we consider seriously a form of "special status" that the péquistes might accept. The approach from now on had to be aimed directly at the people of Quebec; the battle for the hearts and minds (and votes) of Quebecers was joined. The péquistes were henceforth to be considered as diehard antagonists with whom one could not expect to negotiate.

The battle of the statistics

In this developing struggle it was clear to the péquistes that the weakest link in their armour was the economic issue, the cost of separation. They set out to try to defuse or confuse this issue in several ways. One was the courting of Ontario; Jacques Parizeau and Claude Morin had long-established friendships with the senior Ontario bureaucracy, and the flow of people between Queen's Park in Toronto and the Legislative Assembly in Quebec City was greatly intensified after November 15. Premier Davis of Ontario took a cautious public line urging his people to give the new Quebec government a chance. In New York, Jacques Parizeau, in reply to a banker's question about the possibility of Quebec forming an economic association with the new Canada, after separation, is reported to have said "We have discussed it at great length with Ontario; there are no obstacles." Premier Davis's visit to the Quebec winter carnival in early February appeared to give a further blessing to the idea. The péquiste pitch, to anyone who would listen, was "Quebec and Ontario are so interdependent in trade, that it would be unthinkable for them not to do a deal after Quebec leaves Confederation."

The second attack by the péquistes was on the federal thesis that Quebec is a net gainer from Confederation through equalization grants, transfer payments (unemployment benefits, for example), federal spending and tariff protection for Quebec industries. Late in March, Minister of Industry and Commerce, Rodrigue Tremblay, scored a propaganda coup. Mr. Tremblay, an economics professor, triumphantly produced statistics, originating with Statistics Canada, which showed that between 1961 and 1975 Quebec paid $4.3 billion more into the federal treasury than it received. René Lévesque himself endorsed the figures, saying "this is one of the most . . . significant documents . . . ever issued, in the area of economics, to the population of Quebec."

Most of the Quebec press were completely taken in by the figures, and gave the story a big play. In succeeding days, however, it became clear that the published figures revealed only a part of the story. The federal government brought out a modest little white paper of its own on April 6, "Preliminary observations on the economic accounts of Quebec." Among other things the federal statements showed that, in the fifteen years in question, the $4.2 billion allegedly paid by Quebec to Ottawa was almost exactly equal to the customs and excise taxes collected at Quebec ports of entry, but paid for by the ultimate consumers of the goods in other provinces. Mr. Tremblay had no effective answer. Moreover, the paper pointed out that no allowance had been made for Quebec's benefit from federal expenditures common to all Canadians, such as defence, foreign aid, the Finance Department and the Bank of Canada. No allowance had been made for federal payments in Ottawa to employees resident in the Outaouais region, estimated at "over $100 million." My own calculations of the benefit from Quebec's proximity to the capital, taking into account direct federal salaries and wages paid to Quebec residents, employment of Quebec workers in federal construction projects on both sides of the river, and indirect earnings from sales to or work done for federal civil servants (housing, for example), suggest that in aggregate they amount currently to over $500 million a year.

The Treasurer of Ontario, Darcy McKeough, and his officials, were outraged by the Tremblay figures, which suggested that Ontario particularly had benefited at Quebec's expense. In his budget brought down on April 19, 1977, an appendix (Budget Paper E) was inserted which dealt with "Federal Fiscal Redistribution Within Canada," and which used three different methods of calculation to show how much Quebec had benefited: "The $6 billion in equalization payments that have flowed into Quebec over the past decade alone represents a rock-bottom and incontrovertible measure of that province's financial gain from Confederation."

In another supplement to the Budget, "Interprovincial Trade Flows, Employment, and the Tariff in Canada" it was shown conclusively that in manufactured goods in 1974 Quebec's dependence on the Ontario market (20 per cent of its manufactures), was much greater than Ontario's dependence on the Quebec market (11 per cent of such output) although the trade between the two provinces was in rough balance.

Clearly the honeymoon between the Quebec and Ontario provincial governments was over. Premier Davis had become increasingly resentful of being used by Lévesque for internal propaganda purposes, and said on April 21 that "it would be absolutely foolhardy for Quebec to believe it can be independent and still have an economic association with the rest of Canada," and, referring to a Parizeau speech in Toronto, "Who is he to say . . . to any Canadian that the debate (on Quebec separation) is over, the discussions have ended, the time for negotiations have passed?"

Premier Lévesque replied to Davis and McKeough, calling the statements and figures "pure propaganda," citing recent polls which suggested that Canadians across the country were in favour of negotiation for an economic union if Quebec becomes independent. But on May 5, the four western premiers met, and issued a statement that they were totally opposed to any economic association with an independent Quebec.

There the matter rests, at least at time of writing. The Quebec government undoubtedly got some publicity by being first out with figures; separatist supporters still refer to the Tremblay statement as having "destroyed the myth that . . . it would be suicidal for Quebec to renounce the benefits of being a Canadian province." No doubt the confusion created about the figures will also benefit the péquistes, even if simply to muddy the waters. Against this must be set Quebec's loss of credibility with the other provinces, and with the English press, and the collapse of its fragile entente with Ontario.

Notes

1 Pierre Dupont, *15 Novembre '76 . . .* (Montréal: Edition Quinze, 1976), p. 35 (French version).

2 As reprinted in P. E. Trudeau, *Le Féderalisme et la Société Canadienne Française* (Montréal: 1967). An English version appeared in 1968, *Federalism and the French Canadians.* (Toronto: Macmillan Company of Canada). Most of the quotations are from the English version, except where I disagree with the translation.

3 Lord Acton, *Essays on Freedom and Power* (Glencoe: 1948), p. 184.

4 *Ibid., passim.*

5 Krech, Crutchfield and Levson, *Elements of Psychology* (New York: Knopf, 1969).

XVI

The language legislation – launching pad for a holy war?

On April 1, Minister of Cultural Development Dr. Camille Laurin brought out the long awaited, and much internally debated, péquiste white paper on language policy. I had been put off by Lévesque's New York speech, and shocked at the abuse of statistics by Mr. Tremblay and Premier Lévesque, but the long white paper horrified me. It seemed to me to be a regressive document, more concerned with righting past wrongs to French Canadians and with curtailing the use of English than with pursuing the entirely proper goal of encouraging a greater use of the French language in Quebec. I reacted immediately with a special article which appeared in the *Toronto Star* on April 5, and in the *Montreal Gazette* a few days later:

> There is a whiff of the Prussian jackboot about it, an aura of coercion, racism, revenge. There is no explicit statement, 'English get out,' but it is writ large between the lines. Quebec is to become a unilingual province, if the péquiste zealots have their way; the French fact will be made clearly visible – at work, in communications, and in the countryside . . . 'The use of French will not merely be universalized to hide the predominance of foreign powers from the French-speaking population; this use will accompany, symbolize and support a reconquest by the French-speaking majority in Quebec of that control over the economy which it ought to have . . . There will be no longer any question of a bilingual Quebec.'
>
> How sad it all is, how reminiscent of the chauvinistic European nationalism of the Victorian era. How against the trend of the times in

a Canada, which, slowly and belatedly it is true, has begun to learn to accommodate to the French fact.

Is it all really necessary? The white paper thinks so: 'Is the situation serious enough to warrant vigorous intervention? In North America, French has been increasingly threatened since the Conquest. It must be defended at all costs . . .'

I have always been sympathetic to the survival argument – the emotional and cultural imperatives of *'la survivance.'* An old friend of mine from Quebec, however, recently gave me pause. He is a French-Canadian politician, with nationalist leanings, but he said: 'You English have been conned by this 'threatened culture' argument. All through Quebec history it has been used by the élite of the time – the clergy, those in the professions, the politicians – to strengthen their grip on the province, to improve their own economic position.'

There is a new élite in power in Quebec, heavily weighted towards academe, the bureaucracy and the professions. As a group they are the least likely people in the province to be affected by any adverse economic fall-out from these language proposals; few people in Quebec society have been more protected from competition, from the vicissitudes of the real work-a-day world. Many members of this péquiste government have in fact had surprisingly little contact with the English whom they say so dominate Quebec society.

All this shows in the manifesto, a strange blend of idealism, naiveté, cleverness, and a ruthless twisting of facts and history to support their case. Consider the evidence adduced in the paper that French Canadians are excluded from the higher echelons of business in Quebec, unless they learn to function in English. It is no accident that the bulk of their quotations come from the Laurendeau-Dunton Commission on Bilingualism – the material is fifteen years old.

I have worked a large part of those fifteen years in Quebec, and I have seen enormous changes taking place in business and in federal government offices and Crown corporations. In head offices or principal branches of companies national or international in scope, English has to remain a kind of lingua franca, but any French-Canadian businessman will tell you that very substantial progress has been made. The use of fifteen-year-old data, and fifteen-year-old opinions, to buttress the argument that the position of French is 'slowly deteriorating,' is an unconscionable abuse of truth. . . .

The Montreal Board of Trade, in its brief on Bill One several months later, gave the results of a survey which supported my opinion.[1] It showed that 59 per cent of management positions in Montreal-area firms were held by francophones, compared with 37 per cent ten years ago; during the period the number of non-francophones declined. The figures were not so favourable for head offices, with francophones currently holding 32 per cent of top management jobs, 41 per cent of middle management, and 54 per cent of first line supervisory jobs. However, at almost every level of comparison – officer, middle management, first line supervision – and type of business – head office, regional office, and plant – there was a rise in the number of francophones greater than the increase in the number of jobs. The decline in the number of non-francophones was particularly pronounced in the regional offices and plants.

Further support for my conclusions was given in the Bill One brief of the Quebec Chamber of Commerce, prepared by the SECOR firm of French-Canadian economic, social and political consultants.[2] Among the assumptions in the language charter, attacked by this study, was the statement, widely accepted in Quebec, that most French Canadians have to work in English; even in the upper levels of business in Montreal 68 per cent of the francophones work in their own language, and about 50 per cent of the top management jobs are held by French Canadians, according to SECOR's analysis. Their study, acknowledging that there was still some French-Canadian under-representation in business, suggested two causal factors in particular: the gravitation of francophone university graduates to the Quebec government or to its agencies (over 95 per cent francophone); and the lag in the production of commerce or business school graduates by francophone universities.

A second assumption in the white paper, that French Canadians are forever condemned to an economically inferior condition in the face of anglophone domination, has been challenged in a number of recent studies. The historic income gap between Quebecers of French and British origin was shown by François Vaillancourt to have narrowed from a British excess of 55 per cent in 1960 to 32 per cent in 1970.[3] All recent evidence suggests a continuation of this gap-closing trend. Mr. Laurin also said in the National Assembly in June, that francophones alone have had to carry the burden "of learning a second language," and that 60 per cent of them were already bilingual. A research paper by one of his own employees showed that francophone bilingualism has been declining steadily for twenty years, while that of anglophones was rising. Of men of working age, francophone bilinguals dropped from 45 per cent to 40 per cent between 1951 and 1971; the anglophone percentages over the same period rose from 43 per cent to 53 per cent.

Dr. Laurin's capacity for misreading statistical evidence was becoming widely known as the months went by. Even late in June Laurin was saying in a speech that it is only by Quebec government intervention that the "anglophone exclusion of French Canadians from the upper ranks of business" can be stopped!

In any event, figures put forward to show discrimination against French Canadians in the upper ranks of Quebec business must be subject to substantial qualification because of the presence of head offices of Canadian or multi-national companies. For example, chairman Earle McLaughlin of the Royal Bank noted on April 18, 1977, in his speech, "Why Am I Here?" to La Chambre de Commerce of Montreal, that 90 per cent of the bank's business was done outside Quebec (only half of Quebec's 10 per cent is with francophone firms or individuals). But the fact that only about 10 per cent of the bank's board of directors are French Canadians is frequently brandished as an example of anglophone prejudice! If there is still under-representation in some companies, the trend towards appointment of more francophone directors has been pronounced the past few years.

The white paper also proposed allowing children access to English schools only if one parent (or a sibling) had attended an English school in Quebec; an intensive "francization" program was outlined for businesses of fifty employees or more, to be policed by internal committees (one-third of committee members to be appointed by unions or employer associations); quotas of francophones were to be established at every level up to and including the boardroom. All of this activity would be under the surveillance of a new and powerful bureaucratic organization "Office of the French Language." Failure to meet the established norms would expose the company to loss of government business, fines, and public excoriation. All English signs in the province were to be removed, except in a few special cases. All businesses had to acquire a French name, and inside Quebec use it *only*. English municipalities had to keep minutes in French, and use only French in correspondence.*

Dr. Laurin invited comments from Quebecers – including the English minority – on his *chef-d'oeuvre.* The reactions were not slow in coming. The péquiste followers were ecstatic. Jean-Marc Léger, removed from the *Le Devoir* editorial board in 1967 for his separatist sympathies, had a long, worshipful piece in *Le Devoir* (See also pp. 199):

> The document . . . which marks a capital moment in our history, is characterized essentially by its lucidity, cohesiveness, its generosity, shown by the many exceptions, which lead to a singular, almost excessive, tolerance . . . One searches vainly elsewhere in the world for a formula more equitable, more tolerant . . . That a law so healthy and essential in principle, so liberal in expression, provokes from so many 'others' and – hélas – from certain of our own, virulent reactions, and

*The white paper was followed in a few weeks by Bill One, and that in turn replaced in July by Bill 101: this latter Bill became law on August 26, 1977. A summary of the main provisions in the final legislation is given in Appendix Four.

> even (it's too much) accusations of intolerance, just confirm the mentality of the first, the colonizers, and of the second group, the colonized.[4]

Except for some French-Canadian businessmen, and spokesmen for some of the professions, there appeared to be a considerable measure of support for the white paper across francophone Quebec. The fact that it seemed likely to produce more jobs for francophones unquestionably strengthened its appeal for them, quite apart from emotional considerations. Municipal and educational leaders, unions and other organized groups welcomed the bill as finally giving the French language its proper place in Quebec society. Laurin himself became a travelling salesman for the new language policy, and was generally listened to by rapt francophone audiences, individual members of which often thanked him personally for affirming "the pride of French Canadians in their language and culture," to quote a Mme Taillefer. One wonders how many of them had read the lengthy bill, or understood its full implications.

The French-Canadian press was very supportive, with only Claude Ryan coming out solidly against the policy, and with the *La Presse* editorialists apparently split. Most French papers reprinted the white paper in its entirety. In reporting favourably on it, francophone reporters kept referring, to its "tolerance and respect" for minorities; many pointed out that the anglophone minority in Quebec will have more rights than other minorities "in any country in the world." Apart from the implication that Quebec is already an independent country, and disregarding the fact that the English are the majority in Canada, the statement is patently untrue. Consider for example, the rights of Swedes in Finland. And what country in the world bans English signs, as the paper proposed to do?

Ryan's attack on the white paper was trenchant. He called it "exaggeratingly pessimistic" about the state of the French language in Quebec, likely to be very divisive, and naive about the role the state can play in language use. He accused the authors of the paper of using selective or misleading statistics, and provocative and inflammatory language, and said that the paper reflected a rigidity and inwardness of thought.

Dr. Laurin counter-attacked bitterly in a long letter which *Le Devoir* printed in full. His attack on Ryan was in part personal; he implied that Ryan has lost his objectivity, and he has returned to this theme frequently since. Laurin clearly views the state as the only instrument for achieving its linguistic goals; the skepticism displayed by Ryan towards the role of the state, was viewed by Laurin as a symptom of weakness; "I think it frightens him to see that the role of the state is much more marked than was the case with any political movement before us."[5] On another occasion Laurin suggested that Ryan was afraid of losing his role of "interlocutor" between English and French Canada. Laurin's attacks on Ryan were picked up and echoed in even more virulent letters to the paper, some of which were printed on *Le Devoir's* editorial page.

The two main English papers in Quebec, Montreal's *Star* and *Gazette*, both reprinted the 20,000 word white paper in full. Their criticism grew stronger as the weeks progressed, and as the reluctance of the péquistes to consider even reasonable changes became clearer. Of the businessmen, the most outspoken comments were those of W. Earle McLaughlin, in the April 18 speech referred to earlier. He put the case that head offices around the world function largely in English and that if the new legislation made this very difficult head offices would not be encouraged to establish "or even to remain" in Montreal. He observed how some of the white paper's proposals abridged freedoms – language of signs, forced use of French by English school boards – and said "If the government may forbid an English sign, is it so far a step to forbid an English book? And if an English book how about certain French books?"

Mr. Laurin called the speech "humiliating," and accused McLaughlin of "intimidation." He said that the banker's use of English before a francophone audience, after having lived most of his life in Montreal, was clear proof that tough new measures were needed. (In fact, McLaughlin had been invited the previous September to present the Chambre's one English speech of the year).

A statement sent to Premier Lévesque by 115 prominent English educators, businessmen and professionals, accepted most of the principles in the white paper, but challenged the analysis that French is threatened, and deplored the philosophy implicit in the paper, which "sees the survival of the majority culture as requiring the restriction and compression of the minority." The group urged the government to adopt the route of incentives and encouragement rather than restriction. Leading francophone businessmen and professionals put forward the same arguments against coercive measures; Dr. Laurin countered by calling some of them "*roi nègres*" (black kings), the traditional Quebec phrase for French Canadians who become, as some see it, the paid lackeys of the conquerors.

In the weeks which followed the issuing of the white paper Dr. Laurin was very much to the forefront in the news, appearing almost to take over the leadership of the government. In fact he seemed on the way to fulfilling his mother's earlier prophecy. When asked what her son Camille was doing in school, she replied proudly "He's studying to be a pope." Premier Lévesque seemed to fade into the shadows; his own doubts about the language legislation appeared profound. He said "I'm worried . . . I find it humiliating to have to legislate French-language rights."

One péquiste I know suggested that Lévesque was letting Laurin make the running on this particularly controversial issue, partly in order to avoid being tarred with it himself. He also suggested that if Laurin fell on his face René wouldn't be entirely unhappy; there is no doubt that he sees Laurin as very ambitious, a potential threat for the leadership of the party.

Bill One, "Charter of the French Language," was read for the first time in the Quebec Assembly on April 27, 1977; in statute form, its content was practically unchanged from the white paper. Laurin did not eliminate the possibility of changes following the proposed committee hearings in June, but said that they would have to be based on "hard facts, hard evidence," no doubt to distinguish them from the selective statistics and fuzzy evidence on which Bill One appears to have been based.

If Dr. Laurin bowed to no one in his capacity to abuse with personal attacks those he felt threatened his campaign, in general he sailed serenely on, seldom appearing angry or upset, treating objectors more as a psychiatrist deals with a confused patient who doesn't know what's going on around him. The accuracy or otherwise of his statements didn't seem to disturb him. He kept repeating that under Bill One, the anglophone minority would be better treated than the francophone minority in any other province. Other ministers made the same point; yet this is a patently false generalization in respect of access to French schools in Ontario and New Brunswick, the only provinces with substantial francophone minorities.

In speaking to audiences of believers, Laurin cloaked himself in the garb of the "collectivity" – the rights of the French majority to protect its language and culture by legislating a unilingual Quebec. He told such audiences that those who "accuse us of being racist, vengeful, coercive, totalitarian," were doing it to conceal their real motive, "the continuing anglophone economic domination of Quebec." Several times he referred to his deep hurt that "some people have even compared the bill to the final solution used by the Germans . . . I was profoundly offended inside – in my inner conscience as a civilized and humane person." Laurin reportedly was cheered when he promised that most English-language signs and company names would disappear within a year. If such signs offend, it is not a very long step to viewing displays of English books and newspapers as equally offensive. Earle McLaughlin may have touched a sore nerve with his comments about the implicit threat to books, of all languages.

I began a column on Bill One *(Toronto Star,* May 2) in this way:

> The opening words of the preamble to Quebec's new language bill is enough to tell you the kind of legislation it is: 'The National Assembly, being aware that French has always been the language of the Quebec

people, and that it is, *indeed, the very instrument by which they have articulated their identity . . .*'*

Yes, according to this bill, a Quebecker is not just a resident of Quebec, but a French-speaking person with deep roots in the French culture of the province. No other residents qualify, not even if their Quebec ancestry goes back five or six generations. English Quebeckers, under this bill, are to have few rights, only privileges; for most purposes of this bill they hardly exist.

Is it any wonder that the English-speaking population of Quebec, forming over 20 per cent of the province's population, and over a third of Montreal's, feel threatened under the péquiste government? . . .

A few days later Prime Minister Trudeau was reported as saying,

> The kind of nationalism to which I am opposed is that which defines a nation as an ethnic group, as a linguistic or racial or religious group. Quebec is making this error now, even in its language legislation, when it speaks of 'Québécois' instead of saying Québécois who are French-speaking. This is why I define separatism as a countercurrent to the history of mankind, which would move – and has moved – toward the greater liberation of the individual . . . I dread a policy which is based on the notion of ethnicity.

The *Montreal Star,* in an April 30 editorial, called Bill One a "Journey into the quagmire": "It is individuals who are the victims of Bill One, and the whole province which is humbled by a law of that nature. Tragically it can only harm what it seeks to protect, and strengthen what it is intended to oppose."

McGill University, the English community it serves, and Bill One

The arrival of the péquiste government on the scene with its independence goals and language legislation was viewed understandably by McGill as a threat to its survival in Quebec. For one thing, the university was heavily dependent on the province for money; three-quarters of its operating budget came from Quebec. But the language legislation posed an even broader and more fundamental threat, that to the whole anglophone community in Quebec, the community with which McGill had had such close ties over its century and a half of existence.

I think McGill's feeling of concern is more than justified. McGill has never been one of the most popular institutions in the province among many members of the francophone community. In my work with the

---

*Quotation revised slightly to use the exact words of the official translation; the words italicized are those changed.

Quebec government in the 'sixties, several Quebec officials, including Jacques Parizeau, had raised with me the question of the large proportion of McGill students who came from outside the province. The number of Americans in the medical school had been particularly remarked upon. What brought the question to a head then was the rapidly rising provincial share in the ballooning costs of all universities, McGill included. The Quebec government's attitude, not an unreasonable one, was that it subsidized universities because they turn out people whose later work in Quebec contributes to the province's economic well-being and growth. McGill could justifiably argue that its international recognition was in part the product of the wide dispersal of its graduates, but the province had a point.

I decided to pass the comment on to the McGill authorities. After all, if they wanted more provincial money they would be better armed if they understood the mainsprings of Quebec's reluctance to be as generous with McGill as with Laval and Université de Montréal. In a 1965 letter to McGill principal Rocke Robertson, I linked the problem to the composition of the board of governors, then almost totally WASP, long on businessmen and lawyers from downtown, and said "Are these the men to encourage the Quebec government to meet your needs for ever-increasing amounts of money? I have very great difficulty in understanding why McGill has failed to begin to make some gesture towards putting a few people on its board that might have some understanding of the new directions in Quebec, and might be more acceptable to the Quebec government." I also raised the issue at a meeting of the Ottawa Valley branch of the McGill Graduates Society, but no satisfactory response came out of the university.

Still, changes had begun to occur, and within a decade had been reflected in almost all facets of the university's activities. McGill's board of governors is of radically different composition today than when I wrote my 1965 letter. The board's role for one thing has changed; it is not only less powerful but has eleven of its members nominated by the academic senate, the students, and the non-academic staff. Of the thirty-two "traditional" members, the university says that twenty-two "are more or less WASP," five are Jewish and four are French Canadians. The student body has changed: anyone walking the campus today will hear French spoken as often as English – admittedly mainly because of the aroused anglophone interest in becoming bilingual. But 15 per cent of students now are of French mother tongue, and the percentage is rising annually; 75 per cent of McGill students are from Quebec.

McGill's involvement in the francophone community and with its universities has shown a similar transformation. In law and medicine there had been working arrangements at the staff level for many years. In law, one factor at work has been the very high regard which the francophone legal profession held for Frank Scott, former dean of the McGill law faculty. In medicine, there has been close co-operation between McGill and the francophone universities, dating at least from the war. They have worked together on research projects, and made many joint approaches to the Medical Research Council for funding. Many other examples of co-operation and interchanges were cited in an appendix to the brief on Bill One that McGill submitted on June 3, 1977 to the Quebec government.

Yes, the new McGill's right to exist in Quebec does not rest solely on its historic links with the Montreal anglophone community. But, as its brief points out, McGill University does feel threatened by many provisions of Bill One, and it believes that parts of the Bill are incompatible with its ideals: freedom of enquiry, of opinion, of speech, and of criticism, and "of maintaining the orderly continuity and advancement of learning and culture and of the institutions of its community dedicated thereto."

The Bill's restrictions on the right of new arrivals into Quebec to choose English schools will accentuate the falling enrolment in the English school system. McGill estimates that by 1986 this enrolment would be no more than 43 per cent of its present size; it is from these schools that McGill draws 60 per cent of its students. "A university such as McGill, with McGill's present commitment, could not operate successfully on a continually shrinking English-speaking population base, especially if the flow of students and faculty from outside Quebec also is restricted by consequences of this Bill, as it inevitably will be."

The validity of McGill's concerns about a shrinking anglophone population has been confirmed by a number of demographers, notably by Richard Joy, author of *Languages in Conflict.*[6] In a long article in *Le Devoir* Mr. Joy questioned the central assumption back of Bill One, that Draconian measures were necessary to assure the continuing existence of the French language; he wrote that all the evidence indicated rather "that it is the English language that is in danger of disappearing from Quebec while the use of French increases steadily." Among the reasons he put forward were these:

- Between 1971 and 1976, 160,000 people emigrated from Quebec; family allowance address changes in 1970 and 1971 showed that two-thirds of family heads moving were anglophone. Of the 130,000 immigrants in this period, about half were francophone or bilingual.
- There has been a steady rise in the proportion of unilingual French, and a corresponding fall in unilingual English, over four decades.

Joy cited a number of other Quebec demographers in support of his final conclusion:

> In my judgment, Quebec is getting closer and closer to a situation where it will be unilingual francophone, regardless of which party is in power. Measures like Bill One are worse than useless. They will have no other effect than to speed the departure of Quebec anglophones, which is not desirable from the point of view of the Quebec economy, and will damage relations between Quebec and the other provinces.[7]

Joy's analysis was reinforced by two prominent Quebec demographers, Jacques Henripin and Réjean Lachapelle in *Le Devoir* on July 16 and 21, 1977. Their figures suggested that the government analysts, on whose projections the language policy had been based, had biased their figures by the use of assumptions favourable to the growth of the anglophone community in Quebec. This overplayed the threat to the survival of the francophones. A few weeks later, Henripin and Lachapelle were in turn attacked by demographers associated with the government figures. One might have thought that the launching of a policy with such far-reaching consequences as that of the language legislation might have been preceded, rather than followed, by a debate about the validity of the demographic assumptions.

Debate on Bill One

The omens for a conciliatory government approach did not appear that good. Dr. Laurin reverted to his favourite *ad hominem* approach when 326 prominent French Canadians, mainly in business and the professions, sent in a letter critical of various aspects of Bill One. Laurin lashed out – not against the contents of the letter – but against the signatories as "loyal to the English establishment," and "identified with federalists and the Liberal party."

Another letter favouring the Bill was received the same day from a different group of 160 prominent French Canadians, mostly in academe, the arts, or heading up various nationalistic organizations. (Yes, it included some old favourites of mine, François Albert Angers, Richard Arès, and Jean-Marc Léger). Laurin fawned all over them, "rejoicing unconditionally" in their support. As Michel Roy noted drily in a June 6 editorial in *Le Devoir:* "On one side are the good Quebecers who share his (Laurin's) views; on the other are the bad Quebecers, who, in expressing reservations, are clearly in the pay of the enemies of the people. . . . It is not what they think and say that captures his attention, but rather who they are." Roy went on to describe Laurin's attack as "one of the aspects the most disagreeable, most disquieting, of the debate now under way; those who dare put forward reservations and criticism are perceived as servants or accomplices of the anglophones, which in the eyes of the accusers is synonymous with the rich, the dominant, the oppressors."

During the legislative committee hearings, which ended on July 7, 1977, a clear government strategy emerged: each day one or two briefs attacking the bill would be balanced off by several seeking to make the provisions of the bill even tougher. Interspersed would be a few "moderate" presentations, which would contain technical points of particular interest to Dr. Laurin. The effect of it all was designed to put the good doctor in the apparent role of mediator, and the bill itself as representing a balance between conflicting forces. Despite the strategy, however, Dr. Laurin's own biases showed through clearly, in the warmth of his reception of the hard liners, and his tough, at times unfair, questioning of the Bill's opponents.

On July 12, the government brought in a new "Bill 101," in a move to cut off further hearings, opposition debate and questions on Bill One. This new version of the language legislation contained several changes, including the elimination of the clause that gave language legislation precedence over human rights, the re-wording of the preamble to remove the impression that only francophones were Quebecers, the broadening of appeal procedures, and the dropping of economic sanctions against firms delinquent in francization. There were no changes in the right of access to English schools.

To the extent that these modifications removed a few of the grossest injustices and coercive methods, they were welcomed. But in some respects the new Bill was even tougher than the old; one example was that Bill One gave Quebecers the right to demand to be served or informed in French; Bill 101 created the obligation for firms, unions or other bodies to provide services or information generally in French. Further details of the final version of the Bill are given in Appendix Four.

In the discussion on Bill 101 in the Education Committee, the Liberals and Union Nationale opposition attacked on a clause-by-clause basis, and it soon appeared that the debate would continue for months. In mid-August, the government stepped in, suspending normal sitting hours to provide unlimited time for debate, and on August 23, 1977, finally announcing closure of the Assembly debate. Bill 101 was quickly passed and assented to on August 26, 1977.

The language legislation — summing up

Trying to appraise all the implications of the language legislation in the late summer of 1977 has been a bit like trying to gauge the scale of a hurricane from within its eye. One knows there will be damage, but how much? My own position was made clear in this chapter and can be summarized in the following four assertions:

(1) *It is unnecessary:* The evidence put forward by Dr. Laurin to justify the need for coercive legislation is largely out-of-date, selective, biased,

and challenged by recent data. There is a mass of current analytical material to show that the use of the French language, and the role of francophones in business, have been making astonishing gains in Quebec during the 'seventies.

(2) *It will not work.* The many problems faced by the federal government in trying to apply its bilingual program to its own public service would be multiplied a hundredfold. The issue of schools is bad enough, but when it comes to language of work, the matter is simply too sensitive, too personal, to permit coercive measures to succeed. The incentive approach, which had been working well, is the only possible route; this was noted by the special group of businessmen which the government had sent to Europe in June, 1977, to study the linguistic practices within European head offices.

(3) *It will do serious economic damage.* Quebec's economy was hurt by the impact of the language proposals, but if the Bill is enshrined in legislation, even the attempt to apply regulations and penalties along the lines set out in it would bring about an exodus of many head offices, businesses and jobs from Quebec, and restrict further private investment and job creation.

(4) *Its divisive consequences may be most serious of all.* One Laval University professor, Vincent Lemieux, suggested a motive that may be the real reason behind the provocative nature of the language proposals. "Whether the PQ leaders planned it or not, the Charter runs the risk of provoking a state of crisis which is absolutely indispensable to them to win the referendum." He believes that certain radical proposals were deliberately inserted to produce more tensions between Ottawa and Quebec; in any such federal-provincial conflict, Quebecers tend to support their provincial government.

Unquestionably the péquiste language policy is dividing the French and English in Quebec, and in this country, more deeply than ever before, more even than during the two conscription crises. The threat to the nation is much more than the economic damage that separation – real or apprehended – will do to Quebec and to Canada. It is that a large and well-organized Quebec movement, with political power, is deliberately setting out to revive ancient animosities and resentments, to exploit ethnic and language differences in order to drive a wedge between the two language groups, to pick at old scabs and revive old wrongs, to twist facts and history, all to help it achieve its independence goal. This is no political battle on which the péquistes are embarked, it is a holy war.

Notes

1 Brief presented to Committee of National Assembly studying Bill One, by Montreal Board of Trade.
2 Brief presented to Committee of the National Assembly studying Bill One by the *Chambre de Commerce de la province de Québec.* Brief prepared by SECOR (Société d'Etudes et de Changement Organisationnels).
3 *Globe and Mail,* June 27, 1977. It cited another study to the effect that income of unilingual anglophone males in Montreal rose by $1,100 between 1961 and 1971; income of unilingual francophones rose by $1,900 in the same period. See also *Globe and Mail* editorial, April 7, 1977.
4 *Le Devoir,* April 7, 1977.
5 *Montreal Star,* May 4, 1977.
6 Richard Joy, *Languages in Conflict* (Toronto: McClelland and Stewart, Limited, 1967).
7 *Le Devoir,* June 9, 1977

XVII

Separation – An emotional obsession collides with economic realities

Events in the first months of the Lévesque government did not give much aid and comfort to optimists about the future of Quebec and the present Confederation. The debate and committee hearings on Bill One, and its slightly amended successor, Bill 101, only appeared to further polarize opinion, already deeply divided on language policy. The péquistes, elected on a "good government" ticket, seem determined to use every divisive weapon available to build support for their independence referendum, even at the risks of aggravating the present weakness in the Quebec economy and of alienating investors whose capital they need. The Liberals in Quebec, leaderless and rudderless, appeared unable to provide an organized opposition to the péquiste juggernaut. Many members of the francophone information media, with some important exceptions like Claude Ryan, suspended their normal critical faculties in early judgment of the new government and its policies. By July however there were signs of a more critical media attitude developing, and even the battered Liberals were showing signs of revival, particularly after Bill 101 was tabled.

Is Quebec's independence as inevitable as the péquiste leaders tirelessly argue? Not at all; I think the basic Quebec economic situation has deteriorated so much in recent years, and its dependence on federal aid become so necessary to its survival, that the péquiste government could neither win its referendum nor, if it did, begin the separation process without creating economic chaos within Quebec. In fact, I suggest in this chapter that the real issue is not separation, but the emotional feelings and responses generated in Quebec and across Canada by the *attempt* of the separatists to achieve their goal, by the racially divisive policies they are attempting to implement, by the atmosphere of grievance, revenge and hate which seems to be built into many of their proposals, and by the inflammatory language of some of their spokesmen.

What we are seeing now in Quebec is a gigantic propaganda campaign, well directed and orchestrated, unscrupulous in its twisting and distorting of facts, a massive attempt to persuade French-speaking Quebecers that their language is threatened, and that all the problems facing them are due either to federal discrimination against Quebec or Anglo Saxon domination of the Quebec economy. It is in many respects, as I suggested earlier, a call to arms against the English-speaking oppressors. The search for a scapegoat is a distractive device that everyone uses at one time or another; elevated to the level of a government and involving the singling out of a particular language or ethnic group, it has much uglier connotations. When an unemployed English-speaking manual labourer, protesting the charge against him as an "exploiter" of the French, is told by Dr. Camille Laurin, that "it is not necessary that a large percentage of a group be exploiters" for the group to be so designated, and that "he must assume the burden of his collectivity," that's racism.

Who are these péquistes anyway?

A considerable amount about the péquistes has been revealed in recent chapters, in which their opinions and actions are discussed. For one thing they are a dedicated group, with a cause. Educated zealots, many of them, with all the virtues and faults of people seized with the certainty of their convictions; more a movement or religion than a party. In their thinking and method of operation, if not in their theories, very close to the Marxists or evangelical Christian sects. Truth is anything which coincides with or supports their doctrine.

I made fun of this aspect of the péquiste movement in a column in April, suggesting that their *prophet* Lévesque was a blend of "Messiah, Moses, Mohammed and Mao," that his *Option Quebec*, along with the party program, was the *scripture* of the new religion, that its English *devils* lived variously in Westmount, Ottawa and Toronto, and also served as *scapegoats. Paradise, the promised land,* is of course an independent Quebec. I think the religiosity of the péquiste movement has been underestimated by English Canadians; it serves to bind the movement together, it allows members to suspend disbelief in the interests of the cause, and the fervour it generates helps recruit new members, particularly among the young and impressionable.

In her book *Le Parti Québécois,* McGill professor Vera Murray, provides some interesting figures about the social and educational background of party members. Of PQ candidates in the 1970 and 1973 elections, roughly 39 per cent were from the traditional bourgeoisie – professionals and businessmen – and 53 per cent from the new middle class. The largest single group of members comprises teachers and students, who made up over one-third of delegates to the 1969 péquiste conference. Another large group – 27 per cent at the same conference – were white-collar employees in the public sector or service industries. Regionally, of the PQ members in 1971, 62 per cent came from Montreal; by age, 60 per cent were under thirty-five.[1] A membership not quite as Lévesque described them in his New York speech: "Our thousands of party members, who now represent, as no other party can, most of Quebec's regions and walks of life."

The Lévesque cabinet, average age forty-two, reflects the party's middle class origins. All but one member are university graduates; many have multiple degrees. Over half were full- or part-time professors or teachers; included in this group are two psychiatrists and several of the half dozen lawyers. Three public servants, the two media representatives, Lévesque and Lise Payette, plus one stockbroker, Guy Joron, round out a list of individuals with impressive intellectual credentials. But there is a lack of balance. The shortage of people with business experience, or who otherwise have been exposed to the day-to-day world outside academe, the government, or the professions, is beginning to show up as a major weakness in the péquiste government. It also helps explain the tremendous preoccupation of the cabinet with the intellectual, if navel-gazing, study of the language question, and the naiveté of some ministerial statements which reveal an astonishing lack of awareness of the world outside Quebec, or the anglophone world inside it. In some cases naiveté is not the appropriate word; "statements designed for purposes of péquiste strategy or tactics" might be better. I propose to examine now various elements of that strategy.

The strategy of the PQ government

The designer and co-ordinator of that strategy, in the view of most observers, is Minister of Intergovernmental Affairs Claude Morin. Long time senior official at the centre of Quebec's federal-provincial operations, Morin is credited (or blamed) by federal politicians and officials for most of their problems with the successive governments of Lesage, Johnson, Bertrand and Bourassa; he left Bourassa in 1971 to teach and to work for the péquistes. My own experiences with Morin during the 'sixties were uniformly pleasant, perhaps because we were on the same side, Quebec's. But there was no doubt of his intelligence or his conviction; a born intriguer, he plays a skilled, tough game, using a good deal of finesse to achieve his nationalistic goals. I have no difficulty at all in seeing him as the planner behind péquiste grand strategy. And, as I noted earlier, he is credited with the referendum proposal that took some of the curse off his party at the polls. A friend who knows Morin well suggested that his techniques are pure Marxist – one bite of the sausage at a time – all in a very disciplined and orderly way.

What has been the direction of péquiste policy since November 15, 1976? Several clear lines seem to be emerging. In discussing these I make little distinction between péquistes' beliefs, misconceptions or convictions, and their argumentation. There is nothing of which I am surer than that they have few scruples about using or abusing any statement, fact, or statistic which helps their independence case; propaganda or faith, it's all grist to their mill.

"Inevitability" of independence

This "bandwagon" concept was prominent in Lévesque's New York speech:

> So independence for Quebec now appears just as normal, to a very quickly growing number of us . . . almost as inevitable as it was for the American States of 200 years ago . . . To me it would be a bit like King Canute trying to stop the tide, to waste efforts in order to delay the final outcome of something which appears as natural and inevitable as growth itself. . . . the important question . . . is not whether Quebec will become independent, nor indeed when exactly it will happen, but rather how, in due time, Quebecers can be expected to take full charge of their own political affairs.

No doubt this speech was aimed more at the TV audience in Canada than at those present in New York, and the "inevitability" argument has been used frequently since by Lévesque and senior ministers in their efforts to win converts. As any politician knows, people often swing their votes to the party they think will win.

One of the basic assumptions behind Lévesque's assertion that independence is inevitable is the strength of péquiste support among the young. Older Quebecers tend to be more cautious, conservative, or, if you like, "sensible." As Lévesque put it, "The law of nature says that young people become adults and older people kick off." Professor Richard Hamilton of McGill challenges the logic of these conclusions, citing several parallels. In the United States, the older age groups have always been disproportionately Republican, yet this party continues to win its share of elections; since the war even in losing it has seldom been much short of half the votes. In Sweden, the Social Democrats (so much admired by the péquistes) in the 'fifties and 'sixties had an abnormally large share of the votes of the young. However during the last five elections their share of the national vote declined, as did their share of the youth vote; they lost the last election. Clearly two factors were at work: some shifting of allegiances as people grew older, and a change in attitudes among the young.

Hamilton cited polls in 1972 in Quebec which showed a drift from the separatist option with aging, with "the highest percentage of ex-separatists within the thirty-five to thirty-nine age category." Professor Hamilton noted:

> One can anticipate that Parti Québécois leaders will attempt to continue to stress, whenever possible, the argument of inevitability. To the extent that one can convince others of its validity, to that extent the argument does become meritable. It is a tactic which, here and elsewhere, is used to break one's will to resist.[2]

Inevitability conforms well with other qualities possessed by most of the péquistes, such as certainty and religious conviction. It is in the main line of clerical and authoritarian nationalism going back through Canon Groulx, Philippe Hamel, Henri Bourassa into the early nineteenth century. As I noted earlier, Canon Groulx's recorded speech to the 1967 Estates General conveys a sense of destiny and inevitability, and the imminence of a Quebec decision to go it alone.

Tribal drums of emotion

Certainly, much of the péquiste success to date can be attributed to their skilful exploitation of emotionally charged issues. They pursue a number of main themes which interweave: the threatened French language and culture; the need to regain economic power from the English; priority of the collectivity over the individual; discrimination against Quebec by the federal government; the assimilationist attitude of English Canadians; the humiliating and paternalistic attitudes of the English business rulers of Quebec; the wrongs done French Canadians from the Conquest on; and the endangered position of French Canadians in other provinces. Most of these, as we have seen, came together in the language white paper and in Bill One, and in the péquiste explanation for and defence of them.

This approach finds fertile soil in Quebec. There are many reasons – deep historical roots, pride in the survival for two centuries, against heavy odds, of their language, culture and traditions, personal grievances against the English and a desire for revenge, generalized inferiority feelings, an ingrained preference for provincial rather than federal solutions. Besides, many French Canadians find the restrictive and oppressive aura of the language proposals less morally offensive than do the English, perhaps because of their long conditioning under the authoritative régimes of the ultramontane Catholic church in Quebec, and of the Duplessis government; the popularity of corporate state proposals has always been high in Quebec, notably among the nationalists. As we observed, this found particular expression in the 1967 Estates General.

The péquistes have been particularly good at coining slogans with a gut appeal to francophone Quebecers. One such slogan became prominent at the time of the discussion about Bill One: "We want to make Quebec as French as Ontario is English." This sounds eminently fair and reasonable. Yet like many péquiste slogans it doesn't really stand up under close scrutiny. The size of the minority, for example: Ontario's francophone population is 6 per cent of the total; Quebec's anglophones form 20 per cent of the population. Even this doesn't really reflect the disparity, because Quebec outside of Montreal is for all practical purposes (excluding the use of English to serve tourists) as French now as Ontario is English. But Montreal's non-francophone population is close to 35 per cent of the total, and it is this group that is the main target of the language legislation.

Montreal, as we observed in Chapter II, was half English at the time of Union in 1841. Its anglophone roots are deep, and the attempt of Bill One to force such a large minority into a different language mould is almost unprecedented anywhere in modern times. Ontario's move towards bilingualism has not been exactly rapid – except for federal action in Ottawa – but it means giving new rights or privileges, not taking them away.

One interpretation of the phrase "as French as Ontario is English" is that the French would like to see the anglophones in Quebec reduced in numbers to the level of Ontario's 6 per cent francophone minority. This would require a net migration out of some 600,000 anglophones, as Richard Joy noted – comparable to the exodus of the French "pied-noirs" from Algeria. Joy suggests that the psychological warfare of Dr. Laurin will certainly speed up the flow out – already significant. [3]

Is it surprising that anglophone Quebecers are beginning to feel the pressure? Canadians from other provinces are quick to urge them to "stay and fight," and some of them intend to. Many of the older ones are tied to jobs and homes, and are relatively immobile. The younger ones, however, are leaving in large numbers. But even some of their elders are having second thoughts, such as "I'll lose some money if I sell my house now, but it may be unsaleable if I wait" or "Jobs are tough to find in Ontario or the west, but what will the situation be like if the current stream of emigrants becomes a torrent?" Few anglophones have much confidence in the tolerance and generosity of Dr. Laurin and his associates in their treatment of the anglophone minority.

The emotional appeal of the péquiste call to arms in aid of the collectivity is a difficult one for federalists, or threatened Quebec anglophones, to counter. Their reasoned arguments can be skilfully turned by the péquiste leaders to appear as self-serving propaganda. Any anglophone criticism at all of Bill One was labelled immediately by Dr. Laurin as just another attempt to defend the status quo, the privileged English position.

One of the more effective forms of federalist counter-attack was that directed at the defensive, ethnocentric nature of the philosophy behind the language bill. On May 5, 1977, federal Health Minister Marc Lalonde accused the PQ government, in its white paper, of creating a "siege mentality . . . The enemy is at the gates; minorities become the object of suspicion, particularly if they share the same race or language as the enemy. Everything must be regulated; diversity must give way to homogeneity, and to assure this homogeneity, the trumpet must be sounded and the people summoned to the ramparts. Situations must be dramatized – the debate must be provoked and theatricalized."

Senator Maurice Lamontagne, in a speech at the University of Montreal on April 6, 1977, touched on the two main streams in Quebec philosophical thought. The one, the nationalist, in which most péquistes fit comfortably, emphasizes the group or nation, its way of life, its great collective projects; it incarnates, consciously or not, the ambition of certain élites for power. It is often intolerant of foreigners, and demands sacrifices from individuals in the name of the overriding interests of the nation. Its origins in Quebec go back a long way.

Senator Lamontagne described the other stream as having a humanistic tendency, centred in the individual, his needs and aspirations. The nation is perceived not as a master but more of a servant. It is pluralist and open; independence is seen simply as one option among others, to be judged by the contribution it can make to the liberty and development of the individual.

Lamontagne ranges himself squarely against the nationalists – particularly the extremists, the "black" nationalists as he calls them, who have distorted and misinterpreted historical events to support their case. He refers to the Conquest, which Quebec historians speak of as "our" defeat, and which has been largely responsible, he believes, for the inferiority complex which for so long has haunted French Canada. Yet in fact, he notes, France, not French Canadians, lost the Seven Years War, and at the Treaty of Paris in 1763 France could still have kept Canada had it not been more interested in Guadeloupe sugar than in Canadian furs. What would have happened without the Conquest? Stagnation, Lamontagne argues, further delay in creating a democratic society, and probably assimilation by the U.S. But England provided a much broader market, first for wheat, then for lumber and ships; Lamontagne says that the Cession at least made possible the economic and social survival of the French-Canadian people during a very difficult readjustment period.

And, as we have noted earlier, it was the growth of Ontario and western Canada during the century following the Union of the Canadas in

1841, which spurred the growth of Montreal. The jobs created made it possible for hundreds of thousands of French Canadians leaving the farms to remain in Quebec, instead of emigrating south to the U.S. where they would be assimilated.

But let the words of Jean-Marc Léger speak for the exaltation of the "black" nationalists:

> It is an imperious collective obligation of the Québécois to ask themselves about the substance, the implications, and the responsibilities in the imminent, inevitable (ineluctable) sovereignty. I take it for granted that the Quebec people, if properly informed, enlightened and fully in tune with . . . their era, will want to grasp this doubtless unique opportunity to finally assume their destiny, or rather to endow themselves with a destiny. Without it, there is no future other than an accelerating deterioration into mediocrity; all this we have known for more than a century . . .
>
> Every great collective project presumes the mastery of the key elements of cultural, social and economic policy, a mastery that only national independence can assure. A 'province' can only provide scraps or baubles, and above all illusions, to a people resigned and aging, simple tenants in their own country . . . In the Quebec about to be born, a citizen will naturally lose his sense of alienation with the liberation of the country. At all levels, and in all types of activity . . . consultation and dialogue will go on normally, and the participation of everyone will be the foundation of collective progress. The extraordinary powers of creativity which this people harbours within themselves will finally blossom. It will be a matter of reinventing a sense of civic responsibility and raising it to the level of humanism. We must define a new form of relationship between the state and citizens, so that they feel simultaneously making cause with, and accountable to, the state . . .
>
> In the case of Quebec, the consumer society is another form of colonisation, more dangerous possibly because it imperils fundamental values and above all of the society's identity. And our people cannot survive for long with a loss of the sense of the spiritual. National sovereignity is the sole assurance of salvation. This is what gives the referendum its depth and historic significance, it will be, for our people . . . a matter of life or death.[4]

This is pretty heady stuff, and I'm not sure that my translation has done it entire justice. In style and content it is very similar to the message of the great Protestant preachers and evangelists in pointing out the only road to salvation. But I wonder how many Quebecers Jean-Marc Léger will convert to his dream of a new paradise on earth?

A different view of these dreams of glory was given by a Jesuit priest,

Jacques Monet, in a speech given in March 1977, and quoted at length in *Le Devoir* on June 30. He discussed the historic leaning towards unanimity of the élite of Quebec's nationalist movement, who were dominated in the nineteenth century by two reactionary movements, those of Counter-Reform and of ultramontanist authoritarianism. "Unanimity comes easily in Quebec" he said, and "arbitrary (solutions) remain our greatest temptation." As an example, he quotes George-Etienne Cartier as strongly warning Quebecers against organizing a Catholic party, which would force the Protestants to band together: "instead of peace and harmony which exist today . . . you will bring about war, a religious war, the worst of all wars."

Monet is concerned about the developing unanimity in Quebec around the language issue and unilingualism. Formerly the preoccupation of university "obscurantists" and nationalists of the Société Saint Jean-Baptiste, the interest is now widespread, he said, among all parties and classes. Like the ultramontanism of the nineteenth century,

> it accentuates our penchant for national introspection, it pushes our leaders towards rigidity and arbitrariness, contempt for civil rights, and the rejection of individual liberties. 'Having rejected the dogmatism of the ultramontane intellectuals, we are attempting to replace it with another.'
>
> Unilingualism is the denial of dialogue, a wall that limits our minds . . . it will reduce us to the sterility of a monologue . . . it will detach us from the partners that history, geography and economics have placed in our midst and all around us. It will be the end of the Canadian experiment; but it will also be our suicide as French Canadians.

But the seductive appeal of the language issue to the emotions of Quebec francophones, and the creation of a "siege" mentality, has other dimensions than the exalted prose of Léger, or the invocation of the "survival" argument by Laurin and others. A péquiste tactic which became more obvious as their months in office progressed was the use of provocation, intended to serve two purposes. One is to build a case for separation; and the second, to provoke angry retaliatory comments from the rest of Canada or the Quebec anglophone minority. These could then be exploited to show francophones in Quebec how unwilling the anglophones are to relinquish their historically privileged position.

If the divisive emotional game is a dangerous one – the starting of fires that may burn unpredictably, in direction or intensity – the péquistes have not hesitated to exploit it, and with some preliminary success. The weakest link in their independence case, however, remains the economic issue: what will it cost?

The economic debate

Lévesque's original thesis, as outlined in his 1967 *Option-Quebec,* always assumed that independence must be linked with some kind of an economic association with Canada. Ten years have gone by since that was written; it is an impressive comment on the vagueness of the formulation that over the decade péquiste economic theorists and experts have been unable to put much flesh on its bones. Phrases like "monetary union," "customs unions," "free trade association," "common market," are tossed around with abandon, are picked up and then discarded. Loose analogies are made with the European Common Market, Benelux, the Nordic countries, the European Free Trade Association. To the best of my knowledge no péquiste has yet spelled out publicly in detail what such an association might entail.

One hypothesis is that perhaps they haven't thought about it much. This is consistent with a related hypothesis that the purpose of the "association" argument is simply to allay fears of francophones about the economic consequences of independence. The vaguer the formulation the better; for one thing, if the bird is fleshed out and given wings, the people might conclude that it couldn't fly. And if independence is achieved, the fewer the public commitments about association that have been made, the better. Alternatively, the péquistes may have examined the various approaches and don't like what they see any more than do anglophone economists and politicians. All the more reason for confusing things as much as possible.

If the details remain vague for good and sufficient reason, the underlying theory that an association is bound to develop after separation has become hard-core péquiste doctrine. The theory is supported by a number of assertions:

(1) Quebec is a good market for Canadian goods ("they need us").

(2) English Canadians are practical people – business is business (emotions are for francophones).

(3) Anyone who attacks the proposed association is simply trying to blackmail or threaten in order to defend the status quo.

(4) Without close economic ties with Quebec, the residual Canada would be swallowed up by the Americans.

Lévesque in *Option-Quebec* had a number of interesting things to say about association. Some of his theories don't square with the facts; for example, in referring to trade between Quebec and the other provinces in manufactured goods, he suggests that Quebec buys twice as much as it sells: "we had at first – with the support of certain experts (presumably including Parizeau) – set the disproportion at three dollars, to one dollar." "The Quebec market . . . is rather important to the rest of the country . . . [it is] an extremely profitable market for the rest of Canada . . . This is not the kind of business that practical minds would accept losing or jeopardizing, unless an entente with Quebec were really unthinkable."[5]

The facts? In 1974[6] Quebec sales of manufactured goods to other provinces were $6.7 billions, its purchases $5.6 billions. Of Ontario's total output of manufactures 11 per cent went to Quebec; of Quebec's, 20 per cent went to Ontario. What makes the Lévesque case even weaker and more suspect is that Quebec's manufactured products are protected by the highest average tariff of any province, 9.9 per cent (Ontario's is 8.4 per cent). Quebec as a source of manufactures is that much less attractive. Who needs whom?

Another interesting assumption of Lévesque, in his brief discussion of the possibility of a monetary union with Canada, is that the control of monetary policy would be that between "equal" partners.[7] The Bank of Canada, with its top jobs alternating between the two new states, would manage the common currency, administer reserves and national debt, and protect "the stability of the two states." Not a word about why the three-quarters would grant an equal voice to the one-quarter!

The key to the péquiste approach is that everything could be worked out afterwards with "serenity," a word used by them as much as "inevitability." Everyone will behave in a gentlemanly fashion; things will be settled democratically without any fuss; Canada, for common sense reasons, will welcome an economic association with an independent Quebec. As Lévesque noted in his New York speech "After our 'quiet revolution' we are entitled to expect 'quiet independence' in the near future . . . evolution (of constitutional change) is going on . . . in an atmosphere of remarkable serenity . . . Quebec intends to continue, as in the past, to be one of the most stable societies in the world."

The importance of this quietly serene stance is obvious: if Quebecers can be persuaded that nothing will change except that they will be independent, the achievement of it will be very much easier. Jacques Parizeau and Claude Morin have hammered this point again and again in their talks with Ontario: "We need each other." As we have noted, however, the reaction has not been quite what the péquistes had hoped. In April and May their argument was shot down first by Premier Davis of Ontario, and then by the four western premiers. Still Lévesque clung to his faith that the practical anglophones would come around. In the National Assembly on May 6, in reply to a question about the western reaction, he said "No matter how dogmatic" current political statements are "it is written in the geography, in our mutual interest, that will be an association, no matter what the form." He didn't add, as he should have, "no matter what the terms," because as we will note later, this is where the real crunch would come.

Almost everyone outside the ranks of the péquistes who has looked at this idea of "association" dismisses it on a number of counts. One is that the economic rationale makes no sense. One western cabinet minister said to me, "Why the hell would we go on buying Quebec products if they become independent? We're being screwed enough as it is – we westerners have always resented the protection afforded eastern manufacturers – but to compound matters, it seems that every time one of our manufacturers bids successfully on a Quebec government tender, it gets thrown out on some technicality in favour of their own boys."

Simon Reisman, former federal deputy minister of finance, said on January 31, 1977:

> (economic union) . . . breaks down under any kind of rational analysis. Indeed it is a contradiction in terms. Would an independent Quebec with one-quarter of Canada's population and a fifth of Canada's economy expect to negotiate with the rest of Canada as an equal in setting commercial policy, monetary policy, fiscal policy, equalization grants, energy subsidies, government procurement policies? Why would the rest of Canada with quite different economic problems and goals accept this? And if the bargaining process and outcome reflected proportional population or economic power what in reality would be left of Quebec political independence?
>
> Lévesque points to the European Economic Community (EEC) as his model, but misses the essential point. States that enter a customs union have to make some pretty basic compromises. Most of Quebec's secondary industry – for example textiles, garments, boots and shoes – depends heavily on the highly-protected Canadian market. Other Canadians are prepared to accept this cost only to the extent that they can believe it is part of the cement that binds a nation together. A customs union has to involve major elements of give and take, and the members have to see these as being equitable in their broad interest, or justifiable in terms of some major ideal. Those great idealists such as Jean Monnet, who conceived the EEC, were creators, not destroyers. They saw the community as a step towards European federalism.[8]

An equally devastating criticism is that the compromises forced upon an independent Quebec by an association in which it had only one-fifth or one-quarter the votes might lead to "a greater servitude," as Maurice Lamontagne noted in the speech referred to earlier, than the constraining situation it believes itself to be in now. Robert MacIntosh, executive vice-president of the Bank of Nova Scotia, pointed out another hurdle: there are many forms of provincial protection now practised within Canada, such as preference for internally produced goods, which would be inadmissable if "Quebec were separate but continued as a signatory to the

General Agreement on Tariffs and Trade." And hardly a week goes by that some péquiste minister does not promise new protection or "buy-Quebec" policies to help Quebec industry.

The combined impression of the commentaries is that if an association with Canada were possible following Quebec separation, at best it would be on a basis not very different from the kind of federation we have today, but subject to a variety of other and newer compromises that would limit Quebec's freedom to act independently. Much more likely is that Quebec would find itself in a poorer bargaining position than it does as a province in negotiating with Ottawa now. Worst of all is the strong possibility that the emotional climate would be such as to make an association impossible, regardless of possible economic benefits to both parties.

But even apart from the question of feasibility of working out some kind of post-separation arrangement is the complexity of trying to disentangle the existing links between Quebec and the rest of Canada. Lévesque cited the example of the Norway-Sweden divorce in 1905, and subsequent economic association, but those countries were separated for most of their length by a high ridge of mountains, and the main means of communication was by sea, to which both retained access. If nominally joined in 1815 by the Congress of Vienna, they had remained in many ways separate countries. And, in terms of business and economic and financial affairs, life in 1977 is infinitely more complex than it was three-quarters of a century ago. Our complicated omelette would take some unscrambling.

There is in fact no parallel in the modern world to such a division as that proposed by the péquistes. The India-Pakistan division was that of two underdeveloped countries, and the cost in human lives, hostility and disruption to the societies, is still being paid. The African experience is similar. The questions posed by a Quebec-Canada split seem endless, technically complex, and not susceptible to rational solution, even by people with the greatest goodwill in the world.

Goodwill? If Quebec (or some Quebecers) might bask in the euphoria of "independence at last," Canadians would be going through the trauma of seeing their country cut into two parts. How tolerant would they be towards Quebec during this period? One of the great blind spots in the péquiste vision of the glorious future is their reluctance to acknowledge that many Canadians feel for Canada what they themselves feel for Quebec. Some of this was reflected in the reaction of provincial premiers, and leading federal spokesmen. Admittedly there may be a tactical element in this – why provide Lévesque with weapons to use internally in Quebec? – but there are growing overtones of anger in the reaction to the casual separatist assumption that "association" is inevitable.

How would Quebecers vote if association cannot be guaranteed? Polls suggest a strong rejection of independence pure and simple, unadorned by special deals that allow life to go on unchanged. Of course, in the event Quebec did separate, it would be most unlikely for all that trade to halt abruptly, but it would be carried out on terms set by the majority. And it would be difficult to prevent the anger and mutual hostility generated by the independence attempt from leading to acts of violence.

The péquistes themselves may be building a second line of defence, in case their first and preferred line doesn't hold. The economic accounts launched by Industry and Commerce Minister Tremblay on March 25 – and which have been vigorously attacked by Ontario and the federal government – were clearly designed to serve two purposes. One was to show that Quebec had been discriminated against by federal expenditures, and thereby generate anti-federal feeling. Another was designed to show how Quebec could really go it alone; the price tag, in terms of loss of federal subsidies, would be clearly not that great.

There is a third line of defence, still not much talked about, that of the hard line péquistes. It is "independence at any price, to save our souls and our culture." Understandably this is not aimed at the Quebec masses, but if necessary it will be dragged into play if all else fails. Not many referendum votes in it, however.

But what of the short term?

Many of the economic issues discussed above are scenarios about what might or might not happen after independence. But for many observers, the real economic issue is not the viability of an independent Quebec over the long term. Few doubt that it could survive; the questions that matter relate to the resulting state of its economic and social stability, its levels of income, and its growth prospects. What may be more relevant to current discussions is what will happen to the Quebec economy in the near future, and during the period leading up to the referendum.

For the price of independence, real or apprehended, may well be paid largely before the decision is taken. Part of that price is being paid now, through a gradual slowing down in the Quebec economy. (My June 5, 1977 column on this subject is attached as Appendix Five). Planned investment decisions are being cancelled; a few businesses are shifting part or all of their operations elsewhere; new business is not attracted to Quebec because of the climate of uncertainty and the language bill. If the outward move of head offices in recent months has not been quite so precipitous as the official figure suggests – many are simply investment companies with few job implications – the threat of a massive outflow is real.

For example, the SECOR study referred to earlier (p. 180) did a detailed analysis of large corporations in Quebec, taking into account head office location, proportion of sales and employment in Quebec, and the degree of bilingualism at management levels. Assuming that the firms most likely to leave as a result of the francization measures in Bill One would be those with the greatest share of their business outside the province, and the least degree of present management bilingualism, it calculated that there would be a direct loss of some 15,000 jobs, over a third of management calibre. Another 15,000 jobs would be lost by the multiplier effect.[9]

A weakening Quebec economy – few new jobs being created in the private sector, and others lost as businesses leave – is only one dimension of the problem. A more serious threat may be that posed by the fears of individual Quebecers, francophone and anglophone, about their own future. Frightened people tend to think first of their investments (the saying goes, "first their assets, then their asses"), and shift their bank accounts and securities to other provinces or countries. They sell their homes and rent. They buy houses in Florida or Vermont. They borrow in Quebec against their fixed assets, personal or business. The extent to which this has occurred to date is not known, and it may be largely limited to the wealthier and better informed Quebecers.

What happens when the little guy gets the message that troubled times are coming? Will *he* continue to hold his Quebec Savings Bonds, or will he opt for Canada Savings Bonds? Will he leave money in the Caisse Populaire of Ste. Cécile de Masham, or deposit it with the Royal Bank in Ottawa? Can the Caisses Populaires system – with no Bank of Canada backstop – survive a run that is province-wide? These are questions for which no clear answers are available, but runs on banks tend to spread like prairie grass fires. People care about preserving what they have, however small it may appear to others.

Not just banks are affected. What about insurance policies with Quebec companies? Loans and cash surrender values could be a major source of embarrassment, if people suddenly begin to fear that Quebec is in danger of becoming unhooked from the larger, wealthier and more stable Canada.

It can be argued, of course, that frightened people will vote against independence. They well may, if they have a chance. But what about a referendum environment in which the province is approaching an economic breakdown, a state of chaos? Would the péquiste party, if still in power and with media support, be able to persuade the voters that "they" – English Canada – did it to "us," Québécois? And, finally, what about the possible exploitation of chaos by unscrupulous, authoritarian-minded leaders to seize absolute power without reference to the people's will? It is a pattern with many parallels in history.

This may be an overly pessimistic scenario. As the summer of Bills One and 101 dragged on there were signs that the Lévesque government's emphasis on language, at whatever cost in terms of justice, minority rights, economic growth, jobs, and social stability, was hurting its public image. The press was becoming less idolatrous, more questioning. If René Lévesque was still high in the opinion polls – as was Pierre Trudeau – many of the PQ ministers had been severely criticized for their lack of competence, and even for their personal behaviour. The picture that René had presented proudly to his TV audience in November, of a bright, shiny, intellectual cabinet, ready to take on and solve Quebec's problems, was beginning to acquire a jaded, confused look. Several prominent French-Canadians told me, not without a certain satisfaction, "Just give these fellows enough rope; they'll hang themselves." Camille Laurin may yet find himself in the unexpected role of saving Canadian unity by the excesses of his own language policies.

Another French Canadian put it this way: "Look, the accession of the péquistes to power may prove to have served a very useful purpose, like the lancing of a boil. The emotional forces behind the independence movement are strong, and something simply had to break out into the open at this time." Instead of remaining in opposition, heroically fighting an establishment in disrepute, their theories unchallenged by practical concerns, the péquistes have been forced into the limelight, and the inconsistencies and unforeseen effects of their policies revealed increasingly as the days go by. Light, after all, is the sovereign antiseptic.

This analysis is comforting, but overlooks some potentially dangerous consequences of the péquiste legislative activities. The language battle is a divisive one, splitting French-Canadian families, pitting English against French, shaking external confidence in Quebec. Even if the language bill proves unworkable, the referendum and subsequent election held and lost by the péquistes, deep scars will remain. Quebec has been on an emotional binge since November 15, 1976 and the hangover, when it comes, could be of monstrous dimensions.

Notes

1 Vera Murray, *Le Parti Québécois* (Montréal: Editions Hurtubise HMH Ltée. 1976).
2 *Montreal Star* and *Le Devoir,* June 8, 1977.
3 Joy, *op. cit.* (See note 4, Chapter XVI).
4 *Le Devoir,* February 4, 5, 1977.
5 Lévesque, *Option-Quebec, op. cit.,* p. 38 (English version).
6 *Ontario Budget* 1977 Supplement: Interprovincial Trade Flows (Source, Ottawa: Statistics Canada).
7 Lévesque, *op. cit.,* p. 44.
8 Simon Reisman, *What's Gone Wrong With Canada?* Speech to Canadian Club of Toronto, January 31, 1977.
9 See p. 180, and footnote 1 to Chapter XVI.

XVIII

Good-bye, René . . . but I remember the good years

An open letter to Prime Minister Lévesque

Cher René,
Is it really fifteen years since we met? That meeting led to my involvement in that project dear to your heart, the nationalization of the power companies, and to my subsequent role as an adviser to the Lesage and Johnson governments in the 1960s. The face of Quebec in those days was being rapidly changed by the "quiet revolution" in which you played so important a part, and Quebec was an exciting place in which to work. But the pace wasn't fast enough, or nationalistic enough, for you, and in the fall of 1967 you left the Liberals to found the *Mouvement Souveraineté-Association*. Your goal was the separation of Quebec, followed by some kind of new economic association with Canada.

Do you remember the open letter I wrote you at that time? You will, I think, because you quoted a few sentences from it later in *Option-Québec*. The letter began like this: "We have been friends for many years, and there is no one in public life for whom I have more respect. You entered politics as a knight on a white charger . . ." However, I went on to argue, in my more-in-sorrow-than-in-anger letter, "the financial and economic consequences of Quebec separation would be catastrophic." I urged you to "draw back from a policy of potential disaster," and closed with the suggestion if the decision to separate or not is largely an internal one for

Quebec, "the matter of how much it will cost will be determined largely by those outside Quebec."

Nearly ten years have passed and nothing which has occurred in that decade leads me to change my mind. In fact, Quebec is more dependent than ever on borrowed capital, and on federal transfer payments and equalization grants, to keep its economy alive, if in a sickly state. Despite the higher unemployment, wage levels, pushed by aggressive unions in the public sector, have reached levels which the province's output cannot sustain; aroused expectations continue to produce unreasonable wage demands.

My purpose in writing, however, is not to debate or discuss Quebec's economic problems of the moment, but rather to comment on the performance of your government in its first months in office. Let's begin with the election campaign which you fought – and won – on the grounds not of independence but of good government. During the campaign you knew well that the independence issue was a liability, not an asset. Apparently it was something to be played down, concealed, saved only for meetings of the faithful.

And yet, with the exception of the cautious Parizeau budget, most actions of your government since November 15, 1976, appear to have been more a back door approach to independence than a move towards good government. You killed the Anti-Inflation Board's Quebec operations, you dismissed the charges against those involved earlier in illegal strikes, you raised the minimum wage, in a province with 10 per cent unemployment. Your "anti-scab" legislation, Bill 45, strengthened the bargaining power of unions whose aggressiveness in recent years has contributed to the troubled economic environment in the province.

Still, in the first few months I, like most observers, was ready to accept mistakes as a normal consequence of a new government taking power. In my weekly columns I defended the historic demand of Quebec to be treated as a nation within a country, a province not like the others, but one deserving of special status to defend its unique culture and threatened language.

And then came your dinner speech in New York, which I attended as a guest of a French-Canadian investment dealer. You had been invited as prime minister of Quebec, to tell the assembled American financiers what you proposed to do to clear up Quebec's economic problems. You spoke instead as the head of a movement, proudly announcing its avowed intention of pulling Quebec out of Confederation. You cited the opening statement in an American Declaration of Independence, presumably to show the similarities between your battle today, and theirs of two centuries ago, against the "English" oppressor.

How could you have so misjudged your audience? The last thing

Americans – and particularly the investors in Quebec bonds – want to see is an independent Quebec, isolated, vaguely socialist, neutral, certainly facing new economic difficulties and creating all kinds of new problems for American defence policies. I canvassed U.S. opinion that evening and the next day, and reported my findings in my column in expurgated form; some of the things the Americans said about you couldn't be repeated in a family newspaper. Yet when I said your speech was a disaster, I was attacked by your péquiste followers as a biased and frightened Canadian anglophone. Even *you* tried to suggest that American antipathy was really generated by a Canadian "fifth column" at the dinner.

You started to lose me then, René, and forced me to rethink my position. Clearly there was not much hope to be derived from rational discussion with you péquistes. Dissent from péquiste dogma only invites invective and an impugning of motives. Events and facts are viewed by your followers through péquiste-coloured glasses.

And then came that extraordinary presentation of figures towards the end of March by your Industry and Commerce Minister, Rodrigue Tremblay. Figures which purported to show how much Quebec had lost by Confederation, and which you proudly endorsed. It was a great propaganda victory, all will agree, even if simply to confuse the true situation. Like most such triumphs, however, a price has to be paid. The figures were obviously suspect, and a challenge to common sense. As Ontario Treasurer Darcy McKeough pointed out in his budget papers, the $6 billion equalization payments to Quebec this past decade represent a "rock-bottom" measure of Quebec's gain from Confederation.

By the time your April 1, 1977 language white paper appeared, I had acquired a certain scepticism about any public statements or releases of you or your ministers. It seemed as if facts acquired validity only if they supported your cause. I was tempted at one point to use the word "péquonomics" to describe a newly discovered branch of economics, peculiar to your movement, which deals with the science of proving with impeccable logic that up is down, that deficits are surpluses, that Quebec is the real workhorse of Canada, carrying everyone else along on its back.

The language white paper, and Bill One which emerged four weeks later, hit a new low. I had no quarrel with the general objectives of the language legislation, which seeks to establish the primacy of the French language in Quebec. Even some of the proposed measures relating to access to English schools did not offend me, although those touching on language of work in business and public agencies, the exclusion of English signs, and on francization programs, I found regressive, coercive, and bureaucratic, if not racist – and probably largely unworkable. But let that aspect pass for the moment. What I personally found most repugnant about the white paper was its Chapter One – "The situation of the

French language in Quebec." In attempting to provide a rationale for the whole language policy, it set out an array of "facts" that purported to prove that the French language in Quebec is in fact seriously threatened.

And what facts did it pick out? Long quotations from the Bilingualism and Biculturism preliminary report of 1965, citing figures which are now fifteen years old, and many statements by English "assimilationists" from remote parts of Canada. Figures cited out of context from the more recent Gendron Report – deliberately creating a false impression – and distorted population and immigration statistics. Not a word about progress made in the last ten years in French language use and in the hiring of French Canadians in the federal public service and in business in Montreal. No recognition in the paper of the special need for English in national and multi-national head offices. Nothing about the failure of the francophone school system, until recent years, of turning out graduates prepared for business careers.

What a monstrous tissue of twisted facts, misleading statements, and biased analysis! Yet it is on this superstructure, René Lévesque, that Bills One and 101 were mounted; it is with such products of devious minds that it has been defended, justified, rationalized. This legislation, which even you yourself admit to finding humiliating, and which could prove to be the most divisive ever produced in this country, polarizing and envenoming opinion, pitting English against French, splitting Quebec families. This legislation, which any objective observer of the Quebec scene knows is unnecessary.

You would do well to feel humiliated by the language charter, but not for the reasons you give that, for all its strictures, "it is needed." What any good péquiste should feel humiliated about is that your government should go to such lengths to try to prove that the French language in Quebec is threatened, when all the evidence is that its position has never been stronger in the last 100 years, its place never more secure. But péquiste doctrine is not based on facts, but on religious beliefs; language and culture has a place on the high altar replacing the Cross of old. The language charter, the gospel according to your resident psychiatrist and minister, Dr. Camille Laurin, which he defends with all the certitude that comes only from profound religious conviction, has been brought into the world surrounded by a bodyguard of lies. That indeed is humiliation.

As for the coercive and repressive measures in your language legislation, their purpose may be to so alienate the English that either (1) they will leave, reducing the vote against the referendum, and presumably providing more jobs and cheap houses for French Canadians, or (2) they will react angrily, allowing you and your people to exploit their complaints as typical and historic anglophone rejection of legitimate French-Canadian aspirations – intellectual blackmail and terrorism. I can see your back room boys working it all out, making the case that you can't lose. No doubt this made Laurin's extreme position more acceptable to your less fanatical colleagues.

But what of the other side of the coin, your case for association with Canada, after independence? You are already beginning to see some blacklash from your activities to date, and the language issue will inevitably worsen French-English relations in this country. Think of the impact of the thousands of anglophone Quebecers, now scattering across this country, made to feel like second class citizens, forced to leave a Quebec homeland, whose government they fear, giving up jobs and friends, compelled to sell their houses at cut-rate prices? What story do you think each of these latter-day Acadians will be telling the dozens or hundreds of people they meet? Forget the newspaper polls of early 1977; if you honestly believe that association would be possible after the great divide, you had better start reshaping your thinking. Your government's language policies will be the kiss of death for it.

If, however, the purpose of the "association" argument is simply to quieten the fears of francophone Quebecers that they will lose out economically if Quebec separates, then you should be shining up a new propaganda weapon. Even péquiste supporters in the media will be unable to conceal the truth from the average French-Canadian worker, who is more interested in his daily bread than in being a pawn in a struggle for power and glory by the intellectually élite group which surrounds you.

"For they have sown the wind, and they shall reap the whirlwind." That's where you're heading, René, and the wind is rising faster than I thought possible. Maybe your continuing expressions of concern about the language legislation, and your dissociation from the debate on it reflected your unease about where the extremists are taking you, and the government. But leaders are expected to enunciate, or at least support, agreed government policy, not grumble from the side as if they were not involved in the decision. Or is the leader exempt from playing the game of cabinet solidarity according to the usual rules? Maybe you are just reverting to the old René, who as minister under Jean Lesage so strongly resisted cabinet discipline. A less charitable explanation sees you as reluctant to give up the respect of those many Quebecers who believe, as you may well do, that Bill 101 is one of the most regressive pieces of legislation ever put forward by any government in Canadian history – all while you try to appear to your loyal followers as giving it your support.

But no matter what you do now to escape the walls closing in on you, most of the blame for what happens will be yours, in your dual role as Prime Minister and party leader. You are no longer a knight in shining armour to me, of course, and I may have succumbed too readily to your natural persuasiveness. Still, I remember the good years, when the things we did were based on solid economic sense, not on perverted religious doctrine; when the Hon. René Lévesque was more concerned about improving the quality of life in Quebec, and giving good government to the people, than in aspiring to be the George Washington of a new, unilingual, ghetto-like state. Perhaps you yourself are wondering if you made the right choice ten years ago. Could it be that you will look at yourself in the mirror, one of these mornings, and say to yourself, "My God – what have I done to my beloved Quebec?"

En amitié –
(As ever)
Doug Fullerton

APPENDIX ONE

Exchange of correspondence, Lévesque – Fullerton, prior to Lac-à-l'Epaule meeting, September 1962. (see pp. 44-45).

Department of Natural Resouces
Province of Quebec
Minister's Office

Montreal, August 31st, 1962.

Mr. D. H. Fullerton, President,
Fullerton, McKenzie (sic) & Ass.,
140 Wellington,
Ottawa.

Dear Mr. Fullerton:
I would appreciate very much your professional advice on the bond-market implications of increased borrowing by the Province of Quebec with particular reference to the possible effect upon the Province's credit of the nationalization of a number of private electric power companies.

Yours very truly,

(Signed)

RENÉ LÉVESQUE,
Minister.

Fullerton Mackenzie and Associates
2055 Peet St. Montreal

Montreal, September 1, 1962

Hon. René Lévesque,
Minister of National Resources,
Quebec Hydro Building,
Montreal, Que.

You have asked for our professional opinion about the bond market implications of substantially increased borrowing by the province of Quebec, with particular reference to the possible impact of the financing of the purchase of the outstanding stock of five large private electric power utility companies in the Province.

We understand that the amounts involved in this latter purchase could be of the order of $350 million. It is also assumed that the current rate of borrowing by the province in its own name is expected to continue at an estimated annual rate of $200 – $250 million, and borrowing by the Hydro at about $100 million annually. The outstanding debt of the privately owned utilities is in excess of $250 million. Assuming that payment for the utilities would be effected over the next two years, the net debt of province (direct and guaranteed) would therefore be increased by about $1,250 million in this period, although $250 million of this would not be new borrowing but a change of status of existing bonds. This would increase the net debt from approximately $1,500 million to $2,750 million, or from $280 per capita to around $500 per capita. This latter figure is close to the present net debt of Ontario and of Manitoba. B.C.'s per capita debt is about $740.

If these figures are of the correct order of magnitude, the question you ask then resolves itself into several parts:

(a) Could Quebec borrow $1,000 million over the next two years?
(b) If so, what changes if any in marketing or sources of funds would be necessary?
(c) What would be the effect on interest rates paid by the province, both absolutely and relatively to other borrowers?

It would be foolhardy for anyone at this stage to give an unqualified yes or no to these questions. What we prefer to do is to set out the factors which would affect the ability of Quebec to raise sums of this magnitude, and then to suggest a programme of action that in our view would be most likely to make the borrowing possible at the lowest cost to the province. It follows from this that we believe the money can be raised, given favourable circumstances and some modification of existing debt management procedures.

We would like to make first two general points about the bond market. One is that if any borrower – government or corporation – increases its annual demands upon the market its relative borrowing costs are almost automatically raised. The rise in Quebec borrowing during the past two years has meant that interest rates paid by the province have risen slightly in relation to those of provinces such as Ontario and Alberta which have not shown the same sharp increase in borrowing. The adverse consequences of increased borrowing can be modified, however, by opening up new sources of money and by other possible changes which are outlined below. It should also be noted that the per capita debt of Quebec is now lower than the provincial average, and that the new programme would be bringing the level up to the average (and to the Ontario level) and not raising it substantially above it. We must also emphasize that buyers regard indirect or guaranteed debt on precisely the same basis as direct, so that it is the aggregate which counts. "Debt-free B.C." as a slogan may have some political mileage inside that province, but investors know that the per capita debt is double the national average.

The second general point concerns the effect of a government's nationalization programme on the attitude of institutional investors (and investment dealers) towards its bonds. Most financial institutions and corporate pension funds, which form the largest market for new bond issues, have a bias towards free enterprise and against government ownership. Socialism is a bad word, and if a government appears to move in that direction its securities to some degree become suspect. This happened in Saskatchewan and more recently in B.C.

The B.C. example is a useful one because the total amounts involved are approximately the same, and the background situation quite similar. There is no question however that the sharply adverse reaction to the B.C. take-over was not caused primarily by objections to the principle but by the arbitrary and ruthless manner in which it was carried out. The consequences of that action a year ago have seriously affected the province's credit and indeed contributed to the decline in confidence abroad in Canadian securities.

We do not think the credit of Quebec would be damaged to anything like the same extent by the proposed power nationalization programme. First, one has to make the assumption that any expropriation would be handled in a much more equitable, just and legally defensible manner than in B.C. Second, the market, in Canada at least, is now emotionally prepared for the take-over; surprise was a factor in B.C. Third, although the aggregate dollar amounts involved are almost identical, the per capita debt implications for B.C. are more than three times as great. It must be noted that the equity outstanding in the Quebec utilities is more than double ($350 million vs. $170 million) that of B.C. Power, so that the *new* money required to be borrowed is that much greater in Quebec. In summary, however, if the Quebec nationalization is carried out fairly and with dignity, the adverse psychological effects on buyers of Quebec bonds is likely to be held to a minimum.

It is against this background that we comment on the adequacy of existing debt management procedures to meet the new challenge, and put forward suggestions for changes that in our view would improve the province's borrowing capacity.

(1) **New sources of funds needed**

Almost all of the borrowing by the province in the past two years has been in Canadian dollars and along traditional lines, that is by the sale of issues to underwriters who distribute them to investors. A large proportion of these bonds has been sold to Canadian institutions, although there has been some retail distribution and some modest institutional sales in the United States. We do not believe that this system *alone* is adequate to raise the additional sums required to pay for the nationalization programme. Indeed we suspect that the doubts raised about the borrowing capacity of Quebec have arisen mainly because of the widespread feeling that Canadian institutions would not be prepared to take up the additional bonds. Many institutions have preconceptions about the desirability of diversification and about holding a maximum amount of the bonds of any one province or city. They are prepared to modify their preconceptions at a price, but even if interest rates are pushed up sharply there are limits beyond which they will not go. For these reasons we suggest that Quebec will probably have to look elsewhere for a large part of the additional money it would need. We suggest below several alternative sources which might be exploited:

(a) *More U.S. dollar borrowing*

With the Canadian dollar at 92 cents, and the current spread in interest rates between U.S. and Canada wide, the U.S. market would appear to be very attractive now for Canadian borrowers. The chief obstacle is the withholding tax, but with the obvious change of heart in Ottawa about such U.S. borrowing, it may be that the tax will shortly be reduced or removed. (Representation from the provinces on this would no doubt help). We believe that the U.S. market could absorb without difficulty $100 million annually in new Quebec-U.S. pay issues providing foreign confidence in Canada and in Quebec is not impaired by new adverse developments. Such U.S. borrowing would reduce the pressure on the Canadian market and improve the marketability of Quebec's Canadian-pay issues.

The rate which would have to be paid in the U.S. would depend in part on market conditions but more importantly on whether or not the withholding tax remains. Under present conditions a large U.S. pay Quebec issue would have to carry a 5½% coupon; with the tax removed it might be done at 4¾%. Borrowing in the U.S. does mean that the province would have to accept an increasing foreign exchange liability, but it is much less hazardous now to borrow with the Canadian dollar at a discount than it was in the 1950s during most of which the Canadian dollar was at a premium.

(b) *New forms of borrowing in Canada*
(i) *Quebec Savings Bonds*
In the three years 1959-61 annual sales of Canada Savings Bonds in Quebec averaged $200 million. We see no reason why part of this could not be diverted to Quebec Savings Bonds, and in fact believe that Q.S.B.'s would attract new money from savings deposits in banks and even mattresses. How much is difficult to say, but $50 – $100 million in the first year does not appear unreasonable and $50 million or more thereafter. One of the main attractions of introducing a Q.S.B. programme at this time is that the strong nationalistic feeling in Quebec could form the basis for the publicity campaign, and could also be linked to the utility takeover.

There is considerable opposition to the sale of provincial savings bonds. One view is that it is demand money, and hence dangerous. We think that this criticism is valid only if the bonds are sold through the money market, and become concentrated in institutional and corporate hands. The B.C. parity bonds fell into this category, and created difficulties for B.C. when short term rates rose sharply. So long as sales are limited to individuals we see few problems; the total outstanding of Canada Savings Bonds has risen annually, and Saskatchewan and Manitoba have not experienced the type of large scale redemptions which caused trouble for B.C. We should add that all bond dealers are inherently opposed to savings bonds, no doubt in part because they benefit more from the sale of market issues. One other objection may have some validity, that Q.S.B.'s would compete with caisse populaire deposits and hence cause some resentment throughout the province. We do not know how true this is.

(ii) *Quebec Treasury Bills*
We believe that the province should tap the short term market by a regular issue of treasury bills, say $5 to $10 million a week for thirteen weeks, and then continuing on with each issue redeeming the one brought out thirteen weeks earlier. This would raise $65 to $130 million in new money, but would not of course provide any further money after the first

thirteen weeks. Similar objections have been voiced to treasury bills as to savings bonds, that they are a short term liability and subject to pressure in periods of tight money. This is a problem, but providing that no province overextends its short term borrowing we believe that the economy and availability of money from the short term market outweighs any possible disadvantage. We note that the federal government is increasing its treasury bill offering in the first week of September from $115 million to $130 million. The federal government bill market is of course supported by the requirement that the chartered banks hold bills as part of their secondary reserve. We should also note that several finance companies have as much as $100 million constantly outstanding in short term liabilities.

(2) **Centralize sinking funds**
One of the best ways to improve the market for the bonds of any borrower is to operate an efficient sinking fund system to support the market in outstanding issues. Often it is the 10% floating supply that damages the issuer's credit, and these bonds can be siphoned off by skilful sinking fund management. We therefore suggest bringing all the provincial sinking funds under centralized direction with the annual supply of funds for this purpose augmented by a budgetary allotment of $25 million. I have in mind the Quebec Hydro general and pension funds, the funds of the Workmen's Compensation Board, Minimum Wage Commission and the Autoroute, overall provincial superannuation funds, and the province's own statutory sinking funds. Eventually Hydro could be hived off as has been done in Ontario, but the urgent need now is to mobilize all funds for the primary purpose of making a good market for Quebec bonds. We are convinced that efficient sinking and purchase fund management can greatly facilitate new borrowing, and can reduce its cost. The purchases to date by the various Quebec provincial funds has (sic) improved the market for Quebec issues, but one's general impression is that the buying has been haphazard and uncoordinated, and that excessive prices have sometimes been paid.

These are preliminary comments prepared in some haste, and we are quite prepared to elaborate on any particular point that you think needs further clarification. One overall question that cannot be adequately covered here is the state of the market at the time the borrowing is done. If money is as tight as it was in August 1959 or in June 1962, borrowing difficulties would obviously be greatly increased. At the present time, however, the market is surprisingly buoyant for a period of alleged "austerity" and the immediate prospects are that borrowers will have little difficulty raising money from the sale of bonds. Given a continuation of these conditions we are firmly of the view that the province could raise the money needed to purchase the private utilities, providing (a) it is prepared to undertake some changes in the sources of its borrowing; (b) the nationalization is carried out in such a way as to minimize the effects upon buyer attitudes; and (c) that sinking funds and other funds available to the province are mobilized to support the market for Quebec issues.

Yours very truly,

D. H. Fullerton,
President

Note: I sent several minor changes along to Lévesque a few days later; these changes have been incorporated in this September 1 letter.

APPENDIX TWO

Memorandum on public versus private development of Hamilton Falls Power, prepared by D.H. Fullerton for Quebec cabinet on February 3, 1964. (see p. 66).

A note on private ownership

We do not know if it is appropriate for us to interject the question of public versus private development of Hamilton Falls. In studying the figures, however, we could not help but become aware of the very heavy additional costs of building, financing and operating the Hamilton Falls development as a private company. These costs arise in many different ways, but the most important are the payment of federal taxes on annual income, and the much higher servicing costs of equity (and debenture) financing compared with government bonds. These additional costs amount to close to one mill per KWH, or about 40% of the estimated selling price of the energy at the Newfoundland border. We regard this as quite a price for Quebec (and any other buyer) to pay in order that Brinco may be adequately compensated for its expenditures to date and its 99 year lease on Labrador power. To the extent that Canadian governments receive taxes from Hamilton Falls Power Corporation, of course, the additional burden for Canada *as a whole* is reduced.

Apart from costs, however, there are other considerations which lead us to think that public ownership of the project should be considered. The first is that one normally associates equity ownership with the assumption of risks, and with growth prospects arising from the development and exploitation of markets for goods and services. Both these factors are absent here. The operation is entirely wholesale, there being but one buyer for the project. The bulk of the output is sold to a government on a long term contractual basis. There may be risks involved – although we find it difficult to foresee any apart from the failure of the 735 KV system to function – but these risks are just as great for the bondholders as for the common shareholders. The project cannot *partially* succeed or fail, and the physical assets are not much good for any other purpose than the generation of power. We might add that such risks as there are in the project as presently conceived appear to be borne by Quebec.

Our second point is that the building of a gigantic hydro-electric development by private capital is out of step with the trend of the times. We know of no other large hydro-electric project, except possibly in the United States, which is being, or has recently been, developed under private auspices. Even in the United States there has been a pronounced trend towards public control of important hydro developments (Bonneville, T.V.A. etc.), although some of the energy thus generated may be sold to private utilities for retail distribution. The Columbia development, of course, will be carried out by public authorities on both sides of the border. If a Quebec contract makes a private Hamilton Falls utility possible, the Province will be open to the charge in some quarters that it has fostered an expensive anachronism.

The third point verges more on the political than the economic. Many people in Quebec have never become reconciled to the 1927 Privy Council decision that established the Labrador boundary on the "watershed" basis. It appears to us that development of Hamilton Falls by a public agency or corporation in which the Quebec Government participated to a substantial degree would be much more acceptable politically in Quebec than the proposed private company arrangements. Certainly public ownership would fit comfortably into the suggested "condominium" compromise for joint Quebec-Newfoundland exploitation of Labrador; if Hamilton Falls is privately controlled then almost inevitably the condominium would become a troika with Brinco as the lead horse.

We realize that there are obstacles to a sudden move at this time to force public control of the project. Mr. Smallwood has apparently committed himself to Brinco, and to private development of the area, and he would hesitate to repudiate the agreements he has made. Brinco has been spending money on Labrador for many years without much tangible reward, even if its actual investment (less than $10,000,000.) has been less than current publicity suggests. The reaction in United States financial circles might affect the market for Quebec bonds, although if as a result Con-Ed would buy its power at 3½ or 3¾ mills, rather than the proposed 4, Wall Street's disapproval of a new Quebec move towards "socialism" might well be tempered.

In any event we think that all of these obstacles can be overcome with money. Brinco could be recompensed with a lump sum of say $25 million ($25 for each Hamilton Falls Power Corporation share it owns, or over $4 per Brinco share) *plus* a royalty of say .1 of one mill on power generated at Hamilton Falls for the next 15 to 25 years ($3 million a year, which is $3 per Hamilton Falls Power Corporation share or $.50 per Brinco share). If Brinco accepted such a proposal gracefully, then neither Mr. Smallwood nor Wall Street could have much to complain about. Finally we must emphasize again that Quebec has a strong hand; we find it difficult to visualize a user of 32 billion KWH annually establishing an industry on the Hamilton River, and no scheme has yet been devised for transmitting electrical energy cheaply by air or water.

D. H. Fullerton

APPENDIX THREE

Letter appearing in English in the *Toronto Star,* and in French in *Le Devoir,* on October 6 and 7, 1967

An open letter to René Lévesque pleads Canada's cause

Cher Réné,
We have been friends for many years, and there is no one in public life for whom I have more respect.

You entered politics as a knight on a white charger, and few knights were ever more badly needed or more warmly received. To me, your recent manifesto is an honest document written by a man deeply troubled about his people and their problems. If there were any doubts in English Canada about the intensity of your feelings on these matters, they were resolved the other night when you appeared on television with Eric Kierans and debated the issue of Quebec independence – the main conclusion of your search for a fresh answer to Quebec's relationship with the rest of Canada.

Certainly there is much that you said with which I agree. No man could work closely with the Quebec élite, as I have been fortunate enough to do these last few years, without becoming profoundly aware of the strong French-Canadian will to survive. For indeed it is *"la survivance"* which dominates today so much of French-Canadian nationalism, and which underlies everything written in your document. The tides of Anglo-Saxon culture are washing in over your shores, and I can only sympathize deeply with your fear that someday soon – to quote Claude Morin – you will be forced to *"baisser pavillon."*

And yet you force me, on your central argument, to "stand up and be counted." If emotionally I can accept the depth of feeling behind your plea for independence, every reasoning bone in my Scots-Canadian body tells me that the financial and economic consequences of Quebec separation would be catastrophic for the province in the short run – and I leave the long run to look after itself.

In other words, the case that Kierans, Bourassa and others are making is a strong one and I can only add my voice to theirs in urging you to draw back from a policy of potential disaster.

Let me try to put a little flesh on the skeleton of my argument, although I do not believe it possible to make a meaningful dollar-and-cents calculation about the cost to Quebec splitting itself off from the rest of Canada. Yet certain trends have been evident of late which bear on this issue, and Quebec must face also other inherent disabilities which would affect its ability to survive alone.

DEBT

1. Debt problems

For five years Quebec's borrowing has run over $500 million a year, the amount needed to cover social capital expenditure and deficit spending. Today Quebec provincial and municipal bonds cannot be sold in Canada outside Quebec; in fact a substantial selling of outstanding bonds has been avoided only because investors are reluctant to sell and show large losses. Record high interest rates, together with the large volume of Quebec borrowing, have pushed bond prices down as much as 20 per cent. The province's credit has been sustained by the buying of the Caisse de Dépôt and of United States institutions, although American buyers are becoming less receptive lately to Quebec issues – or perhaps more sophisticated about Canadian problems.

The deterioration in the market for Quebec bonds has been in part due to heavy borrowing, but an important factor has been investor fears about nationalism, and uncertainty about Quebec's future. What would be the consequences of Quebec independence? I suggest that the initial effect would certainly be heavy selling of Quebec bonds – at any price – and a complete breakdown in Quebec's credit.

This would have an impact directly on provincial finances, but the indirect effects on investment and business spending in the province might be even more severe. Eventually things would get sorted out, but investors have long memories. It took Montreal fifteen years to purge its credit of early wartime bond defaults, but even if default were avoided by Quebec, the effects of a market breakdown would be similar.

2. Tax revenue and federal subventions:

Kierans sees this loss in revenue at close to $500 million per year, from the surrender of federal equalization payments and the decline in other tax revenues. I cannot appraise the accuracy of the calculation, but I suspect that as a "have-not" province, Quebec has been doing much better out of Ottawa than either side will admit (even if the Atlantic provinces get more on a per capita basis). Declining tax revenues would mean either or both of two things – less spending and fewer jobs, or more taxes. This latter prospect is not appealing to outside investors or entrepreneurs; the former is not palatable to Quebeckers.

INVESTMENT

3. Direct investment:
Capital hates uncertainty, and the conclusions of the study by *la Chambre de Commerce,* that there is a widening gap between the rate of new direct investment in plant facilities in Ontario and in Quebec, does not contradict such fragments of evidence as cross my path. The uncertainties not only relate to Quebec's political status, but to the potential impact on the fabric of the system of abrupt and painful split.
4. Geography:
Quebec has many assets – the people, Montreal, the river, primary resources, but for a modern industrial state it has some surprising deficiencies. Industry is increasingly market-oriented, and Ontario is much closer to the main centres of North American populations. In fact 90 per cent of Quebec is a barren, cold black-fly ridden land, remote from population centres and unattractive to colonists. Modern industry increasingly needs trained people and here again Quebec is behind most of the other provinces. Montreal is well-located, particularly for shipping and entrepot trade, but how much of that has stemmed from an east-west oriented Canada? My point is that Quebec may well have been exploited by outside capital, but its geographical assets are not promising.

ASSOCIATION

5. Common market:
You suggest that separation might be followed by setting up of some kind of a new association between the former component of the old Canada (A divorce followed by a common law relationship?) It sounds like a possible, logical and mutually beneficial proposal, but I have some nagging doubts.

First is the psychological consequences on English Canada of the split. The "Lévesque wrench" would be harder on them than the "Chinese water torture." English Canadians would tend to see themselves, rightly or wrongly, as the guiltless partner in the divorce proceedings – and would blame Quebec for tearing the country asunder. I wonder how amenable they would be in these circumstances to your "common market" proposal?

I wonder also how English Canadians would react to the economic dislocations caused by the actual act of separation. Canada west (Ontario to B.C.) would gain fiscally, which might offset the short run losses in economic efficiency, redeployment of resources etc., caused by the split, but the Atlantic provinces would be in desperate straits.

I feel myself that English Canada has the will to survive, but that there would be a strong feeling of betrayal – (the woman walked out on me – I don't want to see her again!). In summary, I don't think that your calculations about the costs to Quebec if it separates should underestimate the impact of English Canadian backlash. Some of it, in a mild form, is being felt today in industrial decisions.

FLIGHT

6. The exodus:
How great a flight of capital – and people – there would be from Quebec is difficult for me to guess. Probably any such flight to date has been largely limited to liquid balances in banks and the movement of securities out of safekeeping in Montreal. Recent downward price movements in stocks of many companies with headquarters in Quebec (e.g. Consolidated Paper, Royal Trust, Ogilvie, Bell) may have some significance. However, I think that any serious outflow of people or money would reflect itself quickly in Montreal property values. I have no data on this but there are some signs that a decline is in fact beginning to occur.

Separation would be a different matter – even if a common market were quickly established. I suspect the loss of capital and skilled people would pose serious problems for the Quebec economy. This of course is speculating on future developments, and my judgment on this is no better than anyone else's.

PAYMENTS

7. Balance of payments and money:
Almost all the previous points have some bearing on the balance of payments of an independent Quebec, on both current and capital accounts. The money flows would be strongly against you, at least in the short run, and initially trade would certainly be disrupted.

In these circumstances, can one conceive of a monetary union with the rest of Canada, with one partner in a more serious deficit position than the other? I don't see how it could work, for a kind of Gresham's law would be at work – bad money replacing good. Without monetary union, the Quebec dollar would depreciate more than the (new) Canadian dollar. If you asked me to put a figure on it, I could see the Quebec dollar at .70, and the new Canadian dollar at .80 – in terms of U.S. currency. A new equilibrium would eventually be reached at the lower rate, but the disruptive consequences in the intervening period would be severe.

Finally what kind of grass-root support for separatism is there in Quebec, particularly if the public at large were made aware that the price-tag might be high? What about the impact on their own personal "rising expectations," which are more financial than nationalistic? I think that to be entirely honest with the people you must now come forward and talk about economic matters – and possible costs. Bourgault at least did that. You of course are free to differ with anyone's figures or projections, although you will have as much trouble as any of us in coming up with meaningful data.

But what I think you must accept is that if the decision to separate or not is largely an internal one for Quebec – and I support this view – the matter of how much it will cost will be determined largely by those outside Quebec. I can only beg you to spend as much time on this difficult and awkward problem as you have on articulating *"indépendance et association."*

En amitié.

Douglas H. Fullerton

APPENDIX FOUR

Summary of Main Elements of Quebec
Bill 101
Charter of the French Language
(Assented to August 26, 1977)
232 sections – 45 pages

TITLE I – Status of the French language

Chapter I Makes French the official language. (1)

Chapter II Provides "fundamental" personal language rights – to be communicated with in French by government bodies, unions and business firms; to speak French at meetings and at work; as consumers to be informed and served in French; to receive instruction in French. (2 – 6)

Chapter III "French is the language of the legislature and the courts in Quebec." (7) The legislature: French to be used, bills drafted in French, only the French text official, English version published. (8 – 10) The courts: corporations must plead in French, unless all parties agree to plead in English; all documents to be in French, if demanded. Judgments to be in French or "accompanied with a duly authenticated French version," – which is official. (11 – 13)

Chapter IV The Civil Administration – defined as the government, its agencies, municipal and school bodies, health. Social services: French names only, documents to be in French, communication with governments or corporations, and internally, in French; contracts, signs and posters to be French; health and social services to be available in French; language tests (provincially supervised) for employees appointed or promoted. Certain exceptions relating to safety, public health, English municipalities, schools and health services. Traffic signs – French only. (14 – 29)

Chapter V The semi-public agencies, that is, public utilities and professional corporations: services to be available in French, public notices and printed matter in French only; communications with government and corporations in French (but may reply to individuals in English); French names only; French language qualification for professionals (with some temporary exemptions). (30 – 40)

Chapter VI Labour relations. Employer must communicate with employees in French, including offers of employment or promotion; employment ads in English papers must be matched by simultaneous ads of equal size in French papers; collective and labour agreements and arbitration awards must be in French; no one can be fired, demoted or transferred "for the sole reason that he is exclusively French-speaking or that he has insufficient knowledge of a particular language other than French" (Section 45). The following section is related, and quoted in full:

> 46. An employer is prohibited from making the obtaining of an employment or office dependent upon the knowledge of a language other than the official language, unless the nature of the duties requires the knowledge of that other language.
>
> The burden of proof that the knowledge of the other language is necessary is on the employer, at the demand of the person or the association of employees concerned or, as the case may be, the *Office de la langue française.* The *Office de la langue française* has the power to decide any dispute.

Employees can claim a grievance for contravention of sections 45 or 46 under the Labour Code, or through their union for arbitration. This chapter (sections 41 – 49) is "deemed an integral part of every collective agreement."

Chapter VI Commerce and business. Labels, menus, wine lists, catalogues to be in French; no toys or games using non-French vocabulary unless French version is available "on no less favourable terms." Contracts, employment application forms, order forms, invoices etc. to be in French (minor exceptions allowed). Signs, posters, and commercial advertising to be in French only; firms names in French only; ethnic groups, firms with four employees or less, hospitals and social services may use own language in names if French version also given. (51 – 71)

Chapter VIII Language of instruction. Provides for education in French, except where this chapter allows otherwise; the main exceptions are children whose father or mother received elementary education in English in Quebec, or if parents domiciled in Quebec on August 26, 1977, outside Quebec; children who were in English school during the 1976-77 session, and their younger siblings. Verification of eligibility is required by the Minister of Education. Appeals are allowed. Children with serious learning disabilities exempted. No secondary school leaving certificate issued to student without "speaking and writing knowledge of French" required by the province. Special provisions for native peoples. (72 – 88)

Chapter IX A miscellany of clauses providing for making of regulations, general priority of French, and exemption for native peoples. (89 – 98)

TITLE II – *Office de la langue française* and francization (Office)

Chapter I Interpretation. (99)

Chapter II "100. An *Office de la langue française* is established to define and conduct Quebec policy on linguistics research and terminology and to see that the French language becomes, as soon as possible, the language of communication, work, commerce and business in the civil administration and business firms."

This chapter covers the organization, powers and location of the five-member Office. Its purpose is to standardize French terminology, establish linguistic research programs, set regulations for and manage the francization program; for these purposes it is empowered to set up committees to carry out its work. (99 – 121)

Chapter III The *Commission de Toponymie.* Purpose is to establish standards and rules of spelling in place names and to name, and change the names, of places. (122 – 128)

Chapter IV Francization of the civil administration. Concerned with the francization program in the civil administration agencies "to ensure the generalized use of French." Programs to take account of persons nearing retirement or with long service. Programs to be carried out "under the authority and with the assistance of the Office." (129 – 134)

Chapter V Concerned with francization of business firms and public utilities. Firms with fifty employees or more must obtain a "francization certificate" from the Office, attesting that it is carrying out an Office-approved program, or has reached the desired level of performance. Purpose:

141. The francization programme is intended to generalize the use of French at all levels of the business firm. This implies:

(a) the knowledge of the official language on the part of management, the members of the professional corporations and the other members of the staff;

(b) an increase at all levels of the business firm, including the board of directors, in the number of persons having a good knowledge of the French language so as to generalize its use;

(c) the use of French as the language of work and as the language of internal communication;

(d) the use of French in the working documents of the business firm, especially in manuals and catalogues;

(e) the use of French in communications with clients, suppliers and the public;

(f) the use of French terminology;

(g) the use of French in advertising;

(h) appropriate policies for hiring, promotion and transfer.

Special allowance for persons near retirement or with long service, and for firms with activities outside Quebec, and having regard to "the particular case of head offices."

Firms with a hundred or more employees must "before November 30, 1977" form a francization committee of at least six persons; one-third of committee must be designated by unions or employee associations, or elected at large by the "whole body" of employees. This committee is to analyse the firm's language situation and report, through management, to the Office, which decides if a program is needed or not. If it is, the committee will initiate and supervise the firm's program.

The Office may, with ministerial approval, require firms with under fifty employees to carry out a program. Certificates may be granted temporarily suspending firms from provisions of the act; certificates may be suspended or cancelled by the Office for failure of a firm to adhere to its program. (135 – 156)

TITLE III – The *Commission de Surveillance* and inquiries

The enforcement body to deal with violations or failure to comply with the act. Composed of a chairman, investigation commissioners, inspectors and other staff. Inquiries to be carried out (1) when the commissioners "have reason to believe" that this act has not been observed, (2) when requested by the Office (3) when a petition is made in writing by any person or group, accompanied by grounds. "The identity of a petitioner may be disclosed only with his express authorization." (174) An inquiry must be refused by the commissioners if judged beyond their competence, or under another jurisdiction, or if grounds no longer exist, or if "frivolous or in bad faith."

Commissioners have powers and immunity under Public Inquiry Commission Act; if commissioner judges act or regulations contravened "he may put the alleged offender in default to conform within a given delay." If offence continues beyond that delay, "he shall forward the record to the Attorney General for his consideration and, if necessary, institution by him of appropriate penal proceedings." Annual report of all action taken to be provided to Minister, who must table it in the *Assemblée Nationale* within thirty days. (157 – 184)

TITLE IV – The *Conseil de la langue française*
A twelve member council to advise the Minister on language policy and on "any question relating to the interpretation and application of this act." Members drawn from various groups – socio-cultural associations, unions, management, universities, ethnic associations. The Council is to receive observations and suggestions about the status and quality of the French language, to carry out language studies, to review difficulties reported by agencies or firms in carrying out the Act, and to inform the public on French language issues. (185 – 204)

TITLE V – Offences and Penalties
Main penalties are fines: first offence from $25 to $500 for an individual, double that for a company; second offence $50 to $1,000 for an individual, $500 to $5,000 for a company. Firms doing business without a francization certificate, fine of $100 to $2,000 for each day in default. Posters, billboards, signs offending against the act may be removed on court order "within eight days." (205 – 208)

TITLE VI – Transition and Miscellaneous Provisions
Mainly to establish dates for compliance, and to amend or repeal sections of other legislation which are in conflict with the language act. (209 – 232)

APPENDIX FIVE
A 15 per cent income drop when Quebec's 'free at last'
By DOUGLAS FULLERTON

Debate still goes on about whether Quebec benefits or not from Confederation, but even Premier Lévesque admits that during the past few years the province has gained considerably on balance.

A more relevant subject for discussion is the impact of the apprehended, or actual, separation of Quebec upon its present weak and deteriorating economy. This is the issue to which all Quebecers should be giving hard thought.

First, the main weaknesses showing up *now* in the Quebec economy:

• Unemployment close to 11 per cent, well above Canadian average. Impact softened by a rising flow of federal transfer payments – unemployment benefits, DREE and other make-work grants.

• Employment, low as it is, has been artificially shored up by state projects financed with heavy borrowing – for James Bay, Olympics, roads. Total debt of Quebec and Quebec Hydro now over $12 billion, up $5 billion in the three years 1974-1976. Annual interest cost over $1 billion. No income from James Bay power until at least 1980 – and $13 billion more borrowing required to complete the project. Even apart from the impact of lender fears about separatism, this rate of borrowing cannot be sustained – and has already had to be curtailed.

• Quebec taxes highest of any province, despite $1.3 federal equalization payments this year, which is a good measure of below-average tax-raising capacity.

• Weak industrial structure – above-average proportion of jobs are in service industries such as government employment, and large manufacturing concentration in tariff-protected but low-wage and threatened textile, shoe and related industries.

• A rising deficit in balance of trade and services, notably in tourism and farm products, well in excess of $4 billion this year and probably between $5 and $6 billion, taking oil subsidy into account. Gap closed by borrowing in U.S. and Canada, and by federal grants.

• Little benefit from "nationalizing" savings, currently being discussed in Quebec. Chartered bank loans in Quebec are greater than deposits, and insurance company holdings of Quebec securities now are higher than their liabilities to Quebec policyholders.

• An intransigent and militant union movement with above-average lost time from strikes; the highest minimum wages in Canada; the abnormally aroused expectations of Quebec wage earners; the impact of language legislation and other péquiste proposals – all these limit the attractiveness of Quebec for business investment, and creation of new jobs.

That is the Quebec economy today, hardly the best launching pad for independence. An economy, in fact, that is a good deal more vulnerable than it was five years ago. But consider the further damage that would be done by the fears of imminent independence.

• Further disincentives to investment, rising unemployment.

• Flight of capital, more by Quebecers than outsiders, further worsening the balance of payments, coupled with growing inability to borrow to close the rising gap.

• Rising government deficits and new taxes to offset falling tax revenues.

And if, in spite of all this, the péquistes win their referendum vote, and Quebec separates?

The mind boggles at the alternative scenarios, which range from the minimum damage of growing loss of jobs, declining output, loss of federal subsidies, to an exchange crisis and controls, rationing of imports such as cars and gasoline, and threatened economic collapse – perhaps staved off by emergency help from rejected Canada?

Cost to Quebecers: At best an income reduction of 15 per cent, at worst a crisis that would wipe out all personal savings in a currency collapse.

Is this a wager Quebecers would be prepared to accept for independence, a price they would pay? Not if their leaders give them a few hard facts instead of rosy-eyed dreams about the glories of being free at last.

(*Ottawa Citizen*, June 9, 1977,
Toronto Star Syndicate)

Index

Acton, Lord 154-155, 170
Angers, François Albert 95, 97, 188
Arès, Richard 95-98, 188

Barem (Montreal Transit) 10, 158-166
Bélair, Lucien 49, 61
Bélanger, Michel 46-49, 61, 68, 69, 75-78, 83-84, 100
Bernard, Louis 101
Bond syndicates 40, 43, 44, 56-61
Bouchard, T.D. 42
Bourassa, Robert 10, 90-91, 93, 103-104, 158, 167, 194, 225
Bourgault, Pierre 94, 228
Bussière, Eugène 34, 36

Caisse de dépôts 80-81, 105, 225
Canada Council 12, 31-39, 52, 95, 107
Cape Breton Development 112, 118
Capital Study 10, 156-158
Casgrain, Rudy 34, 84
Castonguay, Claude 80
Chapman, Doug 51, 56-57, 60
Chrétien, Jean 111
Churchill (Hamilton) Falls 51, 62-74, 221-223

d'Amour, Marcel 118
Davis, William 175-176, 202
De Belleval, Denis 10, 159, 165, 167-168
de Guise, Yvon 68
Deschamps, Jean 76-78
Desmarais, Paul 76-78, 137
Després, Robert 83
Dorion, Henri (Dorion Report) 64, 72-73, 122-123, 132, 139
Drapeau, Jean 35, 161, 165-166
Ducharme, Claude 49, 53, 58-59, 110
Dufresne, Cyrille 77
Duplessis, Maurice 32, 42, 48, 64, 97, 102, 122

Eddys 136-138
Estates General 95-97

Faribault, Marcel 37-38
Filion, Gérard 77-78, 89
Financial Institutions Committee 83, 85, 99-101, 104-106
Fournier, Jean 66
Frenette, Claude 109, 114
Fullerton, Douglas (DHF) – articles, letters, quotes 88-92, 115, 144, 151, 165, 172-174, 178, 184-185, 205, 215-220, 224-228, 234-235
– BAREM 10, 158-166
– bilingualism 143-153
– correspondence, contact Lévesque 10, 39, 41-45, 87-90, 141, 208-220, 224-228
– costs of separation 90-92, 201-206, 224-228, 234-235
– early years 9, 14-26
– family 16-22, 28-29, 127
– federal employment 26-39, 105, 118
– meeting Trudeau 111-112, 127-128, 155
– stuttering 12, 20-22, 29, 77, 100, 103, 123
Fulton, Davie 37

Gagnon, Jacques 118
Gérin-Lajoie, Paul 38-39, 82, 92
Gignac, Jean Paul 69, 78
Giroux, Roly 35
Goldenberg, Carl 122
Goodman, Martin 87, 110
Gordon, Walter 29-31, 58, 66, 69, 108
Goyer, Jean-Pierre 110, 114
Grandy, Jim 52
Gravelle, André 160, 166
Groulx, Canon Lionel 94-96, 196

Hanigan, Lawrence, 164-166
Hamilton, Richard 195-196
Hamel, Philippe 42, 196
Hellyer, Paul 113-115
Hydro-Québec 41-43, 49, 56, 58-61, 65-71, 78, 80, 90, 97

Isabelle, Gaston 126

Johnson, Daniel 10, 69, 70, 75, 82, 84, 85, 104, 114, 119, 194
Joy, Richard 187-188, 197
Juneau, Pierre 146

Kierans, Eric 49, 58-61, 78, 81-84, 88, 90-93, 113, 115, 224-225

La Haye, Jean-Claude 133, 161
Lalonde, Marc 37-38, 96, 111, 114, 118, 122, 154
Lamontagne, Maurice 30, 34, 38, 107-108, 110, 198, 203
Language legislation 11, 143, 178-191, 196-198, 206, 210-213, 229-233, 235
Lapalme, Georges-Emile 12-13, 39, 45, 95
Laporte, Pierre 102-104, 137
Laurin, Camille 97, 150, 174, 178-189, 193, 197-198, 200, 207, 211-212
Léger, Jean-Marc 95, 181-182, 188, 199, 200
Léger, Jules 151
Léger, Marcel 168
Lemieux, Ed 43, 58-59, 61
Lesage, Jean 10, 31, 38-39, 44, 49-62, 64-71, 75-84, 104, 119, 194, 213
Lessard, J.C. 65-68
Lessard, Lucien 165-166
Létourneau, Roger 49, 53, 61, 65, 67, 77, 80
Lévesque, Georges-Henri 30, 33-36, 39, 46-47, 119

Lévesque, René
- Churchill Falls 65-71, 73
- contact, correspondence DHF 10, 39, 41-45, 87-90, 141, 208-220, 224-228
- elected 167-169
- forms PQ party 94-98
- leaves Liberals 90-92
- nationalization electricity 39-55
- New York speech 173-174, 178, 194-195, 202, 209
- "Option-Québec" 42, 52, 91-94, 193, 201, 208
- other 31, 78, 82-83, 87, 101, 104, 119, 159, 171-177, 193, 207
- sovereignty association 91-94, 105-106, 208, 228

Lussier, Robert 124

Mackenzie, Jack 39, 46-47
Mailloux, Raymond 159, 164-165
Marchand, Jean 31, 108, 110-111, 113-114, 118
Marler, George 39, 44, 48, 56, 59
Martin, Paul 113-115
McGill University 15, 20-26, 160, 185-187
McIlraith, George 118, 126-127, 134
McKeough, Darcy 176/7, 210
Moores, Frank 73
Morin, Alex 134
Morin, Claude 79, 82, 85, 101, 104-105, 119, 122-123, 168, 194, 202, 224
Morin, Jacques-Yvan 31, 95
McLaughlin, Earle 181, 183-184

National Capital Commission (NCC) 10, 105, 112, 118-142, 145, 154-158
Nationalization Electricity 10, 41-55, 112
Newfoundland 16, 62-73
Newman, Peter 87
Nov. 15, 1976 167-169
Ottawa bureaucracy 28-29, 105, 145-148, 154-156
Ouellet, André 158
Ouellette, Jocelyn 158

Parent, Oswald 135-136, 138, 140-142, 158, 168
Parizeau, Jacques 46-47, 80-83, 85, 99-101, 104-106, 168, 175, 186, 201-202
Pearson, Lester B. 79, 83, 107-108, 110-113, 115-116, 117, 119
Pelletier, Gérard 31, 108
Pelletier, Paul 119, 134
Pension Plan - CPP-QPP 79-81
Pepin, Jean-Luc 108, 112
Pigeon, Jacques 37, 118
Pigeon, Louis-Philippe 37, 46-49, 53, 69, 77, 81, 118
Pope Pius IX 154-155
PQ Party (péquistes) 9, 10, 15, 82, 90, 94-98, 193-194, 201
Pratte, Yves 69, 83, 100, 104

"Québec Demain" 103

Raynauld, André 104
Reisman, Simon 30, 124, 203
Roberts, John 147
Robertson, Gordon 154
Rouleau, Claude 158-159, 164
Ryan, Claude 102-103, 164, 174, 182-183, 192

Sauvé, Jeanne 31, 44-45, 115-116
Sauvé, Maurice 30-31, 41, 44, 79, 106-111, 113, 115-116
Smallwood, Joseph 64-68, 71, 73, 74
Spicer, Keith 143, 147
Stanfield, Robert 77
St. Laurent, Louis 32-34, 48
Steel (SIDBEC) 75-78

Tremblay, René 75, 107-108, 110
Tremblay, Rodrigue 175, 178, 205, 210
Trépanier, Victor and Ginette 37, 85
Trudeau, Pierre Elliott
– elected leader 114-115
– joins Liberals 108
– meetings DHF 111-112, 127-128, 155-156
– on Lord Acton 154-155, 170
– on nationalism 112, 169-171, 185
– other 31, 37, 65, 106, 118, 173, 207
Turner, John 113-115, 126-128, 131

Vigneau, Claire and Jean 29

Wagner, Claude 103
Winters, Robert 65-68, 70-71, 110-111, 113-115